Consensus and Controversy

Conflicts and Controversy

Consensus and Controversy

City Politics in Nottingham 1945-66

NICK HAYES

LIVERPOOL UNIVERSITY PRESS

First published 1996 by
LIVERPOOL UNIVERSITY PRESS
Senate House, Abercromby Square, Liverpool, L69 3BX

British Library Cataloguing-in-Publication Data
A British Library CIP Record is available for this book
ISBN   0-85323-571-6 *cased*
         0-85323-581-3 *paper*

Printed and bound in the European Union by
Redwood Books, Trowbridge, Wiltshire

Contents

List of Tables and Map   vi
Acknowledgements   vii
Common Abbreviations   viii

Chapter 1: Introduction   1

Chapter 2: Local Roads to 1945   17

Chapter 3: Consensus and the Politics of
            Reconstruction 1945–51   39

Chapter 4: Consensus Undermined: Old Values,
            New Party Disciplines 1951–57   67

Chapter 5: Militants, Reactionaries and Expulsions 1945–60   93

Chapter 6: Labour Takes Power: Images of Crisis
            and Caucus Rule 1956–61   117

Chapter 7: Political Corruption or Police Partisanship?:
            The Popkess Affair   135

Chapter 8: Controversy and the Arts:
            Building the Nottingham Playhouse   161

Chapter 9: Discord and Harmony: City Policy in the 1960s   187

Chapter 10:   Some Conclusions   213

Appendix   225
Bibliography   233
Index   255

List of Tables

2.1   Committee and patronage distribution
      in inter-war Nottingham   24
3.1   Political parties' strength on Nottingham
      City Council 1945–57 after annual municipal elections   41
3.2   Post-war annual dwelling completions in Nottingham   56
6.1   Political parties' strength on Nottingham
      City Council 1957–66 after annual municipal elections   119
6.2   Comparative percentage strength Labour vote:
      Nottingham and Britain   131
6.3   Swings to/from Labour in the May 1960 and
      1961 municipal elections   132

Map

Council House Building in Nottingham 1919-1966   53

Acknowledgements

The initial research for this book would not have been possible without the help, encouragement and financial assistance provided by the Open University and its staff. For those of us who, for whatever reason, do not follow the traditional routes through higher education or opt to change radically their career path, the University provides an anchor of stability and a conduit for change. In particular, I am indebted to Arthur Marwick for his many helpful comments on the early drafts and his enthusiasm generally, and to Bill Purdue for his encouragement. In similar vein, I would also like to thank Peter Clarke of St John's College, Cambridge for his thoughts and observations. I owe a debt of gratitude to my colleagues at Nottingham Trent University for their support; Colin Griffin especially provided many helpful comments on the final script. An equal vote of thanks goes to Chris Wrigley of Nottingham University for his pertinent insights on the completed text, and finally to John Beckett who took the time to explain to a relative novice the mysteries of the world of publishing.

Secondly, I would like to acknowledge the help I have received from the archivists, librarians and institutions who have aided me in my research, notably the staff of the Nottingham Archives Office and the Local Studies Centre at Nottingham Central Library. A special vote of thanks goes to the Arts Council of Great Britain, which allowed me access to its private files and gave permission to quote from its correspondence and reports. My appreciation also to *Midland History* and the Nottinghamshire Thoroton Society for waiving copyright restrictions on material in part already published in their journals. A general vote of thanks is extended to all those individuals who gave freely of their time discussing the specifics of post-war politics in Nottingham. In particular I would like to express my gratitude to Eric Foster, who unfortunately died before the completion of this work but with whom I spent many enjoyable hours debating council and city Labour policy.

Finally, and above all, my special thanks to my wife, Jane, for her patience, time and energy in reading, re-reading and commenting on the work at all stages of its production. Without her support, both moral and financial, this book could not have been produced.

Common Abbreviations

ACGB   Arts Council of Great Britain
F&GPC   Finance and General Purposes Committee
GPC   General Purposes Committee
GJ   *Guardian Journal*
IAP   In Author's Possession
MRC   Modern Records Centre
NAO   Nottingham Archives Office
NCC   Nottingham City Council
NEN   *Nottingham Evening News*
NEP   *Nottingham Evening Post*
NG   *Nottingham Guardian*
NJ   *Nottingham Journal*
NLSL   Nottingham Local Studies Library
NMLH   National Museum of Labour History
NUMD   Nottingham University Manuscripts Department
PRO   Public Records Office

The terms Labour or Conservative group refer collectively to those councillors or aldermen of each party who each year sat on the city council. The Nottingham City Labour Party was a delegatory body drawn from the individual party membership of the four city constituencies and other affiliated organisations (e.g. local trade unions, the co-operative movement, etc.). Likewise, the Conservatives also had a central City Party, to which each Nottingham constituency elected delegates, who in turn were members of their respective local ward branches.

CHAPTER 1
Introduction

For historians and students alike the post-war period has long since lost any claim to virginal status. This is particularly true of the Attlee years of reconstruction and post-war settlement. Recent years have seen a proliferation of histories and biographies to supplement the well established, but still regnant, polemics from left and right judging the political direction set in 1945. Indeed, that we speak so readily of a pre- and post-war era itself acknowledges that the war is, and was, viewed popularly as a chronological marker and disjoiner, a metaphor for change rather than continuity. Thus are imageable contrasts reinforced: of inter-war slump versus post-war prosperity; of the founding of the welfare state to replace means test and malevolence; of a people's peace honoured in 1945, not betrayed as a generation before. This is one reason, perhaps, why the policies followed in the immediate post-war years remain axiomatic to the still prolific debate on what, if anything, fundamentally ails modern British society. Similar and associated disagreement is equally apparent in judgements on the popular political temper of 1945. Whether or not Labour's victory derived more from a recurrent 'fear of the dark satanic mill' of inter-war depression rather than 'the hope of a new Jerusalem' or 'a tidal wave of left-wing fervour' remains keenly contested.[1]

Yet if our attention wanders from focusing exclusively on Westminster, instead of a field of plenty, we rapidly enter what was aptly described some twenty years ago as 'The Lost World of British Local Politics'.[2] Judged from the standpoint of local histories covering the post-war period, with one or two notable exceptions little has changed in

---

1 K. O. Morgan, 'Post-War Reconstruction in Wales, 1918 and 1945', in J. Winter (ed.), *The Working Class in Modern British History* (1983), pp. 83–98; S. Fielding, 'What Did "the People" want? The Meaning of the 1945 General Election', *Historical Journal* 35 (1992), pp. 623–39; for a recent bibliography of post-1945 histories, see S. Burgess, '1945 Observed—A History of the Histories', *Contemporary Record* 5/1 (1991), pp. 155–70.

2 R. A. W. Rhodes, 'The Lost World of British Local Politics', *Local Government Studies* 1 (1975), p.39; N. Tiratsoo (ed.), *The Attlee Years* (1991), pp. 1, 126.

the intervening years. What we find instead is an expanding literature reflecting the central concerns of social scientists operating in the field of local government: for example, studies of the sociological backgrounds and recruitment of councillors, the nature of central-local relations, and of the representational machinery and identity of local institutions. Few studies offer a detailed chronological perspective or draw extensively on contemporary archive material—that is neither their objective nor operating rationale. This book seeks, in part, to rectify these omissions, offering a detailed, empirically based and local overview of the twenty years following 1945. It takes as its common starting point the election in both Nottingham and Westminster of newly triumphant majority Labour administrations amid the popular rejection of inter-war fatalism.

Spurred by our own contemporary preoccupations, much has also been written recently of a post-war political consensus. Critics of this outline, of whom there are a growing number, attack such a premise on a number of counts beyond disputing a basic policy and ideological congruence. Most common is a challenge to the orthodox chronology operating, particularly in rejecting its founding origins within the wartime coalition (reinforcing the current emphasis on the myth-making processes attached to war itself). It has also been suggested that post-war voter stability and two party alignment is more a measure of active division, not of agreement around a supposed core common agenda predicated loosely as an end to ideology. More radically, the search for consensus has been characterised as merely a nostalgic yearning for an illusionary past where inter-party agreement was purportedly commonplace. Ben Pimlott, for example, suggests consensus to be little more than an artificially constructed product construed only to reinforce the validity of current ideological positions and those values deemed important by historians; in reality, consensus remains 'a mirage ... that rapidly fades the closer one gets to it'.[3] Such an emphasis, aside from its post-modernist overtones, will be immediately familiar to students of twentieth century local politics; a recurrent theme in both the pre and post-war literature laments

---

3 For a useful summary, see R. Lowe, 'The Second World War, Consensus, and the Foundation of the Welfare State', *Twentieth Century British History* 1/2 (1990), pp. 152–82; also D. Kavanagh and P. Morris, *Consensus Politics from Attlee to Major* (1994, 2nd edn), pp. 1–22; D. Kavanagh, P. Morris and B. Pimlott, 'Controversy: Is the Postwar Consensus a Myth?', *Contemporary Record* 2/1 (1989), pp. 12–15.

the passing of a purported 'golden age' of apolitical local government free
from the rancour of party politics.[4]

To this can be added an overarching rationale, the approach to which
lies at the heart of the debate over consensus. If, in offering prescribing
parameters, we seek absolute or near absolute agreement between parties
or politicians, then, as critics suggest, our search is doomed to
disappointment. By its nature and function, party political activity
promotes competition and disparity in both image and substance. Here,
within a modern combative electoral framework, a party's raison d'être
is self-defined, to degrees, as representative of differing interests (and
even ideologies). Indeed, taken to its logical absurdity, a wholly
unadulterated consensus remains anathema to party politicians for it
sounds their death knell.

How then should we define and employ the consensus label?
Proponents make clear its chronologically comparative nature, accepting,
within this paradigm, that, in any stable democratic society, both political
concordance and controversy will be readily evident. What is sought is an
historically unusual measure of agreement (as distinct from compromise)
over key areas of social and economic policy. In itself, however, this is
deemed insufficient. As Paul Addison stresses, in his seminal work of
1975, British inter-war parliamentary politics exhibited a 'species of
consensus', that is:

> a consensus to prevent anything unusual from happening. [But] the
> new consensus of the war years was positive and purposeful.
> Naturally the parties displayed differences of emphasis, and they
> still disagreed strongly on the question of nationalisation. At the
> hustings the rhetorical debate between state socialism and
> laissez-faire capitalism was renewed with acrimony. In practice, the
> Conservative and Labour leaders had by-passed most of it in favour
> of 'pragmatic' reform in a mixed economy. When Labour swept to
> victory in 1945 the new consensus fell, like a branch of ripe plums,
> into the lap of Mr Attlee.[5]

4 For example, see G. M. Harris, *Municipal Government in Britain: A Study of the
Practice of Local Government in Ten of the Larger British Cities* (1939), pp. 46–52; G.
Block, *Party Politics in Local Government* (Conservative Political Centre, 1962).
5 Paul Addison, *The Road to 1945: British Politics and the Second World War* (1975),
p. 14.

The nature of Attlee's inheritance remains central to the current debate on consensus and, de facto, Labour's 'betrayal' of socialist principle. It follows that doctrinal radicalism and pragmatic accommodation are mutually incompatible bedfellows: the stronger the latter, the less polarised the break with the past in 1945. And on balance, recent research has focused more on the road from 1945 when seeking or dismissing the origins of consensus formation. That the parties remained wholly divided ideologically during the wartime coalition is an increasingly common theme. Kevin Jeffreys, in particular, notes the overt hostility, and later ambiguity, to reform from within the Conservative party prior to its humiliating electoral defeat in 1945, while Kenneth Morgan has argued that Labour significantly extended the coalition's plans for social reform—hardly a commendation for existing agreement. In subsequently identifying the limitations of a broader wartime consensual inheritance, deemed anyway to be 'a somewhat ambiguous and deceptive concept', he also points to a created 'facade of [national] unity' within and outside parliamentary circles during the war which masked deep-seated social, intellectual and political division.[6] Arthur Marwick, the first of the 'home front' historians and the most consistent advocate of the correlation between war and social change, likewise stresses Conservative resistance to the social blueprints of the war years and immediately after. Post-war parliamentary consensus, he concludes, 'should not be overstated', being 'most evident' only after the return of a Conservative government. Ideological division, however, did not necessarily preclude a bi-partisan 'harmony of purpose' on the need for fundamental reform, or on its broad objectives, prior to 1945. Historically significant agreement, Rodney Lowe argues, was underpinned and driven by the rejection, across all levels of society, of what he aptly labels 'inter-war fatalism'—albeit based on a popular 'civil illiteracy' surrounding the detail of the proposed alternatives. By 1947 this nucleus of agreement over policy and past

6 K. Jeffreys, 'British Politics and the Second World War', *Historical Journal* 30/1 (1987), pp. 123–44; K. Morgan, *Labour in Power* (1985 paperback edn), pp. 495–99; K. Morgan, *The People's Peace* (1990), pp. 1–28; see also J. Harris, 'Political Ideas and the Debate on State Welfare, 1940–45', in H. L. Smith (ed.), *War and Social Change: British Society in the Second World War* (1986), pp. 233–63; S. Brooke, *Labour's War: The Labour Party during the Second World War* (1992).

failings had expanded to encompass agreement over the broader framework within which the welfare state should develop.[7]

Marwick, somewhat unusually, dates the period of consensus (by which he means a broader social consensus) from 1945–57. The conventional political chronology, however, runs either from May 1940 to May 1979 (Churchill's coalition premiership to Thatcher's election) or June 1944 to September 1976 (from the publication of the *Employment Policy* White Paper to Callaghan's Labour party conference speech renouncing that commitment).[8] In part chronological disparities depend, interpretably, upon which societal groups constitute the consensus-forming body. Not surprisingly, texts on high politics dominate: focusing on policy continuity between governments, or more broadly on the shared objectives (or otherwise) of political and administrative elites. At first glance this would seem the correct emphasis. In their origins and implementation, and indeed through popularist terms like the welfare state and 'Butskellism', statist features remain pre-eminent in defining agreement on economic policy and welfare reform. Dennis Kavanagh and Peter Morris, for example, identify five main areas of governmentalist consensus: a bi-partisan commitment to the mixed economy, the maintenance of full employment, the conciliation of trades unions, agreement over state welfare provision and entitlement and concordance over the key areas of foreign policy. Moreover, a wholly governmental focus allows criticisms which draw on more broadly based evidence (for example, the high levels of party partisanship and class-led voting during the 1950s and 1960s) safely to be dismissed as 'irrelevant'; although, paradoxically, Kavanagh has also cited electoral stability in support of the consensus thesis.[9]

Such a restrictive straightjacket, if legitimate within its own terms of reference, does present certain difficulties. Not least, it devalues the already noted symbiotic (and arguably axiomatic) relationship between a wider popular consensus and governmentalist political convergence, where

7 A. Marwick, *British Society since 1945* (1982), ch. 6, esp. p. 104; Lowe, 'War and the Welfare State', pp. 161, 168–89, 180–81.

8 D. Marquand, *The Unprincipled Society: New Demands and Old Politics* (1988), ch. 1; Kavanagh, Morris and Pimlott, 'Postwar Consensus a Myth?', p. 12; Lowe, 'War and the Welfare State', pp. 156–57.

9 See Kavanagh, Morris and Pimlott, 'Postwar Consensus a Myth', pp. 12–15; D. Kavanagh, *Thatcherism and British Politics: The End of Consensus?* (1990, 2nd edn), pp. 35–36.

the former provided a founding and continuing impetus for reform and policy proscription. This is a central tenet of Addison's founding thesis. It is equally true for those who favour, in part or emphasis, a post-1945 chronological imperative for consensus. Here the despair generated by electoral defeat within a Conservative party raised to hold office, but now doubting its political future, spurred the adoption of a more attractive and consensually oriented agenda (for example, the much cited *Industrial Charter* in 1947) which contrasted markedly with its pre-war emphasis. Thus the unofficial policies of Tory reformers of 1945 became the official policies of the party as a whole in 1951.[10] To Marwick, this re-established consensus in high politics 'was laudable in maintaining social harmony and providing the opportunity for post-war reforms to be worked out'. Morgan, even in doubting the later congruence between the parties on social, industrial and particularly fiscal policy, concluded that if in practice Butskellism was a myth, it probably existed as a state of mind—a circumstantially fortuitous yet 'coherent attempt to maintain a social consensus'.[11]

*

Those working in the field of local government politics have sought to build on this organic relationship between Westminster and a broader social consensus, rejecting a proscriptive governmentalist interpretation. Within traditional legalistic interpretations, where the dominant political tone is anyway centrally dictated, this would seem uncontentious; for here local authorities act primarily as Westminster's executive agents (to whom they remain legislatively, judicially and financially bound). However, recent research into central-local governmental relations has tended to

10 B. Schwarz, 'The Tide of History: The Reconstruction of Conservatism 1945–51', in Tiratsoo (ed.), *Attlee Years*, pp. 149–50, 156–58; A. Seldon, 'The Conservative Party since 1945', in T. Gourvish and A. O'Day (eds.), *Britain since 1945* (1991), p. 243.

11 Marwick, *British Society*, p. 111; Morgan, *People's Peace*, p. 118–9; for a rejection of populist-led wartime reform, see J. Harris, 'Did British Workers Want the Welfare State? G. D. H. Cole's survey of 1942', in J. Winter (ed.), *The Working Class in Modern British History* (1983), pp. 200–14; for support of Butskillism, see T. J. Hatton and K. A. Chrystal, 'The Budget and Fiscal Policy', in N. F. R. Crafts and N. Woodward (eds.), *The British Economy Since 1945* (1991), pp. 52–88; for an opposing view, see N. Rolling, 'Poor Mr Butskell: A Short Life, Wrecked by Schizophrenia?', *Twentieth Century British History* 5/2 (1994), pp. 183–205.

reject wholly deterministic approaches where central government holds a monopoly of power.[12] Local authorities, it is now argued, retain degrees of democratically invested autonomy—which include an expectation to be consulted and certain freedoms to negotiate with Westminster—over policy and its implementation. The outcome reflects the relative power and resources (political, financial and physical) of each tier of government, set generally within the accepted parameters of past practice and, ultimately, Westminster's veto.[13]

It is, of course, misleading to speak of a monolithic local authority structure. Significant differences existed, not only in terms of jurisdiction and wealth but also in the degree of politicisation, between rural, urban and county borough authorities in post-war Britain. Even within complementary bands (for example, comparing the larger county boroughs), studies have suggested noticeable variations in terms of expenditure and provision. This was particularly apparent in areas of spending covered by permissive legislation (ranging through public health and the social services to provision for the arts). Generally, the county and metropolitan boroughs, which were both wealthier and geographically concentrated, were the more generous providers. Even in the area of mandatory basic services, notable inequalities existed between comparable authorities; Labour-controlled councils generally spent more on redistributive and ameliorative services such as education and welfare, just as they were more likely to build larger numbers of houses and offer higher rent subsidies than their Conservative counterparts.[14]

In accepting a flexible linkage and local disparity, a number of authors have suggested that the consensus operating in high politics was still equally apparent locally. This thesis is clearly stated by John Gyford, one of the more prolific and luminous of political scientists writing on local politics. In writing of a stable British political system existing after 1945, he concludes:

12 For an overview of central-local relations, see W. Hampton, *Local Government and Urban Politics* (1991, 2nd edn), pp. 173–89.

13 See particularly R. A. W. Rhodes, *Control and Power in Central-Local Government Relations* (1981); R. A. W. Rhodes, *The National World of Local Government* (1986).

14 P. Crane, *Enterprise in Local Government* (1953); J. Gyford, *The Politics of Local Socialism* (1985), p. 5; N. T. Boaden and R. R. Alford, 'Sources of Diversity in English Local Government', *Public Administration* 47 (1969), pp. 215–19; J. Dearlove, *The Politics of Policy in Local Government* (1973), pp. 13–15.

the majority of the politicians who operated within this system, whether at the local or national levels, inhabited the same 'assumptive world'. They took for granted the permanency of the welfare state and the mixed economy so that partisan disagreements covered a rather narrow range of opinions ... Within local government itself political debate tended to revolve around what policies to adopt within the framework of the welfare state, for example around issues such as the 11-plus examination or rent levels rather than around more basic topics, such as the merits of state education or of council housing. There were few serious ideological strains within either of the parties and little disposition to raise fundamental arguments about the respective roles of local and central government ... It represented one aspect of the mid-twentieth century *rapprochement* between the feudal paternalism of Tory Democracy and Fabian centralism of Social Democracy.[15]

Gyford is stating explicitly the connections which other commentators writing on local government politics take as read; here, municipal consensus is inexorably bound to the triumph, nationally, of social democracy.[16] Indeed, such diffusion and acceptance provides the key stimulus for the much vaunted post-war 'nationalisation of local politics': the homogenisation of local and national political spheres, and of autonomous local characteristics. Thereafter, the impact of local political preference is limited to the variants of existing or decreed provision noted earlier, but within an overall framework of shared values and central constraints. Rarely, it is argued, did local politicians initiate new policy themselves; this function instead is devolved to an increasingly professionalised local bureaucracy, or taken as a response to external

15 J. Gyford, 'The Politicization of Local Government', in M. Loughlin, M. D. Gelfand and K. Young (eds.), *Half a Century of Municipal Decline 1935–1985* (1985), p. 87; see also K. Young and L. Mills, *Public Policy Research: A Review of Qualitative Methods* (1980).

16 See, for example, G. Stokes, *The Politics of Local Government* (1988), p. 8; J. Kingdom, *Local Government and Politics in Britain* (1991), p. 117.

pressures (for example, by central government or commerce).[17] It was only in the mid-1970s that Labour-controlled councils particularly sought to reverse this trend to 'administrative politics' by producing and implementing detailed party policy manifestos for larger local authorities.[18]

There was, course, a wholly physical post-war impetus towards centrally controlled provision: the literal nationalisation of former municipal responsibilities in the areas of health and the utilities. As John Stevenson states, in terms of responsibilities it was 'the period from the late nineteenth century to the Second World War [which] might well be called the heyday of local government'. Nevertheless, a certain ambiguity remains. Lost local autonomy post-war needs to be set against the very immediate centrality of local authorities as enacting agents: the Attlee government arguably being 'the first explicitly to recognise the importance of local institutions in the implementation of national policy ... [where] the task of reconstruction ..., together with ... [an] ambitious social programme ... depended for their success, at least in part, on the effectiveness of local institutions'.[19] Indeed, not all historians accept an inverse correlation between growing national provision and direction, and the declining importance of local factors. Mike Savage has argued recently that it is misleading to view such a relationship as a zero sum where 'the significance of the local is violated by the expansion of national state activity'. Instead, as state responsibility expands, it 'may relate to or bear upon more aspects of local social life, [and] so the local determinants of these aspects take on more political significance.' Savage's primary interest is in working-class political activity, and the linkages between the social/cultural environment and political behaviour; here the 'significance of the local' reminds us that political movements are 'ultimately grounded in the practical politics of everyday life', where

17 Gyford, 'Politicization', pp. 87–89; P. Dunleavy, *The Politics of Mass Housing in Britain 1945—1975: Corporate Power and Professional Influence in the Welfare State* (1981). For a more critical assessment of the national/local party relationship, see J. Gyford and M. James, *National Parties and Local Politics* (1983).

18 C. Fudge, 'Winning an Election and Gaining Control: The Formation and Implementation of a Local Political Manifesto', in S. Barrett and C. Fudge (eds), *Policy and Action* (1981), pp. 123–41; C. Game and C. Skelcher, 'Manifestos and Other Manifestations of Local Party Politics', *Local Government Studies* 9/4 (1983), pp. 29–33.

19 J. Stevenson, *British Society 1914–45* (1984), pp. 307–09; A. Alexander, 'The Decline of Local Government: Does Local Government Still Matter?', *Contemporary Record* 2/6 (1989), p. 2.

local politicians forge (or fail to forge) linkages between this world and that of formal state politics at the local level.[20]

Like other county boroughs in 1945, as a unitary authority Nottingham had specific responsibility for a wide range of services and provision. Aside from ceding, in part, temporary control over local emergency services during the war to centralised control, corporation responsibilities stood at their peak. Revenue expenditure that year on local rate-funded services totalled some £3.7 million (excluding loan charges of £660,000). Within that figure, the city financed—with the aid of some £1.3 million in central government grants—its own comprehensive hospital and specialist clinic provision, social welfare and housing services, a city police and fire force, schools and colleges, roads, sewerage and refuse disposal. It also provided a myriad of lesser facilities: from public libraries, museums, swimming baths and parks to public wash houses, and from court and probation services to car-parks and public lighting. By March 1946, the city also had a nett loan debt of £13.4 million. A little under half of this total (£6.2 million) had paid for the Corporation's expansive inter-war housing programme of some 17,000 dwellings. Of the remaining debt, a further half reflected investment in the city's trading undertaking. Nottingham, like many other large towns and cities, owned its own electricity generating and gas production capacity. Not only were these services sold to the surrounding communities, they also made healthy contributions to the financial relief of the city rates.

Several of these expansive civic functions were soon to pass from direct municipal control to fall under the orbit of other public bodies. In the twentieth century local authorities had taken the initiative in health care and education. However, with the establishment of a National Heath Service, direct city provision was subsequently limited broadly to inspection, home visits and help, midwifery and ambulance services. Similarly, local authorities also lost their only recently acquired responsibility for public assistance. In terms of the utilities, first the nationalisation of the electricity industry, and shortly after of gas, left only city transport and water provision in corporation hands. Both these undertakings remained under municipal authority until local government re-organisation in 1974, when water passed to regional control. However,

20 M. Savage, 'The Rise of the Labour Party in Local Perspective', *Journal of Regional and Local Studies* 10/1 (1990), pp. 2–3, 10–11; see also M. Savage, *The Dynamics of Working-Class Politics: The Labour Movement in Preston, 1880–1940* (1987).

in other areas, city responsibility continued to expand rapidly within Britain's new Welfare State. Nowhere was this more evident in the immediate post-war years than in housing. Ten years after the end of the war, the city's nett housing debt had risen from £6.2 million to stand cumulatively at £19.8 million; a further ten years later this figure stood at £30.8 million.[21] Similarly, by March 1946 cumulative nett loan indebtedness for capital spending on education was £630,000; by 1956 this figure had reached £4.6 million and by 1966 it had risen to £8.5 million. Likewise, annual revenue spending on education in the same years stood at £1.2 million, £2.9 million and £8.2 million respectively. Thus it was that by 1966 the city council's annual expenditure on services amounted to some £20.5 million, a fifth of which went to repay debt charges accumulated by its past and continuing investment in the local community.[22]

*

To the historian, the chronologies of continuity and/or disjuncture have a central, indeed defining, importance. Thus, for example, we are prompted to question the extent to which any newly dominant national welfare ideology supplanted existing local interpretations of municipal responsibilities inherited from the inter-war years. This might be thought particularly apposite given the longevity of office of many elected representatives (and officials) on key council committees–appointments which readily spanned the 1939–45 divide. What value also is to be attributed to independent local motivating–or retarding–forces? The most immediate of these was the impetus for reconstruction; a cardinal if initially unguided response to 'total' war. In fact, with the cross-party adoption of its 1943 reconstruction plan, Nottingham, with other local authorities, pre-empted central social and economic planning initiatives

21 As a guide, the index of construction costs stood at 167.6 in 1955 and 208.9 in 1965, where 1945 = 100; C. H. Feinstein, *National Income, Expenditure and Output of the United Kingdom* (1972), Table 63.

22 NCC, *Epitome of Accounts for the Year(s) Ended 31st March 1946–1966*, Tables 7, 8, 9, 11, 12, 14; NCC, *Annual Report of the Education Committee 1955–66*, Tables 4, 5.

which, because of government divisions within the coalition, at the time lacked clarity.[23]

Recent studies of reconstruction in other cities have, on balance, tended to stress the divisive functioning of the process itself. In particular they have noted the continuing discord over objectives between town halls, central government and Whitehall which impinged significantly upon local settlements and progress. While the diversity of city experiences is readily acknowledged, the overall impression remains that reconstruction promoted disagreement rather than consensus. Local disunity was not always a function of direct party political division, although this was not uncommon. Nevertheless, the priorities of vested industrial, commercial, professional and political interests remained particularly diverse over core issues like social provision, town planning, land reform, industrial and housing policy.[24] In short, whether to return to the status quo or seek new alternatives remained keenly contested. Likewise, in Nottingham reconstruction, as with other parochially harnessed responses in the post-war period, built heavily on subtexts of inherited civic pride, party prestige and personal advancement (tenets equally visible in its local administrative bureaucracies). It was also based on local needs-driven provision, set against pre-war standards of local housing which exceeded nationally set benchmarks. Moreover, the agreed agenda locally in 1945 was far from static; future adherence to its basic outline was to have an immediate and continuing influence on city government and inter-party relations which reflected different political interpretations and priorities.

Of course, national and local chronologies may exhibit a pronounced dissymmetry. Well known is the municipal absence (in Nottingham and elsewhere) of a Liberal revival in 1923 and 1924 to match its parliamentary success. Equally, Labour's rapid recovery locally after 1931

23 Addison, *Road to 1945*, pp. 252–53; A. Cairncross, *Years of Recovery: British Economic Policy 1945–51* (1987), p. 300–03; J. Hasegawa, *Replanning the Blitzed City Centre: A Comparative Study of Bristol, Coventry and Southampton 1941-50* (1992), ch. 2.

24 Hasegawa, *Replanning Blitzed Cities*, passim; N. Tiratsoo, 'Labour and the Reconstruction of Hull, 1945–51', in N. Tiratsoo (ed.), *The Attlee Years* (1991), pp. 126–46; N. Tiratsoo, *Reconstruction, Affluence and Labour Politics: Coventry 1945–60* (1990). For a more positive assessment, see S. Lloyd Jones, 'Working to a Plan—Committee Structure in Plymouth during Reconstruction and Subsequently', *Local Government Studies* (1980), pp. 29–36.

failed to express itself in parliamentary by-elections or the 1935 general election.[25] If electoral disparity was markedly less evident post-war, contemporaries highlighted other factors which, in hindering a local acceptance of national policy, might impose chronological disparity. The supposed militant or reactionary status of local activists in both major parties provides one notable example; if true, this would challenge the foundation of consensual diffusion. Militancy was more popularly associated with Labour constituency activists, whether exhibited spasmodically in the Bevanite factionalism of the early 1950s, or more generally through the overall politicisation of local politics itself. Moreover, it was also readily associated with the later intolerance and dictatorialness of caucus rule.[26] Here, Conservative orthodoxy proclaimed that through the twentieth century (and especially after the Second World War) local authorities had been ensnared by a growing, centrally orchestrated Labour campaign to secure national Socialist objectives at a local level through the deployment of a disciplined party machine. Conservatives only reluctantly abandoned the belief that local government should remain structurally free from party dominance to counter this Labour challenge (notably after the Tory rout in 1945). The political construction of a past age where city politics particularly remained divorced from party political control (locally and even centrally) has subsequently been discounted.[27] In the context of the inter-war period, it had anyway a fraudulent quality which frequently saw the traditional parties, in seeking to resist Labour gains, adopt pseudonymous 'Independent' labels while, paradoxically, standing on an overtly anti-Socialist ticket. Indeed, the anti-Labour hostility immediately after the Great War, and passing into the 1930s, arguably produced the more 'venomous' of inter-party conflicts.[28]

25 C. Cook, 'Liberals, Labour and Local Elections', in G. Peele and C. Cook (eds), *The Politics of Reappraisal 1918-1939* (1975), pp. 166–88.

26 For the seminal party polemic, see G. Block, *Party Politics in Local Government* (Conservative Political Centre, 1962); for a good riposte, see K. Young, *Local Politics and the rise of Party* (1975). For Labour and local politics generally, see, for example, J. Gyford, *The Politics of Local Socialism* (1985); and S. Goss, *Local Labour and Local Government* (1989).

27 Young, *Local Politics*, pp. 29–33; D. Fraser, *Urban Politics in Victorian Britain* (1979 edn), pp. 9–24; J. M. Lee, *Social Leaders and Public Persons* (1963), pp. 174–75.

28 H. E. Smith, 'Party Politics in English Local Government', *Secretaries Chronicle* (March 1955), p. 159. For concealed party allegiance, see A. J. Beith, 'An Anti-Labour Caucus: The Case of the Northumberland Voters' Association', *Policy and Politics 2*

Jim Bulpitt, through his study of Lancashire towns, subsequently sought to classify inter-party frictions and politicisation as a function of internal discipline and patronage distribution. The political tenor, he argued, was set by an individual Labour group's interpretation of the party's 'Model Standing Orders', which had been widely adopted across Britain by 1945.[29] The Orders contained, amongst other things, the principle of caucus rule and the establishment of a whipping system similar to Westminster practice—ridiculed by political opponents for its authoritarian approach when adopted comprehensively within local government circles. The stricter the interpretation, he concluded, the more politicised the atmosphere in the council chamber; for in general terms, Conservative attitudes were viewed as a largely reactive, if more temperate, response to Labour's determining attitudes.

It will become readily apparent that ideological or party-driven considerations were a central feature in the changing landscape of post-war city politics. Nottingham, which by 1945 had a strongly established tradition of party-based activity, first acquired a self-congratulatory reputation for its inter-party co-operative and pragmatic spirit (which built on an earlier inheritance from the inter-war period). Equally, however, in the late 1950s the city earned a national notoriety for the bitterness and animosity which dominated inter-party relations. This transformation rested only partially on differing interpretations of a provision-based agenda within a changing political and social environment. More immediately, it reflected a growing disagreement and disenchantment over the established political practice and structures of city government itself. Noticeably, division arose particularly at times of party political instability, when neither group had decisive majorities on the council. But instability was also a product of changes to Nottingham's own 'rules of the game', that is the formal relationship between the parties themselves, and between members, committees and the full council. So pervasive and virulent were these divisions that they readily corroded a past, if deteriorating, consensual ethos amid Conservative allegations that local Socialist militancy made inter-party agreement impossible.

(1973), pp. 153–65; and for a party-free Independent movement, see G. W. Jones, *Borough Politics: A Study of the Wolverhampton Town Council, 1888–1964* (1969), pp. 205–23.

29 J. M. Bulpitt, 'Party Systems in Local Government', *Political Studies* 11/1 (1963), pp. 11–35; J. E. Maccol and E. C. R. Hadfield, *British Local Government* (1948), p. 95.

Nevertheless, individual issues were to be important in shaping political responses. At a basic level, during the two decades following the war, and irrespective of local political temperature, a clear majority of recommendations put to the city council received multi-party support. This in itself might be construed as one measure of a political consensus, except that—like criticisms of post-war consensus generally—it ignores completely the demonstrably changing tenor of the times, and with it the changing realities of city political life. Equally, there were to be issues over which the parties remained perpetually divided, and indeed over which they united to oppose central policy. In the late 1950s, particularly, the antagonisms invested in two topics—the suspension of the city's chief constable and the construction of a new civic playhouse—so dominated local affairs as to redraw the future civic agenda under the spotlight of national publicity. Here Nottingham, at least in part, set the pace for broader change elsewhere. Such equations rest uneasily with a broader nationalisation/administrative politics hypothesis in which disagreement is limited to matters of little substance, or where the emphasis for consensus rests outside local political cycles.

Indeed, this study concentrates unreservedly on Nottingham: the municipal government of one city and the local party political community tied to it. It echoes Kenneth Newton's sentiment (in the preface to his study of Birmingham) that 'local politics are not simply national politics writ small'.[30] While attempts are made to place local events in a broader national perspective, and to study issues deemed important in post-war Britain generally, no special claims are made to place the city on a pedestal as a model representative of British, or even English, urban society. The central objective of this book is to resurrect the inner dynamics of a local political component; to argue that far from conforming to a national chronology, political consensus in Nottingham, which was meaningful, comparatively, both in its own historical terms and to contemporary observers, peaked in the years of reconstruction immediately following the war. Thereafter, in terms equally discernible to local politicians and for those in the city who chose to look, consensus declined markedly until, having reached its nadir, electoral imperatives and pragmatic necessity determined its revival.

30 Newton, *City Politics: Democratic Processes and Decision-Making in Birmingham* (1976), p. 12.

Finally, a brief comment needs to be made on source material and on local authority responsibilities. Local authorities offer no *Hansard* equivalent to record the details of council debates. Full council minutes merely list the order of business, the motions discussed and, on rare occasions, members' voting behaviour. Committee minutes and reports are more helpful, but frequently provide only an outline of the debate and the outcome. Fortunately, detailed accounts of a generally high quality appeared in the local press (Nottingham had two morning and two evening papers of differing political persuasion in 1945)[31] to help supplement and balance the record. Of the major parties in Nottingham, only Labour kept formal minutes (the Conservative group kept brief notes in the late 1950s and early 1960s). Indeed, it is Labour's records generally which have survived in the greater quantity. Fortunately, Labour was also the governing group in Nottingham for much of the post-war period under study and, as importantly, appeared as the prime mover in the key controversies and in instigating change. For both these reasons, one wholly pragmatic and the other one of conscious emphasis, greater attention is paid to Labour politics than that of the other parties. In terms of locating other sources, the local political historian is, to a large extent, left to his or her own devices: there is no local equivalent system of deposit to that of national government although recently County Archives Offices have made gallant attempts to rectify in part such shortcomings. Perhaps unusually, therefore, frequent reference will appear in the text to documents currently in the author's own possession (subsequently abbreviated to IAP). These, which include a major collection formerly in the keeping of Eric Foster (a past leader of the city Labour group), will be deposited shortly with the Nottingham University Manuscript Department. Suffice it to say that this material was invaluable to the production of this book.

31 The *Nottingham Guardian* and *Nottingham Evening Post* took a broadly Conservative line, the *Nottingham Journal* and the *Nottingham Evening News* a broadly Liberal stance. In 1953 the two morning newspapers amalgamated, becoming the *Guardian Journal*—which was Conservative in inclination.

CHAPTER 2
Local Roads to 1945

Commenting on Nottingham's local political achievements during the Conservative-dominated inter-war period, the prominent left-wing journalist and politician, Tom Driberg, wrote of an era of 'imaginative thinking': 'when the city centre and the boulevards ringing the city were laid out, the Council House built, slums cleared and Newstead Abbey acquired'. This contentious programme, he argued, was implemented because 'the leaders of the two party groups [Wright and Bowles] ..., both of them dominant and vigorous men, once these ambitious projects had been sold to them, formed a personal axis and bulldozed the projects through'.[1] Driberg was writing in 1959, drawing favourable comparisons with past accomplishments to highlight a similar and equally contentious 'revolutionary burst of thinking' in contemporary city politics: this time, he argued, 'by different and more democratic means'. Here the ruling Labour Group, having revoked past power-sharing agreements with local Conservatives, embarked on an expansive programme of civic arts and leisure provision to which its former 'partners' were bitterly and irreversibly opposed. Active democracy now meant more than the process of choice between clearly identifiable electoral party programmes (both the Labour and Conservative groups had offered this throughout the twentieth century); after 1957 it meant the formal separation, by party, of the executive function in committee. It was perhaps ironically prophetic that Driberg uttered these words in a month that was to mark the nadir of modern local inter-party relations following Labour's suspension of the city's chief constable. If a central gauge of consensus is marked by a willingness to compromise—which, like good and evil, has a mirror image—then such antithetical spectres were readily haunting Nottingham's political corridors in the late 1950s.

That a dynamic and purposeful inter-war polity existed, particularly one consensually bound, runs against past academic constructions of the city's history. Moreover, because the consensus label remains essentially a comparative chronological measure, we need briefly to evaluate such

1 Tom Driberg, 'This Proud City', *Reynolds News*, 5 July 1959.

claims. It has been argued that an equally vitriolic and robust antagonism separated the parties before and after the Great War. Nottingham, before 1914, was a bastion of Lib/Lab politics and industrial paternalism: alternatively a city in which 'Progressive co-operation was still a very real feature of local politics', or where socialists, nevertheless, 'made an essential impact ... in establishing the credibility and political reality of independent labour representation'.[2] Both perspectives are open to degrees of reinterpretation. The years preceding the outbreak of war did see a brief period of co-operation between the Liberal and embryonic Labour parties. Not only did the local Liberal press endorse Independent Labour Party (ILP) candidatures, but Liberal ward organisations, encouraged by appeals from local Lib/Lab working-class parliamentarians, agreed to stand aside to allow Labour to challenge Tory councillors. In 1912, however, electoral co-operation collapsed: Labour candidates, who previously had received Progressive endorsement, and who were to form the nucleus of the local post-war Party, were denounced collectively by Liberals and Tories alike as a 'small, noisy band of I.L.P. wire-pullers'; the traditional parties—in the words of Sir Edward Fraser (Liberal Group leader)—'drawing together' to oppose the 'rise of a new force which calls itself socialism'.[3]

It was perhaps not wholly coincidental that the Liberals' short-lived electoral détente with Labour followed immediately their loss of control of the city council to local Conservatives in 1908 after some fifty years' hegemony. It was also noticeable that 'Progressive' disunity (or traditionalist realignment against a radical ILP) was to the immediate benefit of neither the Labour nor Liberal parties. An electoral high point in 1911 saw Labour capture four of the 48 elected seats on the city council. The discord of the following year halved Labour representation: in the six seats contested—all but one winnable by post-war standards—it polled on average only 26 per cent of the vote (although one sitting Labour councillor took a creditable 42 per cent against a Conservative-sponsored Liberal opponent). An already weakening local organisation, the increasing popularity of protectionist policies amid local industrial

2 D. Tanner, *Political change and the Labour Party 1900-1918* (1990), p. 296; P. Wyncoll, *The Nottinghamshire Labour Movement 1880-1939* (1985), p. 161. For a useful overview critical of Tanner's generalisations regarding local and regional politics, see K. Laybourn, 'The Rise of Labour and the Decline of Liberalism: The State of the Debate', *History* 80 (1995), pp. 209—26.

3 *Nottingham Daily Express*, 1 Nov. 1909, 1 Nov. 1911, 24 Oct. 1912, 1 Nov. 1912.

decline, and general government unpopularity does much to explain Liberal failure. Nor were the party's fortunes improved by concerted Labour campaigns to exploit a past reluctance to redress the historically poor condition of city working-class housing against the appeals of the Lib/Lab, medical and civic improver lobbies. Conservatives also made play of past 'Progressive' failures in this respect, and it was they, upon coming to power, who first established a city Housing Committee and a separate Housing Department. If rhetoric exceeded application here, one should also note that reform was all too easily stymied by local and 'powerful forces of inertia': notably a vigorous owners and ratepayer lobby, and an omnipresent belief that bad tenants made bad housing. Arguably, this dictated 'a sophisticated exercise in consensus policy formation' built on a cautionary partnership between the private and public sectors.[4] Nevertheless, in at least formally acknowledging free market failure, Conservatives provided a foundation upon which a younger faction within the Corporation could build in a post-war climate more favourably disposed to interventionist social policy.

The 1919 municipal elections, the first held for six years, saw a significant increase in the number of contests fought by Labour where their share of the vote now averaged 55 per cent. Here the party took seven of the nine seats contested (six Tories and one Liberal being returned unopposed). This increased their representation in council to ten. Nevertheless, local Conservatives, although losing several seats, easily maintained their dominance electorally—an overall if diminishing control which they kept throughout the inter-war period. Considering only local factors, Labour was undoubtedly better placed organisationally and financially than before the war, although this was by no means yet true of all wards. One key factor was the support now offered by the Nottingham Trades Council, 'shedding its past prejudices' and former Lib/Lab sympathy by unanimously supporting Labour candidates at the polls. This new unity built on a spirit of co-operation cemented during wartime campaigning on emotive 'home front' problems of shortages and inequalities.[5]

4 R. Smith, P. Whysall and C. Beuvrin, 'Local Authority Inertia in Housing Improvement 1890–1914: A Nottingham Study', *Town Planning Review* 57 (1986), pp. 420–23.

5 NLSL L.33 *Nott'm and District Annual Trades Council Reports*, 1917–20; Wyncoll, *Nottingham Labour*, pp. 165–77, 184–85; B. Waites, *A Class Society at War: England 1914-18* (1987), p. 221; J. Holford, *Reshaping Labour: Organisation, Work and*

In 1919, Labour focused quite specifically on housing. The issue had a special poignancy locally. Contemporary surveys had revealed the true state of dilapidation: some 7,000 working-class houses of 'mean' character, 'built in congested blocks, intersected by narrow streets, courts and alleys'; a majority being back-to-back and around a century old, with only a pail closet (which was frequently shared).[6] Although even patchwork demolition of slum property had finally been suspended during the war years because of severe housing shortages, in 1918 the Housing Committee instructed that all unfit houses be served with closing orders. This was to be a prelude to an ambitious reconstruction programme combining general needs provision with vigorous slum clearance. Yet so acute was the city accommodation problem that three years later slums already closed were being re-opened. Clearance, anyway, was not a government priority. New construction, however, was. Significant disquiet had already been expressed locally prior to 1914 on the abilities of private enterprise to meet demand for working-class housing. Wartime disjunctures, combining with a patriotic and civic sentiment, a fear of civil unrest and central government encouragement, provided an interventionist agenda upon which the council now acted. Plans were approved to construct some 1,000 working-class dwellings. More expansive proposals, however, to build a further 2,700 houses (to meet the estimated shortfall in accommodation) were subsequently rescinded until Addison himself intervened at the request of the Housing Committee—blocked by a coalition of local laissez-faire recidivism and 'progressive' vacillation. Typical of the latter was Edmund Huntsman, the newly elected Liberal leader, an ardent advocate of the earlier, more limited, proposals and a self-proclaimed civic social reformer. Now he spoke of high costs and the current misguided 'passion of grant and subsidy', of an inappropriate focus on 'garden city' provision and the usurping of council authority by the Housing Committee. In a body historically conservative in interventionist terms, uncertainty underwrote caution in even those whose instincts favoured reform. The *Nottingham Journal and Express*, now part Liberal-financed, was less circumspect in its judgement. Huntsman's objections, it decreed, were 'reactionary'. Commenting later on Labour's electoral success, its Editorial concluded:

Politics—Edinburgh in the Great War and After (1988), pp. 154–63.
6 NCC, Report of Housing Committee, 10 Oct. 1919.

> If a progressive party is to be kept healthy, it must have regular
> constant and suitable exercise ... Possibly the successful onslaught
> which Labour has made on the old regime may be the best thing
> that could have happened ... it was high time somebody imparted
> more vigour and life into the criticism of Corporation affairs. The
> attitude of the City Council towards housing has been a scandal.[7]

Nevertheless, despite a delayed start and continuing internal opposition,
Nottingham's completion rates compared favourably with other county
boroughs under the 1919 legislation. Within this overview lay the basis
for future co-operation between progressive and/or paternalistic elements
within the traditional parties (particularly in the majority Conservative
group) and a Labour party seeking social municipalism and reform.
Indeed attitudes to, and agreement over, municipal housing offers a fine
indicator to future local consensual practice. Housing was, of course, an
essentially innovative and testing responsibility for local authorities in
1918. Thereafter it remained a key focus for state and popular concern,
and an increasingly dominant component of city responsibility, provision
and social policy (despite fluctuations in government emphasis). For all
these reasons it forms a central component of this study.

That inter-party relations, and electoral affiliation, immediately after
the Great War remained essentially fluid is borne out by subsequent
election returns and by the conduct and rhetoric of the parties. Again,
existing accounts focus on the antagonism directed jointly against Labour.
Thus the traditional parties carried forward their co-operative alliance of
the pre-war years, 'banding together to fight a common danger in the
Socialists and their revolutionary doctrine'. And indeed, talk on the
hustings of combating revolution, revolutionaries and Bolshevism
generally was commonplace. Liberals particularly, in now counterpoising
their own financial conservatism, were prone to illiberal hyperbole in
seeking to distance themselves from their former Progressive partners: that
'crowd of leather-lunged, self-assertive people ostensibly representing
Labour' who had 'secured seats ... to the exclusion of able men of ...
civic affairs'.[8]

7 *Nottingham Journal and Express*, 23 Sept. 1919, 3 Nov. 1919.

8 *NG*, 2 Nov. 1920, cited in both C. Cook, *The Age of Alignment: Electoral Politics
in Britain 1922–1929* (1975), pp. 61–62 and Wyncoll, *Nottingham Labour*, p. 193;
Editorial, *Nottingham Journal and Express*, 2 Nov. 1920.

The 1920 election, held again at a time of national industrial unrest, saw anti-Labour rhetoric peak. Yet only a few weeks later, at the city's mayor-making ceremony, Huntsman made the following declaration in support of Herbert Bowles's nomination to civic office:

> It is with the highest degree of satisfaction that not withstanding the peculiar views that the hot atmosphere of a recent election might have forced to growth that they should elect a representative of Labour to the position. They could not expect that Labour should permanently lie like Lazarus outside the house for crumbs that might fall, or might not.[9]

On its own, this might be thought an equally artificial sentiment, albeit one enthusiastically endorsed by the local press. Yet the unanimity surrounding Bowles's election also needs to be set in the context of the high prestige in which the mayoralty was held and the associated competition for nomination, even in supposed radical Labour circles.

The year 1920 also witnessed the election of the first Labour aldermen. The party had been pressing vigorously for an entitlement proportional to party strength. What was finally agreed, however, was somewhat less generous: allocation based not only on party size but weighted to take account of length of individual members' service. As Bernard Wright, the Conservative group leader, commented:

> To prevent unpleasant disputes ... it was felt desirable that some definite working arrangement should be arrived at ... [so] that, whatever occurred, there should remain upon the council a certain number of aldermen of experience who would be in a position to criticise and protect against innovation or experiments which might be contrary to the city's interest.[10]

Nevertheless, the concordat was to form the foundation for the normalisation of inter-party relations in both the inter- and post-war periods. This first six-year inter-party agreement, which also stipulated alternating party entitlement to the mayoralty and shrievalty, was signed in October—immediately prior to the 1920 'Bolshevik' elections.

---

9 *NG*, 10 Nov. 1920.

10 *NG*, 8 Nov. 1920 (also contains the full text of this first agreement).

Undoubtedly this first exercise in acknowledging Labour aspirations also operated to the party's immediate tactical disadvantage. The weighting element particularly was an application in the continuity of traditional power. As Wright went on to explain: 'any party which had recently come into being, ... whose members were inexperienced or who were there as the result of a merely transitional wave of public support, ought not to count equally with parties whose members were of long-standing'. Yet the concordat also formalised Labour's local integration and acceptance: thus, what at face value appears to be a wholly reactionary and defensive instrument, was quickly and 'unanimously' accepted by all three parties. Indeed Wright, under immediate pressure to renege on the agreement following Labour's poor showing in 1920, steadfastly refused, arguing that this would be 'dishonourable' and 'unconstitutional'.

In 1926, the initial two-clause agreement expanded to a proposed seventeen, all designed to enhance inter-party co-operation and lessen friction over patronage placements. Most initiatives and administrative duties, however, were devolved to a multi-party committee system (one reason why direct comparisons between Westminster and local authority politics remain problematic). Each committee held delegatory powers for specific areas of responsibility—limited only by its inability independently to raise finance or levy rates. The city had a strong tradition, dating back to the nineteenth century, of granting liberal authority to its individual committees which historically had heightened the latter's sense of political freedom.[11] The cornerstone of the system, in which considerable power and prestige were invested, was the committee chair. The inter-war period provided many examples of leading members being elected in perpetuity to these offices. Sir Albert Ball, the Conservative group leader from 1931–39, chaired the city's Gas Committee from 1906–46, the year in which he died at the age of 83. Sir William Crane, a builder by profession and perhaps the most influential of these specialists, chaired the Housing Committee from 1919 and, although a Conservative, throughout the Labour dominated post-war era. He was only finally deposed in 1957. In 1926 the committee hierarchy was still dominated by the old parties (Table 2.1), where party tradition, lineage and sometimes arbitrary seniority reinforced Conservative hegemony of the political

11 *NJ*, 3 July 1954; A. J. Burkett, 'Conventions and Practices in the Committee System in Selected Local Authorities in the East Midlands' (University of Nottingham, MA thesis, 1960), p. 156.

initiating process. Yet as its strength grew, Labour increasingly controlled the junior posts within committee. Indeed, Bowles chaired the Estates Committee from 1920 onwards. After 1932, the concordats formally acknowledged that committee offices should be allocated in proportion to party strength (allowance being made for minor posts).

Table 2.1 *Committee and patronage distribution in inter-war Nottingham*

	Chairs			Vice-Chairs			Aldermen			Party Strength		
	Con.	Lib.	Lab.	Con.	Lib.	Lab.	Con.	Lib.	Lab.	Con.	Lib.	Lab.
1913	17	7	-	16	7	-	8	8	-	37	23	2
1920	22	5	1	12	12	2	8	6	2	34	21	9
1923	19	5	1	10	11	2	8	6	2	35	17	11
1926	18	5	2	7	9	6	7	5	4	30	15	18
1929	13	5	9	8	4	12	6	4	6	27	11	26
1932	17	3	7	11	3	12	8	2	6	34	8	22
1935	14	1	10	10	1	12	9	1	6	32	3	29
1938	14	-	10	11	-	12	8	-	8	34	1	29

Informal 'gentleman's agreements' (by word of mouth or exchange of letters) governing patronage distribution were not uncommon elsewhere. Equally, and particularly in the 1920s, local Labour councillors were frequently heavily discriminated against in patronage placements—provoking both bitterness and later retaliation.[12] Theorists have since argued that patronage distribution remained the singularly most contentious issue between political parties in local government circles, disagreement being spurred by the search for individual aggrandisement or party power.[13] What was unusual about Nottingham's concordats was their comprehensive and formal nature. In granting early recognition to Labour aspirations and limiting subsequent patronage disagreement, the

12 G. M. Harris, *Municipal Self-Government in Britain* (1939), pp. 46–52; B. Keith-Lucas and P. G. Richards, *A History of Local Government in the Twentieth Century* (1978), pp. 114ff; R. Hills, 'The City Council and Electoral Politics, 1901–1971', in C. H. Feinstein (ed.), *York 1831–1981: 150 years of Scientific Endeavour and Social Change* (1981), p. 271; H. Keeble Hawson, *Sheffield: The Growth of a City 1893–1926* (1968), pp. 295–98.

13 J. C. Bulpitt, *Party Politics in English Local Government* (1967), pp. 127–28; L. J. Sharpe (ed.), *Voting in Cities* (1967), pp. 12–13.

protocols became a symbol of an equitable co-operative ethos within a competitive party system—one noticeably at odds with pre-1914 patterns under either Conservative or Liberal control. At the same time, the agreements were a recognition of party authority within local government—effectively excluding the independent or individual from the patronage network. For the historian, the fluctuating terms of the concordats also offer a regular benchmark (each usually ran for six years) by which we can judge the improving state, or otherwise, of inter-party relations and consensual spirit in the city.

Joint patronage was not popular with all. Both the left and the Tory right were at times highly critical of inter-party co-operation, in that it sullied political identity and weakened radical authority. In a similar vein, Wright's and Bowles's already noted co-operative liaison, indeed their open friendship, was held by critics to work against their party political responsibilities; Wright particularly, in cultivating 'a policy of collaboration ... caused umbrage to some of his more aggressive followers who thought he carried conciliation too far'.[14] The positive accommodation within the council chamber needs to be set against the almost continuous operation of a formal 'anti-socialist' pact between 1919–38, of the sort common elsewhere. At times, relations between local Liberals and Conservatives were brittle, or even hostile. Yet, with certain years excepted, only rarely did the two parties contest the same seat. More commonly, each campaigned on the other's behalf. This apparent paradox in Tory behaviour—of pact against concordat—can best be explained by separating election strategy from local Conservative realpolitik, a rationale bound to the inverse yet parallel chronologies of rising Labour and declining Liberal power.

Long-term, the pact worked to the Liberals' detriment: as junior coalition partners they remained firmly in the shadow of Conservative rhetoric, policy implementation, recruitment—indeed identity. If in predominantly working-class areas Liberals lost to Labour, middle-class wards became wholly Conservative preserves. Even in former Liberal non-conformist strongholds, and increasingly in wards of mixed social status where the coalition partners alternated candidatures, it was the Conservatives who claimed the dominant role as the key anti-socialist force. In the two years 1924 and 1928, when the pact broke down, of the

14 *GJ*, 15 Aug. 1961, 18 Aug. 1961; also *NJ*, 21 Nov. 1927, 15 Dec. 1932, 2 Nov. 1934; *NEP*, 30 Nov. 1934.

nineteen wards contested in total, in only two did the Liberal poll more votes than the Conservative, and in only one (the party's last regularly contested non-working class seat) did it provide the winning candidate. Liberal protestations during the 1928 elections that the Conservatives had deliberately engineered a crisis, accusing one Liberal councillor of having 'socialist sympathies' in order to stand against him and 'pocket' the seat, led the party to declare that the pact was 'broken ... absolutely and finally'.[15] Yet so politically dependent had the Liberals become that the years following saw the pact operating again, albeit in a rising atmosphere of resentment as Conservatives continued to claim candidatures in former Liberal seats. Local organisational atrophy only further hastened this decline.

The idea that housing particularly provided a central core around which progressive interests within the parties could unite during the inter-war years requires chronological clarification. We have already noted the uncertainty and resistance which threatened to undermine Housing Committee initiatives immediately after the armistice. The local accent on private provision continued short-term: with the Corporation tending to pass central subsidies to speculative builders, or offering municipally built properties for sale as well as rent. As Crane recalled later of the early to mid-1920s, 'there was still a very large reactionary section on the Council at that time.'[16] Nevertheless, under his energetic chairmanship, between 1920–39 the Committee constructed 17,095 houses (or one for every 16 of Nottingham's inhabitants). Of these, almost half were built under the 1924 Wheatley Act (where the city had one of the highest per capita completion rates in Britain) —not a trend associated generally with Conservative-controlled authorities.[17] This latter commitment to rented provision sat uneasily with the government's own later sanitary emphasis. Indeed, after the abandonment of general-needs subsidy in 1933, the Housing Committee went on to erect a further 1,500 unsubsidised dwellings. Local Conservative minimalists argued that if costs had fallen sufficiently to allow such construction at affordable rents, then municipal

---

15 *NJ*, 24 Oct. 1928, 2 Nov. 1928.

16 *Fifth Report from Select Committee on Estimates*, PP (1945–46), Mins of evidence, p. 173.

17 *Ibid.*, p. 172; NCC, *Epitome of Accounts*, 1949; J. H. Jennings, 'Geographic Implications of the Municipal Housing Programme in England and Wales', *Urban Studies* 8 (1971), p. 128; J. Darke, 'Local Political Attitudes and Council Housing', in S. Lowe and D. Hughes (eds.) *A New Century of Social Housing* (1991), p. 163.

intervention in the housing market was wholly unjustified. Nevertheless, in council the proposals were passed 'without demur'. In fact a clear majority of members, actively or passively, supported the Housing Committee's progressive objectives. As one senior Conservative alderman confided, 'there was a time when I regarded Ald. Crane as a fanatic and visionary'; now he thought 'the committee were [sic] doing sound, valuable and useful service'. Indeed one Labour left-winger jibed that he 'was at a loss to understand why Mr Crane is in the Tory Party'.[18]

There were, however, limits to this policy consensus. Conservative housing intervention was subject philosophically to the group rhetoric of continual justification, for within Tory ranks there remained a highly vocal minority that objected strongly to the municipalisation of the city's housing stock. Intervention here was seen at best as a temporary expedient, and certainly not 'to house people who could, in the main, provide suitable accommodation for themselves'. Crane and the Housing Committee, however, subscribed to different criteria, qualitatively and quantitatively. In adhering to the tenets of the garden-city movement, the city acquired a national reputation for its low density suburban housing. Partly this was a response to a shortage of city centre sites, partly because Crane (despite considerable opposition) thought flats and tenements 'un-English', but primarily because the committee saw its civic objective as one of laying down permanent standards for a better future.[19]

In similar fashion, Nottingham was one of the few early enthusiasts for the national slum clearance campaign initiated in 1930, so that by 1939 over 3,600 properties had been demolished and replaced. However, the governing Conservative party then twice refused to endorse Housing Committee requests to clear a further 1,350 slum houses. Opponents cited the growing international tensions as one justification for postponement, a rationale immediately dismissed by the then Minister of Health. More significantly perhaps, they argued for repair rather than demolition, and against property confiscation 'without compensation'. Much to the chagrin of Labour and Crane, senior Conservatives observed that many of the condemned properties were indeed 'beautiful houses', both 'pleasant and suitable for the people living in them'.[20] In fact, the retreat from

18 *NG*, 28 Feb. 1934; 6 March 1934, 7 Feb. 1939.

19 *NG*, 21 Sept. 1937; *NEP* 26 May 1937; R. Unwin, 'Introduction' to T. C. Howitt, *A Review of the Progress of the Housing Schemes in Nottingham under the Various Housing and Town Planning Acts* (1928).

20 *NG*, 1 Aug. 1939; *NJ*, 29 July 1939.

previously agreed objectives centred primarily on the anticipated half million pound cost of the project.

In 1938, city rates rose by 1s 4d, prompting the immediate formation of an independent ratepayer party, the Nottingham Citizens' Association, which was tacitly supported by several prominent Tory councillors. As quickly, the Conservative leadership moved to curtail spending by increasing the powers of the Finance Committee, and abrogating to it the duties of the General Purposes Committee—a past bulwark of inter-party hierarchical co-operation. Conservative disquiet found two other immediate targets: capital spending on housing and the principles of shared committee patronage.[21] A political expedient perhaps, but Conservatives highlighted that the largest spending committees (other than Housing) —Education, General Works and Highways, Public Assistance, Watch and Health—were all chaired by Labour. However simplistic such an analysis—it ignored the scale of committee remits or notably that Conservatives always retained a vetoing majority on each committee and in full council—it provided sufficient incentive, in a year when the inter-party agreement was to be renewed, for many Conservative councillors to call instead for an end to formalised co-operation. Unfortunately for its opponents, the pact ran until after that year's committee placements had been nominated. All Tory abolitionists could offer during the interim council elections, therefore, were leadership pledges of a subsequent radical revision to reduce minority party influence and ensure that in future Conservatives chaired all major spending committees.[22] Yet the reaction against expenditure also provides an important measure of past achievement in municipal provision. To characterise this as attributable wholly to Labour influence would be inappropriate. Undoubtedly, mainstream Conservative intervention was more temporally determined, paternalistic in origin and pragmatic, if largely reactive, in design. Nevertheless, the material gains were significant. Indeed, basic agreement over immediate objectives provided a changing foundation for local consensus, one no longer based predominantly on the political negative of accommodating Labour's growing strength. It was this new agreement which was under threat in 1939 until the war provided a core agenda around which party factions could reunite.

---

21 *NEN*, 4–7 April 1938, 2 May 1938.
22 *NEN*, 25 Oct. 1938, 16 Nov. 1938; *NG*, 28 Oct. 1938, 2 Nov. 1938.

*

As Cecil Armitage, the new Conservative group leader recalled, a temporary political concordat was quickly reinstated to ensure 'during the difficult time of war, a fair representation on the Council according to party strength and to get a united war effort'.[23] This expired in November 1944. In the interim, the operation of an electoral truce and a basic agreement over civic priorities during the emergency cauterised many existing sores. Yet two notable issues, reconstruction and member autonomy, did provoke significant disagreement; although paradoxically, both in their separate ways cemented post-war consensus.

In 1942 the city council, in common with many other local authorities, established an all-party Reconstruction Committee, chaired by Crane, to consider post-war municipal development. After consulting widely, and receiving reports from a number of extraneous bodies, the Committee's report was placed before the council in October 1943. Welcomed by the press for its vision, it called for civic 'energy and far-sightedness': offering an overview of future municipal objectives, and particularly the need for some 18,575 houses over the next twenty years—6,235 of which were required urgently. Similar forecasts were made for each Corporation committee, as was an overall appreciation of the need for future amenities, infrastructure, planning requirements and administrative provision. No general expectation existed that all or part of the report would be enacted immediately, it being accepted that such ideas involved 'a total expenditure by the Corporation which will be exceptional'.[24] Nevertheless, amongst a number of senior Conservative members, its conclusions drew nothing but open hostility. Sir Bernard Wright, for example, publicly belittled the 'purely utopian' idealism of this immature 'little committee' in its attempts to 'bluff and rush' the Corporation into 'great capital expenditure' of little relevance to immediate post-war needs. It was all wholly reminiscent, Crane complained, of objections raised after the Great War when 'senior members of that Council felt the Corporation would be ruined if the Housing Committee were allowed to proceed ... until force of public opinion compelled them to give way.'[25]

23 *NJ*, 8 Dec. 1942.

24 NCC, 'Report of the Reconstruction Committee on Post-War Development', 9 Sept. 1943, pp. 4–9, 32; *NJ*, 30 Sept. 1943, 5 Oct. 1943.

25 Letter from Wright, *NJ*, 4 Nov. 1943; *NJ*, 5 Nov. 1943.

After a particularly acrimonious council debate later that month, acceptance of the enabling cornerstones of the report was deferred. However, the economic expedients of 1919 and 1938 were insufficient restraints, as Crane had predicted, when set against local need and raised socio-political expectation–now more firmly based on past precedent. Shortly after, members agreed in principle to promote the necessary Parliamentary Bill to improve the city's infrastructure, purchase what building land remained in Nottingham, and as a corollary, to seek again an extension to the city's boundary. Opinion remained divided, however, over the pattern of future housing development: whether to extend the inter-war practice of suburban estates (favoured by the Housing Committee) or opt for redeveloping city centre sites with flats and terraces. Again it was a divide wholly redolent of 1919, further exacerbated by the indecision within central government, itself deeply divided over land use and compensation, upon which local physical reconstruction was conditional.[26]

Opposition to particular components of the Corporation's reconstruction compendium remained a latent sore for city party leaders for many years to come. One of the most vociferous of the early critics was Alderman Billy Green, who argued that the city's expansive housing plans were impractical because, without heavy subsidy, increased capital costs now placed economic rents beyond the reach of working-class tenants. Green instead proposed that housing provision be left to the private sector.[27] Such a radical sentiment—in opposition to the strong inter-war emphasis on municipal provision—could only expect limited support even from the Conservative benches. Green, however, was not a Tory. Until 1943, he had been a long-standing and senior member of the city Labour group. Now, however, he formed part of a dissident rump which campaigned, amongst other things, against aspects of the reconstruction package as an imposed product of joint Conservative-Labour hegemonic rule.

The abandonment of the 1939 and subsequent municipal elections until 1945 should have meant that the political complexion on the city council remained static. Sitting members continued in office, while those who retired or died were, by agreement, replaced by co-opted councillors of

26 Addison, *Road to 1945*, pp. 252–53; Lowe, 'War and the Welfare State', p. 165.

27 Green, speaking to AGM, Nott'm and District Property Owners' Ass., *NG*, 19 Nov. 1943.

the same political colour. Yet the war years in Nottingham also witnessed an extended and increasingly publicly aired dispute of older origins in Labour ranks. This centred on a member's individual freedom, as an elected representative, and his or her collective loyalty within and to a disciplined group structure. The party's and hierarchy's emphasis, and ultimately insistence, on the latter led finally to the expulsion of three Labour rebels. Green was one of this number. The dispute also provided the catalyst for a final, and acrimonious, campaign for representational independence. In January 1945 this culminated in a public meeting to form a new Independent municipal party, the declared aim of which was to break the allegedly dictatorial caucus machinery operated by the 'Tory-Socialist' clique that dominated municipal affairs. Present, aside from the Labour dissidents, were prominent city Liberals and other local political notables: libertarians such as Conservative Thomas Lynch, the politically fickle President and National Organiser of the Union of Small Shopkeepers, and former independents from the Nottingham Citizens' Association. In fact, although chairing the meeting, Liberals instead decided to enter into only a loose 'association' with the new 'Independents'.[28]

It was the expulsion of William Cox in September 1940 that sparked the controversy over member autonomy. Relations between the independently minded Cox and the Labour group had been strained for several years, but matters came to a head when he sought to compel male councillors and employees to join the Home Guard. Conscription, as an issue, anyway divided Labour opinion. Having not first cleared his motion to council with his colleagues (which contravened Group Standing Orders), Cox was asked to rescind it. This he resolutely refused to do. His failure to attend a disciplinary meeting sealed his fate and the whip was withdrawn. But it was his later automatic exclusion from committee office—allocations being allotted strictly according to party strength as per the inter-party agreement—which provided a focus for broader discontent. His appeal against this, supported by the one remaining Liberal but also heavily by Tory members, was narrowly lost because a number of Conservatives abstained. Armitage himself opposed any

28 *NJ*, 5 Jan. 1945, 10 Jan. 1945, 13 Jan. 1945. For an analysis of the formation of Independent parties, see W. P. Grant, '"Local" Parties in British Local Politics', *Political Studies* 19 (1971), pp. 203–04; for the broader public reaction against parties, see S. Fielding, 'The Second World War and Popular Radicalism: The Significance of the "Movement away from Party"', *History* 80 (1995), pp. 38–58.

revision, arguing against increasing committee sizes or allocating Conservative places to Cox. A vitriolic protest the following year by George Twells, on Cox's behalf, led to his subsequent exclusion from the Labour group and council committees. With the collapse of Conservative support, the campaign for committee reinstatement became increasingly volatile. Police, for example, had to be called to eject a protesting Twells from a Transport Committee meeting from which he had been debarred. Green was the last to side openly with the rebels, being finally expelled from the group in 1943 for this and 'his attitude during the last ten years'![29]

Indeed, while the dispute was ostensibly about individual freedoms within the group system, there were other roots. Cox, himself, openly personalised the conflict, ascribing its origins to past differences of opinion with Bowles. Green, too, had a history of conflict with the Labour leader dating back to the late 1920s; here a bitter disagreement between the two, when Bowles was his parliamentary agent, saw Green resign his candidature, splitting the local party in the process.[30] Bowles was a skilful but aggressive politician. Both autocratic and belligerent, this self-made entrepreneurial building contractor dominated the City Labour Party and group in a manner that provoked internal dissent. Yet it is impossible to separate the duality of Bowles's involvement as an individual and as the disciplinary instrument of collective group will. Here he had near unanimous group support, not only in the expulsions, but also in the non-allocation of Labour committee places to the dissident trio—party offices of patronage to which they were no longer entitled.

If the validity of caucus patronage was indeed the foundation of the dispute, local Conservative opinion here proved distinctly fickle. However, after four years of increasingly bitter wrangling, Armitage, as council leader, reversed his previous stand and moved for a reinstatement of the three to committee, conceding that the 'clamour' being generated was publicly undermining the 'great work' achieved by wartime co-operation. The debate in chamber is revealing, particularly for the sentiments expressed by Conservatives to party rule and the caucusing principle. Labour's views were neatly defined within the boundaries of the dispute itself. As Bowles somewhat dramatically overstated, when

29 *NJ*, 5 Dec. 1943.

30 *NJ*, 10 Nov. 1943; *NG*, 5 Dec. 1944; NAO, DDPP 7, South Nott'm Lab. Party mins, 1 May 1927, 21 July, 1927.

attacking those whom he regarded as seasoned offenders against group disciplinary structure:

> You [Armitage] and I have some difficult jobs to do. This is something too small to bother about. We are two great parties. You [the Conservatives] are fighting for a principle and we are, too. If the wheels are clogged up by people who do not run with us we get rid of them.[31]

Armitage was visibly shaken by the hostility of this sentiment. Nonetheless, Conservative opinion was openly divided. There was much rhetoric for the three to be granted committee membership to fulfil their broader electoral obligations; others thought it a purely Labour party affair. There was, however, negligible support for the apolitical ideal of an independent voice in council. The Conservative chief whip, Harry Emmony, offered the most enlightening (and honest) insight into Tory thinking:

> I have tried to make the public understand that to whatever party you belong you must have unity, or you will not get anything done. The caucus means that these men get together and agree upon what action shall be taken. Those people who have written long letters to the press should remember that. Even in a club they have a committee, and they were supposed to abide by the decision of the majority.[32]

The city's Liberal press, and its politicians, did indeed proclaim 'the principle at stake [as] one of supreme importance'. As a local editorial boomed, 'Are the Electors to rule or are the party bosses?'; it was a question of 'democratic freedom and democratic rights'.[33] It was left to Bowles and Ball, as council elders, to remind members that it was the Liberal party itself which in the past had most vigorously resisted the wider sharing of patronage.

Indeed, it is tempting to conjecture that city opinions on caucus rule varied inversely to the political fortunes of the individual parties

31 *NJ*, 5 Dec. 1944.
32 *NG*, 5 Dec. 1944.
33 *NJ*, 2 Dec. 1944.

concerned: that decline prompted internal calls for an apolitically based council. In pre-1914 Nottingham, under either Tory or particularly Liberal leadership, patronage distribution, and therefore party administrative dominance, was clearly tied to majority party governance. In gradually and formally broadening this base through the inter-war party agreements, albeit largely upon a mathematically slavish and anti-meritocratic root, greater cognisance was given to overall opinion within the council. It was this increasing diversity, or more particularly growing Labour influence at their own expense, which Liberals had strongly resisted. Indeed, individual and party interest, and specific talents, did play a part in committee patronage selection: for example, Crane's skills in construction, or Labour's penchant for health and welfare issues became, by tradition, their areas of responsibility within the allocation procedures. Nevertheless, Conservative opinion on shared committee patronage and caucus rule was of variable quality. Echoing Emmony's remarks on the value of the caucus, one colleague robustly suggested that after the 1945 municipal elections: 'when the Conservative Party were [sic] returned to power their duty was to keep that power under their [sic] own control'. Here we find strong echoes of a pre-war emphasis on restricting Labour influence within the committee structure; a belief which, although favouring a concordat of sorts, argued that 'it had worked latterly to the disadvantage of the Conservative section of the Council in regards to certain of the "plums" of office'.[34] After the party's subsequent defeats, however, this emphasis changed. Then it too publicly stressed its non-conformist structure, and particularly the greater individual freedoms of expression afforded Conservative members in the chamber. Thereafter the issue remained dormant until Conservatives once again found themselves in opposition. Labour, of course, never sought to hide its own predilection for conducting business along party lines in the chamber, although also openly subscribing to the traditions of joint patronage.

The Liberal campaign against 'the caucus' and for 'democracy' in the council chamber did little to revive the party's flagging fortunes. Independence meant abandoning its inter-war pact with the Conservatives, although local deals were still struck in seats with a tradition of Liberal representation. Electorally, however, little had changed since the inter-war period. Although four Liberals were elected in 1947, no member was to be elected in the post-war period if opposed by a Conservative candidate.

34 *NJ*, 5 Dec. 1944, 6 Dec. 1944.

And in the chamber, little separated Liberal and Tory voting habits. In 1950, the local party split. Its leader, Bill Dyer, took the Tory whip, commending Conservatism to his colleagues as a pragmatic means of defeating Socialism. For James Cottrell, the lone Liberal councillor (St Ann's Ward) by 1938, his term of office ended as it had begun—in a dispute over 'the caucus'. On occasion the lone supporter in council of the rebel three during the war, he claimed that now because he refused to 'toady' to the Conservative party machine, he was opposed by a Tory candidate who split the vote and let Labour in.[35]

The newly formed Independent party failed to contest any seats in the 1945 municipal elections, although Twells stood in the General Election of that year. Cox supported the Conservatives in 1945, stood as an Independent with Tory backing two years later, and thereafter took the Tory whip. Twells by contrast joined the Liberals—the only party, he believed, to be uncontaminated by caucus rule. Active in various local community pressure groups, he continued to campaign against 'reconstruction', and ended his career on the political fringe as a 'Vigilante' candidate (a grouping formed in 1959 to campaign against Labour's dictatorial rule) opposing the working of the inter-party agreement. Green, however, tried to rejoin the Labour party. His application and subsequent attempts to retain his committee status were blocked by Bowles, and he never stood for public office again.

The dispute over patronage did, however, prompt Bowles and Armitage immediately to renegotiate and amend the temporary concordat that governed party relationships in the war years. This was signed on 1 January 1945 (see Appendix One). Essentially, the 1945 agreement was conservative in intent. Building on, and reincorporating the consensual practices developed during the inter-war years, it sought to reinforce and transfer wartime co-operation into a period of post-war uncertainty and reconstruction. Thus, when calculating aldermanic entitlement, the weighting afforded senior members according to length of service was retained. Committee chairs and vice-chairs were again to be allocated according to party strength, as were committee places—clearly a rejection of the line favoured by those Conservatives who sought to limit Labour influence in what they assumed would be a Tory controlled council after the war. The predilection of the party leaders for continuity and consensus also found expression in other areas. The protection granted sitting

35 *NG*, 11 May 1951.

aldermen meant their automatic re-selection at the end of their six-year term of office, unless it could be shown that they were no longer engaged in 'active or material work upon or with the Corporation'. What is also striking are the procedural devices deployed through the agreement to enforce the consensual process by seeking to limit potential inter-party friction over patronage and power. Disputes over entitlement were, in the first instance, to be referred to the party leaders, who were required to act 'judicially and without reference to Party matters'. Even failure here was to be catered for: incorporated within the agreement was an external arbitration procedure to settle serious disputes, should they arise, over the interpretation of the 'true spirit' of the concordat.

That 'true spirit' is relatively easy to discern. The agreement itself specified that the majority party was entitled to choose which committees it wished to chair within the prescribed proportional arrangements. In practice, individual expertise and preferences, coupled with past precedent, continued to be the major selective determinants. In similar fashion, continuity within the committee and aldermanic structure was promoted by avoiding ad hoc changes simply to reflect variations in party strength. This added to committee autonomy by preventing undue and random party inference. Nevertheless, as an agreement between Conservatives and Labour, the concordat quite clearly cemented an existing party duopolistic control over Corporation affairs in advance of any post-war election. To avoid any repetition of the wartime debacle over committee entitlement, 'unattached members' (those belonging to neither major party) were assured of committee placements—but the selection of those places lay in the hands of the main parties. This, like those provisions which set out the governing rights of the majority party, delineates not only the consensual but also the party political root of the concordats; they remained intrinsically confidential, bilateral and hegemonic agreements about dividing political power which ran wholly counter to Liberal and press calls for a local government system run on non-party lines.

Nevertheless, their all-embracing and regulatory nature for governing, and thus limiting, disputes over patronage distribution clearly underlines the intent of both party leaders to promote harmonious inter-party relations.[36] It is possible, of course, that such an insurance was only

---

36 W. P. Grant, 'Local Councils, Conflicts and Rules of the Game', *British Journal of Political Science* 1 (1971), p. 253.

thought necessary because of local political antagonisms: in other county boroughs, inter-party relations were predominantly and successfully governed by ad hoc arrangements which lacked the formal structure or detail of those in Nottingham.[37] Such an interpretation, however, misinterprets the local situation. Elsewhere, agreement over future patronage distribution was at times specifically resisted because parties reserved the right to manipulate appointments to retain power and influence.[38] Nottingham's politicians, at a time of political uncertainty, rejected that course; instead they opted to carry forward a formalised consensual solution firmly rooted in power-sharing. Labour's dramatic municipal victory in 1945, and Bowles's resignation as Group leader two years later, prompted speculation that the party might renege on, or reinterpret, the agreement to its own advantage. No such intention was discussed within the group.[39] Six years later the agreement was renewed on almost identical terms.

37 W. Thornhill, 'Agreements between Local Political Parties in Local Government Matters', *Political Studies* 5/1 (1957), pp. 84–86—Nottingham's agreement is noted on p. 85, item v.

38 Jones, *Borough Politics*, pp. 182–83; Block, *Party Politics*, pp. 14–16.

39 *NJ*, 3 Nov. 1945; NAO LPC Box 10, Nott'm Labour Group mins, Feb.–June, 1947.

CHAPTER 3
Consensus and the Politics of Reconstruction 1945–51

Two headlines from the local press neatly sum up the results of the first post-war municipal election: 'Socialists Rule in Nottingham' testified starkly to the sea change in electoral opinion since 1938; the second, 'Labour will honour Nottingham Party Pact', bespoke continuity.[1] Nevertheless, November 1945 did mark the very obvious beginning of a new era in city politics. Here Labour, for the first time, took overall control of the council. Indeed, in an inversion of inter-war trends, the decades running from 1945 to 1966 saw Labour hold office on sixteen separate occasions. Yet the political balance was somewhat finer than these bold figures suggest. In eight of these years, fewer than five seats divided the parties; so with some sixteen seats contested annually, continuity in office was less than guaranteed. This was true particularly of the first post-war decade. As the early years of expectation gave way to ones of prolonged austerity, so Labour's fortunes also entered a period of relative but rapid decline (Table 3.1). Thus the late 1940s and early to mid-1950s in Nottingham was an era in which neither party dominated—indeed, where political majorities were rarely anything but minimal. Marginality here had a twin edged potential: to promote consensus through policy moderation and joint agreement (building on past co-operative traditions) or to evoke party chauvinism. The political inversion of 1945 likewise offered two likely, if divergent, policy sets: a primary re-ordering of civic priorities (with perhaps a subsequent defensive reaction), against a continuum of broad agreement. For if the problems of reconstruction facing the city were obvious, the solutions and emphases offered varied—particularly after initial enthusiasms faded into a haze of practicalities. This potentially volatile political cocktail was only enhanced by exogenous factors: notably the radical re-structuring of local government responsibilities (in the utilities, for example, and education). All in all, it was a potent test for the newly signed inter-party concordat.

1 *NEP*, 2 Nov. 1945; *NEN*, 2 Nov. 1945.

Undoubtedly, the key local election issue in 1945 in Nottingham, as it was nationally, was housing, with Labour emphasising a single-minded devotion to municipal construction against the broader Conservative rhetoric of deregulation and economic prudence. In practice both parties agreed to concentrate Corporation resources on resolving the housing crisis. No fundamental disagreement existed over the seriousness of total shortages, nor the deteriorating nature of the existing stock. Despite abdicating responsibility for housing save all those living with relatives or in lodgings within the city boundary (or with TB), by June 1945 there were still nearly 7,000 names on the waiting list (65 per cent of whom were ex-service personnel). Twelve months later this total had risen to 10,500 and did not finally peak (at some 12,500) until after 1951.[2] By comparison, waiting lists in the mid-1930s contained around 3,000 names, fewer than half the inter-war maximum but still judged at the time to be unacceptably high. Of these, only around two-thirds would have qualified for registration under the revised post-war criteria. Some 2,875 already condemned properties also remained to be cleared. This, however, was only the visible tip of a much larger iceberg: a 1942 survey, for example, classed around 16,500 of the city's housing stock as obsolescent—a local political *bête noire* largely ignored until the mid-1960s.

Local shortages were not the result of direct damage—fewer than 500 houses had been destroyed or rendered uninhabitable by enemy action. But in Nottingham, as elsewhere, the war years saw rapid population growth, a fall in average family size, and a significantly higher (12 per cent) rise in local marriage rates over and above a rising national mean. Consequently between 1939 and 1951 the number of private families rose by around 15,000—a figure which makes reconstruction estimates of immediate need (6,200 houses) appear wholly inadequate.[3] Local policy then, in building on the progressive dictates of its inter-war policy antecedents, and despite the claims of Nottingham's unreconstructed Tory

2 *NJ*, 5 June 1945, 16 Oct. 1945, 9 June 1951; NCC, MOH Annual Report 1947; NAO CSS 6, Nott'm Social Services Soc. Annual Report, 1946; NCC, Housing Comm. Annual Report, 1967.

3 *Registrar General's Statistical Review: 1940–45* (1946–47); author's estimate for 1939 based on extended rate of growth (allowance made for boundary changes) from 1921 and 1931–34 census figures.

old guard and of subsequent revisionist historians,[4] was pragmatic and cautionary rather than expansionary and idealistic. Nevertheless, judged by its early, yet ambitious, site preparatory programmes, the Housing Committee was eager to recommence construction. Local attempts, however, to resume large-scale construction were blocked by the Coalition government—until, that is, the general election was called.

Table 3.1 *Political parties' strength on Nottingham City Council 1945–57 after annual municipal elections*

Year	Labour	Conservative	Liberal	Independent	O/A Maj.
1945	37	24	1	2	10
1946	42	19	1	2	20
1947	36	22	4	2	8
1948[a]					
1949	33	26	4	1[b]	2
1950	30	31	3	-	0[c]
1951	31	33	-	-	2
1952	34[d]	34	-	-	0
1953	37	31	-	-	6
1954	39	29	-	-	10
1955	33	35	-	-	2
1956	36	32	-	-	4
1957	38	30	-	-	8

Notes: [a] No annual elections were held in 1948, the year the month of the elections changed. Thus elections were held in Nov. 1947 and May 1949.

[b] The Independent was Cox, who shortly after took the Conservative whip.

[c] The Conservatives were deemed to be the majority party, courtesy of Liberal support.

[d] In 1952 an independent arbitrator awarded Labour control of the council.

In late 1945 and early 1946, the Finance and General Purposes (F&GP) Committee met to select priorities from the capital reconstruction projects submitted by the various council committees. Here it was finally

4 See particularly C. Barnett, *The Audit of War: The Illusion and Reality Britain as a Great Nation* (1987 Papermac edn), pp. 242–46. Contemporary government estimates (1944) place national housing shortages at 450,000; more recent estimates range upwards from three to four million; D. A. Aldcroft, *The British Economy: The Years of Turmoil 1920–1951* (1985), pp. 230–31.

resolved to disregard any expenditure which might divert resources from the housing programme. Even then, progress remained painfully slow, absolutely and compared with other cities: by the end of 1946 only some 179 permanent corporation houses had been completed. Local political will simply proved to be an ineffectual counter to severe material and labour shortages. Here, for example, only one-seventh of the local building labour force was engaged on corporation housing, with a similar number working in the speculative and authorised housing repairs sectors (or about half in total of those supposedly employed on housing work). Most of the 'surplus' labour was thought to be engaged in more lucrative unlicensed housing repairs. Equally irritating to the Housing Committee were the large numbers working on local major government contracts covered by Essential Works Orders—which Crane and city officials thought to be singularly less than essential to immediate post-war needs. In particular, they cited the one thousand men (including fifty per cent of all local bricklayers) working on a new headquarters for the Post Office Savings Bank. Scheduled work carried guaranteed earnings payments, particularly attractive at times of acute materials shortages, but which local authorities were reluctant to offer as they sought to restrict costs.[5]

The Housing Committee's response, albeit it a reluctant one, was to turn to systems building, to benefit from its economy in skilled labour and use of alternative materials. The decision to accept 1,000 temporary 'prefab' homes, popular with tenants but described by one senior member as 'little better than dog kennels', had already split the Committee. Shortages, however, dictated that every avenue be explored and they went on to order a further 2,100 steel framed permanent units—900 fewer than intended originally before demand again outstripped supply. Crane was almost apologetic over the purchase; his reservations, particularly over site erection times, being fully justified as the nominated contractors fell so seriously behind schedule that finally the Corporation cancelled the contract. Nevertheless, the Ministry and its regional staff, in offering special grants, allocations and coordinating spare capacities, remained firmly wedded to promoting systems technology—part of an overall strategy to double non-traditional housing production to a level accounting

5 *Fifth Report Select Comm. Estimates*, PP (1945–46), Mins of Evidence, pp. 148–49, 160–72; A. Cairncross, *Years of Recovery: British Economic Policy 1945–51* (1987 Edn.), pp. 337, 395–97.

for half of public sector construction.[6] Again, the reasons for this are easily understood. Across the country, productivity in the speculative sector continually ran ahead of that for local authority projects, as contractors transferred resources to minimise delays on capital invested. On corporation sites in Nottingham, where slow completion rates remained a perennial concern, local builders were anyway fully employed on traditional schemes.[7] So the prompt completion of early projects employing the then under-utilised 'no-fines' technology led the Committee to negotiate a series of extended major contracts with George Wimpey to build two-thirds of its new 7,000 unit Clifton estate. Cost, too, bore favourable comparison with conventionally built brick and other factory-based systems housing, a fact overlooked by at least one housing historian when assessing 'the failure' of post-war pre-fabrication methods.[8]

Primarily, however, it was the sheer scale of the housing waiting list which prompted an increasing reliance on no-fines systems, with overall productivity rates on corporation sites only noticeably improving with the commencement of several large-scale no-fines contracts after 1951. Yet if the pragmatic attraction to 'the speed with which these [no-fines] houses are erected' overcame many reservations within the Committee itself, there remained a vociferous body of external opinion which condemned this departure. This was particularly true of an unholy alliance of economic interests between craft unionism and local contractors, both of whom drew on limited support within the council. Through the 1950s it was the local Trades Council which led demands for a public enquiry into the hidden scandal of 'gerrymandering', 'scamping' and a general lowering of 'standards of craftsmanship' at Clifton, while on a broader front, the Corporation was accused of creating a 'soulless, heartless

6 *NJ*, 5 June 1945, 30 Nov. 1945; NCC Housing mins, Sept. 1946–Sept. 1948, *passim*; Min. of Health, *Housing Programme for 1947* (Cmd 7021), PP (1946–47); P. M. Johnson, 'The Regional Housing Organisation of the Ministry of Local Government and Planning', *Public Administration* 29 (1951), pp. 237–45.

7 S. Merrett, *Owner-Occupation in Britain* (1982), p. 22; Morgan, *Labour in Power*, p. 165; NCC, Housing Comm. mins, 8 Sept. 1950, 8 Dec. 1950, 12 Jan. 1951.

8 S. Merrett, *State Housing in Britain* (1979), p. 241; Direct comparisons are difficult because of the scale, and cross-subsidy, of no-fines operations. Nevertheless, for comparably sized contracts, initially no-fines housing offered savings up to £130.00 per unit over traditional build. Claims for extras also compared very favourably; NCC, Report of Housing Comm., 23 Nov. 1948, 11 Feb. 1949, 10 June 1949, 11 Nov. 1949, 13 Feb. 1953; NCC, Housing mins, 12 Sept. 1952, 14 Nov. 1952, 14 Aug. 1953.

dormitory, devoid of amenities, of uncomfortable, badly heated houses'. Yet if 'general standards of urban design had fallen', an internal enquiry also argued that maintenance costs at Clifton were no higher than on other estates, and a majority of members and officers alike continued to see mass housing techniques as the only practicable solution to the city's shortages.[9]

*

Perhaps surprisingly, the early preoccupation with the housing problem, epitomised by the F&GP Committee's near unanimously endorsed ruling on post-war objectives, was also to have an immediately divisive impact on council policy making, and ultimately committee autonomy, group discipline and inter-party relations. In party terms, Labour adopted a simplistic–almost blinkered–stance on housing that operated to the detriment of the broader objectives outlined in the 1943 Reconstruction Report. Conservatives, by contrast, never engaged in this exclusivity, either when electioneering or within the chamber. Specifically, a single-minded concentration on housing raised the spectre of divided loyalties within the Labour group. The issue at point was whether committee chairs owed an unquestioning (or inflexible) obligation to group objectives which overrode their traditional, and in many cases long-standing, loyalty to committee decisions taken in the inter-party tradition.

A useful test case and marker soon presented itself. The council had for a number of years sought to improve its eighty-years-old College of Arts and Crafts; the Reconstruction Report itself had noted 'the need for remedying [these] handicaps', housed as it was in an 'old and inadequate building'. In December 1945 the Education Committee sought to compulsorily purchase and convert an adjacent factory site to provide much needed basic facilities. Conservatives argued for adequate technical education in an area where student numbers were rising rapidly. Crane himself proposed that a high priority be afforded to developing design expertise upon which the city's lace and textile industries depended.

9 For example, NCC, Report Housing Comm., 10 Nov. 1950; NUMD, TrM Box 2, J. Charlesworth, 'Statement in Respect of the Construction and Installation Work on Certain Council Houses', 1957; *Ibid*, Letter from Martin to Chair Housing Comm., 19 Aug. 1957; Digest of ATV Programme 'Paper Talk', 19 Feb. 1958; Smith and Whysall, 'Nottingham Local Authority Housing', p. 41.

Labour members of the Committee took a similar line in defending the proposals before full council, calling on objectors to inspect the atrocious conditions for themselves. Bowles, however, with majority group support, rejected such pleas. Its construction, he argued, would dilute the housing drive, and while educational expenditure had second call on the Corporation's purse, this should be limited to the primary and secondary sectors, not to the provision of 'luxury training'.[10]

The choice of words is immediately revealing as a local commentary on Labour attitudes to industrial regeneration; although critical judgement should be tempered because the extension received all party support three years later. Equally instructive were the attitudes struck by Labour Education Committee members—many of whom either abstained or voted against their own party line. This was not simply a matter of political leaning. Both the Committee's chair, Walter Halls (an NUR official notorious throughout the inter-war period as a Labour radical) and a senior contemporary, Robert Shaw (an ex-Liberal and lace manufacturer), here publicly opposed Labour group policy, placing committee loyalty and personal belief first. Through the late 1940s Halls continued to promote Education reports which ran counter to the group's housing doctrine, and which, given the party's majority, were destined to be defeated.[11]

However, the tide was beginning to turn. Rather than publicly split the party, increasingly Labour committee chairs bowed to the group disciplinary line, or as a last resort, withdrew reports if committee and group policy conflicted. It was this latter course which Halls took in 1951, when the council met to discuss the construction of a new technical college. Like the Arts College five years before, the project was anticipated in the wartime reconstruction report. Development plans were formalised in 1948, as part of the authority's five-year plan for further education prepared at Whitehall's behest. This reasoned that, although the existing premises were 'totally inadequate', 'the shortage of buildings, and the difficulties in present circumstances of obtaining building priority for educational projects' meant that a new college in the near future was unlikely. When, however, control of the council passed to the Conservatives, the project was resurrected. Not surprisingly, the Labour group continued to oppose a scheme which, they maintained, would drain

10 *NJ*, 4 Dec. 1945.
11 NAO LPC Box 10, Labour Group mins, 31 Jan. 1947; *NG*, 4 Feb. 1947.

the local building labour market at a time when the city's housing programme was again falling behind schedule. Again Crane rejected such arguments. In utilising different forms of construction (steel frame and stone cladding), he suggested, it would not attract labour from the Corporation's housing sites. Halls was again instructed by the group to withdraw the Education Committee's report.[12] This time he attempted to comply, although Conservative absenteeism allowed Labour instead formally to defeat the proposal.

Halls's decision totally surprised the Conservative leadership. Never in living memory, it was recalled, 'had an attempt been made to withdraw a report standing on the agenda without the leader of the opposite Party being informed in advance of what was proposed'.[13] That Halls agreed to adopt this course contrasted sharply with his own recent behaviour as a notable Labour exponent of placing committee autonomy before group authority. This camouflaged deception, intended to prevent Conservative whips from mobilising their own support that night, broke the long-standing traditions of informal inter-party co-operation over the conduct and organisation of business in the chamber. Etiquette was further breached when William Sharp, Labour's Deputy Lord Mayor who was temporarily chairing the meeting, cast his own decisive vote against the report. Although a not unknown occurrence in the 1920s, tradition more recently dictated that the presiding civic member remain strictly neutral in debate and decision making. However, political opportunism that day was evenly distributed. Several Labour members, as council tenants, found themselves temporarily disenfranchised from voting on an equally controversial proposal to increase housing rents. Appeals for a deferment to allow voting dispensations to be obtained evoked little sympathy from the Conservative benches, and it is in the light of this that Labour's infraction of agreed co-operative behaviour is better judged.

Indeed, violation of inter-party custom and practice amounted to little more than a subtle disruptive trend up to 1951. By far the majority of committee reports were passed with the agreed support of both parties and without formal dissent. More immediately local political pundits openly commented on the initial lack of vigorous debate on matters of policy, attributing this to the poor quality of a Conservative opposition unfamiliar

---

12 NCC, *Scheme of Further Education and Plan for County Colleges* (1948), pp. 4, 15; NAO LPC Box 10, Labour Group mins, 29 Dec. 1950.

13 *NJ*, 2 Jan. 1951.

with its new role rather than to post-war consentience. Conservatives, nonetheless, suggested that there were now few locally initiated policies upon which the parties disagreed violently, particularly when much of Corporation activity was determined centrally by Westminster. Yet the revival, from mid-1946, of a more adversarial heritage in council debate itself provides an inaccurate yardstick by which to measure fundamental policy disagreement. Here, disputes most frequently arose over trivial items, unrelated to the underlying substance of an already predetermined and agreed policy which filtered largely unhindered through the joint-party committee structure.[14] Rhetorical interludes, although undoubtedly highlighting underlying political perspectives, had little bearing on overall municipal strategy.

The most obvious civic scheme to arouse Tory displeasure was a new sewage treatment plant costing some one million pounds—opposed on the traditional grounds of inopportune and unnecessary financial extravagance! Labour, however, seeing an obvious linkage between housing expansion and sewage disposal, backed the proposal (which had been under discussion since 1936) and which was now being pressed vigorously by the Conservative committee chair, Arthur Savage. That political division arose over public spending, particularly on large capital projects, should not be ignored. Yet these divergences represented a different and temporary ordering of immediate priorities, highlighted in an era of post-war shortages and large-scale need. Essentially both parties accepted the rationale behind each committee's recommendations. Thus it was that all three projects (the College of Arts, technical college and new sewage works) were eventually sanctioned in line with the earlier 1943 reconstruction report.

Inter-party agreement, however, was not always wholly reflective of a broader consensual impetus outside the chamber. We have already noted that Conservatives tended towards a more catholic view of the city's future economic and social requirements when set against Labour's 'absolutism' on housing—which more closely mirrored local concerns and preoccupations if judged by local and national polls from the period.[15] However, even Labour's position in practice was considerably less

14 *NJ*, 2 July 1946, 6 Dec. 1948; *NG*, 1 Nov. 1946.

15 See local survey organised by Norman Smith, MP, *NJ*, 8 July 1947; BIPO, *Political Quarterly* 16 (Autumn, 1945), p. 379; R. B. Macullum and A. Readman, *The British Election of 1945* (1964 edn), p. 237.

mechanical than its rhetoric of continual self-justification suggests. The most notable example was the decision, taken in late 1945, quickly to improve the city's communications infrastructure. Accordingly, the council's permission was sought to promote a parliamentary bill to complete the inner ring road system. Just why Bowles particularly chose to pursue this course, which ran counter to his other publicly expressed sentiments on housing primacy, remains a matter for speculation. In 1943 the council had decided that the project was to be afforded a high post-war priority in response to Nottingham's chronic city centre traffic congestion.[16] Such benchmarks, of course, had not prevented Bowles opposing similar projects. Indeed, despite assurances to the contrary from council members—and again Crane in particular—opponents of the road scheme were quick to focus on and exploit local fears that resources would be diverted from the housing drive. This was exactly the same utilitarian argument deployed by Labour when opposing plans to improve technical education. Moreover, the ring road proposals meant actually demolishing existing property at a time of severe shortage: when, for example, city slum dwellers were disbarred from registering for rehousing because they already had a home. Bowles's advocacy is best traced through his own history of championing similar road improvements against considerable opposition during the inter-war years. Perhaps, equally, he assumed that this new improvement could likewise be driven through. Indeed, that Bowles succeeded in mobilising bi-party support for the project, with all but one member backing the proposal, is indicative of his personal, and frequently decisive, influence within his own group, and, overall, of the authority vested in senior members of both parties within the caucus system. Outside the chamber, however, post-war pressures now dictated a less than reverent reception for the dictates of Nottingham's planners and politicians.

The promotion of a private parliamentary bill, by which local authorities acquired additional powers, was a flexible but initially complicated device requiring (in the case of borough or urban councils) both the now granted approval of a majority of the council and formal consultation with the electorate. Accordingly, therefore, the Corporation publicised its proposals in order to confer with its citizenry and consider objections. This 'town meeting', open to all voters, backed the proposals. Opponents, however, were not so easily silenced. Accusing city leaders

16 NCC, Reconstruction Comm. Report, pp. 11–12.

of imposing a straightjacket on debate at the meeting the better to overrule dissenting opinion, campaigners now demanded a 'town poll'—a local plebiscite of all voters. To do this they required a petition of one hundred local signatories. In the event, those calling for a vote numbered some three-hundred and polling day was set for 16 January 1946.

It was the self-appointed 'Houses First Committee' that organised both this petition and the subsequent campaign. Although declaratively apolitical, this was far from the case; its active support came principally from those Liberals and others prominent in launching the 'Independent Party' twelve months previously.[17] Bowles, using Labour party and Co-operative Society's resources, contested the Corporation's case as if fighting a municipal election, distributing over 18,000 leaflets, and organising street canvassing and loudspeaker vans. There is little doubt that he took the temporary thwarting of the scheme as a personal slight to his own authority. Nevertheless, despite the resources and prestige invested in the Corporation's name, popular support rested squarely with the dissenters, with electors voting 5:2 in favour of rejecting the new inner ring road.[18]

In itself the result is more interesting as a commentary on the operating rationale of city politics than for revealing well-established popular priorities. Nevertheless, that neither party successfully gauged the extent of hostility is surprising, particularly in Labour's case given its politically attuned rhetoric on housing primacy. In fact it was strictly neither an oversight nor a local example of the contemporary cult for enforced technocratic planning. Its derivation lay with semi-authoritarian civic imposition, generically rooted in the 'city father' tradition where personal prestige and authority were vested in, and exercised by, leading council members. In nineteenth-century Nottingham, local political leadership had been exercised by a self-governing, and largely self-renewing, social elite of Liberal manufactures:[19] now authority was expressed 'democratically' through the party machine by senior members. In this case, the proposals to complete the inner ring road scheme formed an addendum to a prestigious infrastructural scheme initiated before the

17 *NG*, 12 Jan. 1946.

18 Votes cast were 4,029 for, and 10,706 against (seven per cent turnout), *NG*, 17 Jan. 1946.

19 R. A. Church, *Economic and Social Change in a Midland Town: Victorian Nottingham 1815–1900* (1966), pp. 205–06, 218–20.

war. It was this vision that Bowles, and other senior members, still sought to complete.

One supposed safeguard against the imposition of unpopular policy from above lay in the mechanism of truly local representation: councillors, it was argued, because they lived amongst the community, were sensitive to, and reflective of, parochial sentiment.[20] Contemporary local Liberal and Independent opinion—notably that at the heart of the 'Houses First' campaign—ridiculed this view on the very grounds that the city's politics were dominated by a bi-polar, party-orientated dual caucus which overrode local views. Town polls and meetings were also designed to ensure adequate consultation and protect local democracy. However, nationally the system had fallen into disrepute and its abolition sought, primarily because of the cost, the delays involved and a series of well publicised exceedingly low turnout rates. Nottingham's politicians collectively certainly felt justified in attempting to ignore the result, believing their own views to be more objective and public criticism of their strategy flawed. Thus in 1951, with housing waiting lists still rising, the now Conservative-controlled council (but again with all party support) sought to overturn the objections. This time the opposition was better organised and the assembled town meeting rejected the plan. Nevertheless, the council pressed ahead in seeking a referendum to vindicate its position. A full seventeen per cent of eligible voters responded, voting 13:2 against the proposals and trebling the opposition poll.[21] Subsequently, and with little good grace, council members were forced to shelve the plan indefinitely. Clearly those who campaigned against the road scheme were unable to command popular support at municipal elections, particularly on a platform of opposition to the oligarchic domination of local affairs by the two-party system. Nevertheless, on two, albeit very specific, occasions, they were able successfully to mobilise community-based opinion against its perceived governance. It was no coincidence, however, that the issue here was housing: the mobilising focus of reconstruction objectives, of post-war inter-party co-operation and, both negatively and positively in terms of providing policy constraint, the popular foundation for a broader community consensus.

Indeed to speak of a broader unifying consensus here itself requires specific and positive qualification set against certain defining spatial,

20 See K. Newton, *Second City Politics*, esp. chs 1, 2 and 6.
21 Votes cast were 4,780 for, and 30,767 against; *NG*, 25 Jan. 1952.

chronological and sectional parameters. That housing should be considered a unifying factor runs counter to recent interpretations of national bi-party policy and antagonisms. Thus for Lowe, 'housing policy enjoyed little wartime consensus and remained throughout the post-war years at the heart of party conflict'—in part because of this very, and continuing, popular interest and concern.[22] This only adds value to that consensus operating in Nottingham. More obviously, the consensus over local need (and the responses this elicited) was self-defining geographically. As will become apparent, this was perhaps even more true because of concurrent national shortages generally, which strengthened parochial competition between centres, as it did between sectional interests putting forward their own, sometimes conflicting, demands.

One unfortunate consequence of inter-party agreement over municipal housing provision before 1939 was a severe post-war shortage of building land, which left sufficient only for some 5,000 of the anticipated 18,500 houses required. Long-term, the solution remained inextricably linked to an expansion of the city boundaries (finally accomplished in 1951) —the Corporation being naturally reluctant to build on land for which it received no rateable income. More immediately, steps were taken before the war's end, to purchase—compulsorily and from speculative builders where necessary—much of what land remained. Not surprisingly, this stimulated division, the Tory free-marketeering rump objecting vigorously to Corporation attempts to monopolise land ownership. It was with the equally controversial purchase in early 1946 of the substantial 944 acre site at Clifton, then outside the city's southern boundary, that the Corporation believed its most immediate problems had been resolved. This, however, proved to be a premature conclusion.

As we have seen, the construction methods adopted at Clifton were to irritate the economic interests of crafts trade unionism and those local builders excluded effectively from tendering, and raise political doubts over the aesthetic and social consequences of mass housing techniques. Initially, however, objections came primarily from outside Nottingham, for internally the consensus over housing need overrode partisanship. Externally, however, city needs cut little purchase with those neighbouring authorities in whom the granting of planning permission was vested. An appeal to the Ministry of Town and Country Planning proved

22 R. Lowe, *The Welfare State in Britain since 1945* (1993), p.235; H. Pelling, *The Labour Governments 1945–51* (1984), pp. 108–13.

an equally fruitless avenue, primarily because of the agricultural value of the land and the lack of access across the river Trent.[23] This threw city planning into a temporary crisis: by 1948 there was only sufficient land in Nottingham to build a further 3,500 houses set against a waiting list of some 12,000. The Corporation, therefore, had little option but to re-apply for permission to develop Clifton. After some delay, ministers decided to re-convene a public enquiry; its task being not so much to pass judgement on good planning practice but to arbitrate between largely pre-determined and competing interests.

Ranged against the Corporation, besides neighbouring authorities, were the National Farmers' Union and local Agricultural Executive, various rural preservation societies, the Ministry of Planning itself and the Association for Planning and Regional Reconstruction—all of whom favoured developing other sites for Nottingham's overspill. For the same reason the Coal Board supported the application because the alternatives meant sacrificing coal-bearing areas to the north and west of Nottingham.[24] Not all positions were as predictable. Although now opposed to the city's plans, the county council had earlier signified its willingness to withdraw objections if the city likewise abandoned its boundary extension application, allowing the additional rates revenue to accrue to itself.

The crux of the dispute rested on whether other more suitable land was indeed available immediately. Both political parties in Nottingham openly backed the Clifton proposal as agreed policy. City representatives were, therefore, wholly taken aback to find four recently elected Conservative city councillors appearing against them before the enquiry. Here they argued not only for other sites but forcefully restated the right's traditional proposition for the building of city centre flats and terraces (to increase housing density and also address the acknowledged problem of unit under-occupation) to replace the now locally enshrined principle of the garden city suburban estate. Other objectors pointed to the unique and unspoilt rural character of Clifton village, a codicil apparently inapplicable to other self-contained communities put forward for sacrifice.

23 PRO HLG 79/501, Note of Discussion between Powell, Spray and Beltram, 19 Nov. 1947.

24 NCC, Housing Comm. mins, 8 July 1948; PRO HLG 107/136, Min. T&CP Inter-Dept. Planning mins, 18 Aug. 1948; see also PRO HLG 79/501, meeting of Assistant Commissioner and Regional Officers, 20 Nov. 1947.

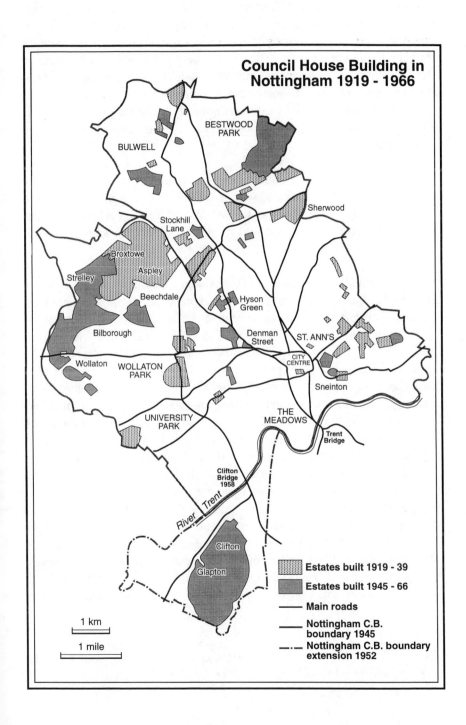

Council House Building in Nottingham 1919 - 1966

BESTWOOD PARK

BULWELL

Sherwood

Stockhill Lane

Broxtowe

Strelley

Aspley

Beechdale

Hyson Green

Bilborough

Denman Street

ST. ANN'S

Wollaton

WOLLATON PARK

CITY CENTRE

Sneinton

UNIVERSITY PARK

THE MEADOWS

Trent Bridge

Clifton Bridge 1958

River Trent

Clifton

Glapton

1 km

1 mile

Estates built 1919 - 39

Estates built 1945 - 66

Main roads

Nottingham C.B. boundary 1945

Nottingham C.B. boundary extension 1952

On pragmatic grounds, the Corporation argued, immediate need ruled out the further delays caused by the compulsory acquisition of new sites. It was, according to the inspector conducting the enquiry, a particularly interesting but extremely complicated problem that could only be resolved after conflicting ministerial interests had been determined. This, unfortunately, was to take some considerable time.

Crane, in his evidence, expressed nothing but contempt for his four fellow Tory members. From the beginning of the discussions on Clifton, he concluded:

> Approval had been unanimous. The matter was raised last week and there was no vote against it ... The very first intimation I had about this opposition was to-day. Would you expect any member of the City Council, without notice, to come here and oppose? If this is not the work of a traitor, what is?[25]

Indeed, mimicking the line of Tom Owen (Deputy Town Clerk) in discrediting the rebels' testimony as representative of city political division, Crane later called on 'everyone who really wants houses to be built to vote solidly' for a motion of censure subsequently moved by Labour.[26] Here it was charged that the four Tory rebels (Hanson, Ball, Rook and Sellars) sought to prevent the Clifton development because they themselves all lived comfortably and/or to the south of the city's boundary. Defending themselves amid charges of 'filibustering', the rebels first asserted that the Housing Committee had been negligent in its search for other sites and in rejecting alternatives to suburban development. As they spoke, most members expressed their displeasure by adjourning for early tea! However, finally the four moved that their actions were justified in terms of 'the strict dictates of their conscience'. Thus the rights and wrongs of the deception to which Crane and Owen, for example, took strong exception were cast aside in favour of a member's right 'to have a little free speech'.[27] This was a party amendment to which Tories and Liberals could, and did, rally; for it was a central, if largely erroneous, propaganda claim of the 1940s and 1950s that a great disciplinary divide separated Labour and Conservative group voting practice. Nevertheless,

25 *NG*, 15 July 1949; for a detailed outline of the evidence see, *NG*, 15–22 July 1949.
26 NCC, Council mins, 25 July 1949; *NG*, 26 July 1949.
27 *Ibid.*

that amendment narrowly defeated, the original motion of censure was then passed easily. Crane, despite a public commitment to vote with Labour, finally abstained. A majority of Conservative members, also inwardly unhappy with the rebels' conduct, followed this lead or voted with Labour.[28]

As an indicator of disciplinary practice, the debate offers some insight into the workings of each party machine. Although supposedly subject to a free vote, the Labour whip at least was in place—although this probably made little difference to the way votes were cast. On the Conservative benches, also, the call for party over personal loyalty was largely heeded. Thus, as one local political commentator remarked, the debate over Clifton underlined that for either group 'there is little difference between a Party vote with the whips on and a so-called free vote.'[29] Nevertheless, had the four been Labour members, their reward for opposing agreed policy would more likely have been expulsion than the public support of their colleagues. In that sense, here, and on other occasions, Conservative members exercised greater freedoms than their Labour counterparts. This was no doubt partly because of their contrasting backgrounds of social and workplace independence, when set against the working-class delegatory traditions of collective obedience within the labour movement. Even here, however, a word of qualification is necessary. Sporadically, as noted, Labour members also prefaced group loyalty with an overriding commitment to committee decisions. In the years that followed, both parties were to become increasingly regimented as political divisions widened. Transitionally, this prompted spasmodic rebellion within the Labour group, as certain senior members held to the belief that, on occasion, their own perception of city interests overrode considerations of party obedience. Nevertheless, individualism remained more a Conservative than Labour group trait, albeit one with a stronger rhetorical base than one exercised in practice.

At the close of the Clifton enquiry, the Ministry promised a prompt decision. After six months had passed, Crane determined to bring matters to a head by publicly proclaiming the consequences of further delays. As he explained:

28 The final vote was 25:10, with two Conservatives voting with Labour and 11 abstaining.

29 NAO LPC Box 10, Lab. Group mins, 22 July 1949; *NJ*, 26 July 1949, 27 July 1949.

We have received an allocation from the Ministry of Health of 1,200 houses for 1950 but we have land on which to build only about 200. When these houses are erected, house building in Nottingham will come to a complete stop.[30]

Owen went further. Even if permission was granted immediately, he argued, the city was still unlikely to meet its building targets for 1950 or 1951; a consequence of the lead-time required for site development work and the temporary dislocation to the Corporation's management apparatus caused by the break in continuity. Essentially, these prophecies proved to be correct (Table 3.2). Even the stimulus provided by the 'no-fines' system failed to raise production to meet overall targets between 1950 and 1952. Final approval for Clifton was granted in January 1951, it being reluctantly acknowledged by the Ministry that only with 'large scale development on one site' could Nottingham hope to match present and future completion targets.[31] Permission, however, was conditional on the site being developed at a high density. This was only possible with the inclusion of terraces and flats, which ran counter both to Corporation plans to construct a 'show estate' and its long-standing housing policy. Although later negotiations somewhat eased density specifications, the Corporation was to come under increasing pressure to raise density levels on future sites by offering similar solutions. It was a course of action resolutely resisted by the Housing Committee, but one which it was eventually forced to adopt. It was also made clear that immediate steps must be taken to secure less agriculturally valuable land for future projects. That this was achieved with relative ease (at Bestwood and Strelley) suggests that, if alternatives had been pursued earlier, disruption to the city's housing programme could have been minimised. Neither site, however, was ideal. Indeed, the 535 acres at Bestwood had been purchased earlier by the National Coal Board specifically to prevent surface interference with underground development and prevent costly subsidence claims. On both, however, housing construction was to be subsequently phased with mining activity to alleviate damage.

30 *NJ*, 25 Jan. 1950; NCC, Housing Comm. mins, 9 Dec. 1949.
31 Letter from Ministry of Town and Country Planning, 27 Jan. 1951, reprinted in *NJ*, 30 Jan. 1951.

Table 3.2 *Post-war annual dwelling completions in Nottingham*

Year ending 31 March	By Corporation	By Private Enterprise	Total
1946	179[a]	31[b]	210
1947	625[a]	232	857
1948	1145[a]	482	1627
1949	1346	189	1535
1950	692	252	944
1951	786	205	991
1952	740	257	997
1953	1534	309	1843
1954	1292	323	1615
1955	1450	402	1852
1956	1045	367	1412
1957	1187	247	1434
1958	815	277	1092
1959	828	260	1088
1960	851	509	1360
1961	722	486	1208
1962	842	349[b]	1191
1963	391	250[b]	641
1964	453	268[b]	721
1965	635	555[b]	1190
1966	670[c]	493[b]	1163
Total	18228	6743	2497100

Notes: [a] Figures inc. a total of 1,000 temporary houses.
  [b] Totals incorporate just under 400 flats.
  [c] Inc. 18 dwellings constructed by a Housing Association.

Sources: NCC, *Annual Epitome of Accounts* Years Ending 1946-56, 1958-66; NCC Annual Reports of the General Works and Highways Committee Year Ending 1946-66; *Housing Returns for England and Wales, Appendix B*, 1946-66.

*

Labour had accused the Clifton rebels of placing personal and sectional interests before those of the city. That this call was acknowledged on the Conservative benches, albeit partially, suggests that members did place weight on bi-partisan appeals to civic loyalties which to degrees cut across the political and social ties naturally promoted by the presence of a well-developed party system. It was a feature of this period that disagreement on key issues, where it occurred, was normally short-lived, that an air of compromise—an essential ingredient for consensus—prevailed. 'Dispensing with political differences ... where the interests of the city were concerned', according to a senior Conservative Alderman, was founded on the distribution of patronage 'without question or dispute, on an equitable party basis.'[32] It was this shared perception of municipal interests which, with agreement over patronage, formed the foundation of city consensus. Nevertheless, this did not prevent even minor or personalised squabbles from acquiring a heavy, if temporary, garnish of party political acidity if it was thought to advance the party cause. This was especially true within the robust atmosphere of the debating chamber. Here the immediate contradictions of a system which alternately sought to marginalise party political considerations within an inherited structure of shared committee responsibility, yet in practice frequently condoned advantages sought for party gain, are most readily exposed. As one bewildered Labour committee vice-chair complained, when facing orchestrated Tory criticism against alleged extravagances during a trip to inspect the Paris abattoir system:

> I am sure that all right-minded members of this council of all Parties will deplore this [criticism] with me. I completely fail to understand how this can be made a Party matter in view of my statement that this was a committee decision.[33]

Yet such contradictions, however temporarily destabilising, could be and were overridden because of this very espoused commitment to the principles and responsibilities of joint government. In this case, the Conservative committee chair vigorously supported his bemused Labour colleague against several members of his own party, precisely because of his own allegiance to that traditional committee ethos.

In part, the cause of local civic consensus was helped because national political policy was considered an inappropriate focus for formal debate. So central, however, were the structural changes in local government responsibilities in the post-war years that total abstinence was neither possible nor likely. This was particularly true of the nationalisation of past municipal utilities. The transfer of the city's profitable gas and electricity

32 *NEP*, 14 Oct. 1948; *NJ*, 15 Oct. 1948.
33 *NJ*, 8 Nov. 1949.

enterprises to central control provoked persistent outbursts for many years from Conservatives that Labour members had capitulated to the dictates of Whitehall on terms that were little better than 'legalised theft'—particularly as the utilities yielded some £86,500 annually towards rates relief.[34] Labour members, whatever their personal views on the compensation terms, balked at formally condemning their own government's policy on an issue for which many, anyway, had campaigned vigorously. Outside the chamber, however, some were more forthright. Speaking in London before an audience from the Association of Municipal Corporations, Bowles was bitterly critical:

> The terms on which the Government are proposing to take these industries away from us are most unfair and something we ought not to tolerate. They are taking millions of pounds worth of assets away from us and giving nothing in return. I don't mind what Government it is, but anyone who attempts to do anything to the mass of the ratepayers should be fought.[35]

Under strong pressure, the compensation terms were eventually to be improved, although never matching those offered private companies and certainly not amounting to the 'full reimbursement' which 'mollified' opposition claimed by Morgan. Nottingham's Electricity Department's assets, for example, were valued at some £9.4 million at cost in 1949, for which in compensation the city received the cancellation of its nett loan debt of £3.9 million, plus an ex gratia payment of £80,000. That year alone, electricity sales had subsidised the rates to the extent of £65,000, plus a contribution to central establishment charges and gains from tax relief. It was hardly surprising that even the modified terms offered provoked local Conservative hostility, just as they stretched Labour loyalty.[36]

Although called upon to explain his comments, Bowles had the support of senior Labour party spokesmen and many of his group when echoing past Fabian traditions for municipal, rather than national, control of local

34 NOA DDPP 2/1, Nott'm South Con. Ass. mins (AGM), 1 July 1948; Nott'm Conservative Ass., *Nottingham Citizen*, 1950 Municipal Election edn; *NJ*, 4 Feb. 1947.

35 *NJ*, 4 Feb. 1947.

36 Morgan, *Labour in Power*, p. 103; for a full breakdown, see C. N. Chester, *The Nationalisation of British Industry* (1975), pp. 316–30; NCC, *Epitome of Accounts*, 1948–53.

utilities. His remarks clearly identified his own underlying political priorities: foremost a fiercely independent loyalty to his perception of collective city interests which was shared by senior colleagues in the years surrounding 1945. In fact, the concept of placing municipal commercial interest before ideological dogma was ably illustrated shortly before the war when the Labour group had supported Conservative moves to purchase gas supplies from private manufacturers. It was a financial pragmatism which had split the local party, and led to unsuccessful calls (eventually taken to national conference) for a return to the system where party delegates, not the Labour group, controlled the implementation of municipal policy.[37]

It would also be simplistically inaccurate to identify the major difference between the parties as one resting wholly on their individual propensity to raise and spend public revenue, as the debates over post-war housing well indicate. Nevertheless, as the 1938 rates dispute also readily indicates, there was a comparative yet underlying philosophical Conservative resistance to Corporation expenditure which expressed itself in a variety of ways beyond that purely of differing priorities. The annual budget debate revealed such disagreement at its most rhetorically obvious. In fact, the council's expenditure estimates were subject to the deliberations of an inter-party sub-committee, albeit one on which the majority party had the greater voice. Because of the cross-party nature of the discussion, custom dictated that, when in opposition, even Labour members were offered a free vote or were requested to abstain in the budget debate. In 1949, the Conservatives broke this tradition by moving an amendment to reduce the proposed rate by one shilling. More usually, Tory opposition to Labour's post-war budgets was purely vocal, limited to arguing that either Conservative efficiency and business expertise would have undercut the rate being set, or that the Socialist taxation levels being proposed 'seriously impinged' upon personal liberty.[38]

These two views fairly summarised much that continued to underpin local Conservative thinking. Education, listed by both parties in 1945 as second only to housing as an expenditure priority, was not excluded from this attack. Debating the annual education report in 1948, speaker after

37 Interview with Fred Orton, 12 April 1989; NOA LPC Box 10, Lab. Group mins, 31 Jan. 1947; W. A. Robson, 'Labour and Local Government', *Political Quarterly* 24 (1953), pp. 39–55; *Report of the 38th Annual Conference of the Labour Party: Southport 1939 Conference Report* (1939), p. 221.
38 *NG*, 6 April 1948; *NJ*, 4 April 1950.

speaker rose from the Conservative benches to denounce the unacceptably high, but still rising, cost of educational provision which threatened to bankrupt both individual ratepayers and the business community. Liberals supported this view. Arguing that present policies were overtly egalitarian, their leader declared:

> You cannot give the same facilities for children of secondary school education to compete for places in the universities as those enjoyed by children who have the privilege of being educated at public schools.[39]

In practice, the aims of the Education Committee were far from an exercise in utopian social engineering. Of the four-fold expansion in the school capital programme that year (rising to £242,000), sixty per cent was allocated to the primary sector to meet demographic change, with less than thirteen per cent being spent on the secondary sector. Expenditure priorities in the five years from 1949 broadly retained this emphasis, with 43 per cent going to the primary sector, although in the latter years secondary and further educational provision expanded exponentially to meet anticipated demographic and economic needs. Even so, individual primary class sizes were higher than at any time since the war, overcrowding dictating that classes were held in cloakrooms, stock cupboards and corridors. By 1955, annual corporation capital expenditure on the schools programme stood at £861,508. Yet despite the early rhetoric, it is important to note that there was no discernible change in spending patterns on primary or secondary education under either Labour or Conservative control.[40] Indeed, there was markedly little debate on the guiding principles behind education policy; the most controversial item politically centred on the provision of free school transport for secondary pupils living fewer than three miles from school. On the more potentially divisive issue of comprehensive education, little was heard until 1954. Here, unexpectedly, Labour members of the Education Committee, who had previously resisted internal calls, came out in favour of its introduction. Its inclusion in that year's manifesto, however, was only a

39 *NJ*, 3 Feb. 1948.
40 NCC, Annual Report of the Education Comm. 1955, Table 5 (total capital spending for the period March 1949–March 53 was primary £1,114,802, secondary £882,265, other £602,381); NUMD, TrM Box 17, Enquiry Report by Nott'm Trades Council, 28 Jan. 1953.

temporary aberration; subsequently dropped, it only re-emerged in the 1960s when it became central to the battle between left and right within the party.

*

A major and traditional function of the city council lay in exercising policy control over municipal trading undertakings. Finally, therefore, it is worth examining briefly the attitudes of both parties to service provision. The nationalisation of gas and electricity left transport, in terms of turnover, as the most important of corporation utilities. The post-war years saw a marked reversal in the fortunes of this once profitable undertaking, where increased costs (particularly vehicle replacement and, with acute labour shortages, comparatively high labour charges) rose by almost fifty per cent between 1939 and 1950 set against fare increases of less than fifteen per cent. By 1949, expenses exceeded income; by 1952 past accumulated profit balances had been exhausted.[41]

Political response to these reversals was generally muted, delayed and lacking in long-term coherent strategy. Chaired alternately by Labour and Conservatives since the late 1920s, and by Labour since 1945, the Transport Committee's primary objective was consistently based on minimising fare increases. Particularly sacrosanct were early morning workman's concessionary rates (to accommodate the Corporation's outlying housing structure); here, Labour members were particularly susceptible to internal group, party and trades union pressure. To maintain this direction, the committee increasingly resorted to savings through increased unit labour cost efficiency, which in turn promoted further under-staffing, increased overtime payments, high staff turnover and labour shortages. Those fare increases approved by full council (and not all were) then went before an exhaustive and bureaucratic public enquiry procedure—notable also for attempting to minimise increases and delaying sanctions.[42]

41 NCC, Annual Report of the Transport Comm. 1949; NCC, Transport Comm. Report, 6 Feb. 1950, 16 June 1952.

42 NCC, Transport Comm. Report on Conclusions of Special Comm. of Inquiry, 12 Dec. 1955; NCC, Report of Special Transport Comm. Presented to Council 6 May 1955; NUMD TrM Box 1-3, Nott'm Trades Council mins, 1949–53, *passim*; letter from Coffey to Morgan Phillips, 12 July 1951, Phillips to Coffey, 31 July 1951, in author's possession (hereafter IAP).

Conservative reaction to fare increases varied considerably. Initially, they argued, raising fares to finance capital expenditure would not only provide Nottingham with one of the dearest transport systems in Britain, but would also be particularly unwise in view of the pending threat of nationalisation. When this threat passed with a change of government, attention focused on the need for the greater productivity reputedly associated with private operators. The party leadership, however, remained largely detached from this pre-1951 impulse: its overriding priority was to prevent the department from becoming dependent on a general rates subsidy. It too, however, tended to favour expenditure and service cuts, which intermittently reinforced Conservative attempts to reject fare increases. The Labour leadership also rejected direct rates support for city transport, but was generally more supportive of the Committee's moves to increase fares. Yet such was the strength of internal opposition here that, despite attempts to manipulate and set opinion, it was not unknown for the leadership to suffer what were rare defeats on matters of policy.[43]

Despite their sometimes stark differences over methodology, however, the party leaders did seek a consensus to fulfil their agreed aim to reject the subsidising of transport trading deficits. Notwithstanding the failure of early attempts to reach agreement, after which mutual recrimination increased significantly, escalating financial problems demanded a planned pragmatic response which both parties acknowledged could only be found outside the realms of short-term political expediency. The consensual device selected to resolve this temporary impasse was, as at other times, a bi-partisan committee of inquiry, consisting of three members of each party, to which was added a single voice from both the Chamber of Commerce and Trades Council. Retrieving the debate from the party political domain held a certain universal appeal: as one Labour Transport Committee member commented, 'clearing the air, which has been poisoned by a certain amount of political feeling'.[44] That the then controlling Labour group was prepared to submit to external assessment (albeit reluctantly at first) in an historically sensitive policy area was both an acknowledgement of a pragmatic desire to manage municipal services on other than ideological grounds and a measure of the problem itself.

43 *NG*, 30 July 1946; *NJ*, 2 July 1946, 7 Feb. 1950, 3 Oct. 1950; *GJ*, 28 July 1953; NAO LPC Box 10, Lab. Group mins, 2 July 1948, 15 June 1952.
44 *GJ*, 2 Nov. 1953; see also 8 July 1952, 6 Nov. 1952, 28 July 1953.

Indeed, the dilemma rested on the incompatible twin aims of commercial viability set against escalating expenses and the maintenance of low fares—to which each party in turn had subscribed. The outside consultants appointed by the committee of inquiry pointedly recommended that in future fares policy be wholly determined by costs.

Despite the differences surrounding the overall strategy, it is important to understand that both parties viewed city transport provision as a community service, albeit one operating without external subsidy. Much of the opposition to increased fares from both sides rested on this premise. Illustrative of the limits of this underlying agreement was the move to grant concessionary fares to the elderly. Temporarily rejected by Labour in 1949 because of the financial health of the department, it nevertheless continued to be promoted by individual members partly, it must be admitted, to test the sincerity of those Conservatives also advocating a similar policy. A Conservative majority, the following year, referred the matter to the F&GP Committee. Not surprisingly it rejected the concept of 'free travel', arguing that it would cost the department some £35,000 a year in lost revenue. Yet an inter-party commonality of purpose, if not of conceptual language, did exist. As the Conservative leader (who also chaired the F&GP) acknowledged in agreeing to again review the matter, there was a concern on both sides of the chamber that 'old age pensioners were not getting a fair crack of the whip', there being a 'gap in the Welfare State that local charity had to bridge'.[45] That Littlefair chose to view concessionary travel as charity is in itself revealing of local Conservative ambiguity when called upon to extend the parameters of welfare activities at a local level beyond any statutory responsibility. Yet in this instance, paradoxically, it was to be central government, through its agent the Licensing Authority, which vetoed the Transport Committee's attempts to extend its concessionary fares structure—an initiative which by then had local cross-party support.

Over certain Corporation activities, however, there was no consensus over even basic objectives. While Conservatives generally accepted, and even fought vociferously to retain, local control over services historically operated by the Corporation, equally they rejected any expansion of municipal trading into non-traditional areas of responsibility. It was within this zone of battle between private enterprise and municipalisation that political ideology found its full voice. Thus Conservatives opposed

45 *NJ*, 6 Feb. 1951.

granting powers enabling the city to sell furniture directly to its tenants, and rejected any extension in the activities of the Civic Restaurants Committee. Labour, likewise, fought against the closure of Civic Restaurants, regarding them as an integral part of the local welfare State, not an emergency response to wartime need. Such vehement disagreement, however, operated only on the margins surrounding Corporation polity. The potentially divisive exception to this rule—because of the scale of building activity—was direct labour, but as a policy this always lacked support within the Labour group. The pragmatic reality was that a broad underlying political consensus not only existed but was actively sought in the conduct of municipal affairs. The period after 1951, however, was to see a gradual undermining of this agreement in major areas where previously inter-party policy was cohesive.

CHAPTER 4

Consensus Undermined:
Old Values, New Party Disciplines
1951–57

The move from a formalised system of inter-party co-operation towards what was later dubbed by critics Nottingham's 'Tammany Hall phase' of 'Socialist Dictatorship' was posted by Labour's 1956 manifesto declaration to impose a regime based on single party rule if returned to power after the May elections.[1] Here all committee chairs were to be taken by the majority party. Abolished at the same time was that protection previously awarded sitting aldermen—no longer could they claim the right to automatic re-selection. Dropped, too, was the inter-party arbitration clause and recognised rights for minority members (see Appendix). Clearly a major structural and psychological break with past practice, it was also a formal acknowledgement of the growing authority of parties in city government at the expense of the once more apolitically orientated committee system. Labour, as instigators, advocated single party rule as an extension of the democratic ideal, where electors chose between, and were governed according to, the precepts of competing party programmes. Opponents proffered less sympathetic hypotheses: it was mere political opportunism—reflecting the party's enhanced prospects at the forthcoming elections—or a desire by Labour to extend the dictates of caucus rule to all aspects of city government.[2] How these changes functioned in practice will be discussed in the following chapters. Of more immediate concern are the reasons underpinning this transformation.

The first point to clarify is that in rejecting joint party rule, Nottingham was only belatedly following a post-war trend; at the time of the proposed changes locally, in a clear majority of other major towns and cities the larger political party automatically took all committee chairs. In fact, Transport House actively encouraged Labour groups to monopolise

1 *GJ*, 20 March 1956, 4 June 1957; *NEP*, 11 May 1960; A. Howard, 'The Power Behind the Throne', *New Statesman*, 21 Aug. 1964.
2 *GJ*, 20 March 1956, 11 May 1956.

committee offices when in power (partly reacting against past discriminatory practice before 1945) and to refuse office when in a minority.[3] The timing of any change locally was also largely predetermined. Inter-party agreements covering patronage elsewhere overall were of a less structured nature, potentially variable from election to election. In Nottingham this was not the case. Here, agreements predominantly covered a six-year period. Both political leaderships, sometimes under trying circumstances, readily accepted their obligations to honour existing concordats wherever possible, ignoring the somewhat questionable legal status of the documents. Change, therefore, was tied to the expiry date of the existing agreement in December 1956. All that can be said with certainty is that in 1951 both parties reaffirmed their commitment to the traditions and practices of power-sharing, although again in retrospect this was more than Conservatives had offered prior to the outbreak of the war.

It might be expected that the critical catalysts for local change rested within the instigating party between those years. And indeed in part the answer does lie with Labour's already noted greater propensity for collective accountability, uniformity and a disciplined structure. Having already restricted the number of committee offices each Labour member could hold in an attempt to curb individual power, in 1951 the group sought to restrict committee autonomy by insisting that all committee decisions and minutes be ratified by full council—or in effect the controlling political group. Conservative members, with one exception, opposed the motion. So did Tom Owen (now the Town Clerk) who—much to the annoyance of Labour members—openly supported criticisms that the proposed change would be inefficient and time-consuming. The dissenting Tory member was the former Liberal, Bill Dyer. In a debate, which to Labour eyes centred on group authority, Dyer proved a reluctant and ironic advocate. As he admitted, in pressing for wider access to committee information, he was speaking with 'some

3 W. Thornhill, 'Agreements between Local Parties in Local Government Matters', *Political Studies* 5/1 (1957), pp. 85–88; survey by author of past town clerks of largest 50 county boroughs in Britain; Keith-Lucas and Richards, *History of Local Government*, pp. 120–22; F. Bealy, J. Blondel and W. P. McCann, *Constituency Politics* (1965), pp. 369–70; H. V. Wiseman, 'The Working of Local Government in Leeds: Part II., More Party Conventions and Practices', *Public Administration* 41 (1963), pp. 137–56; Sharpe (ed.), *Voting in Cities, passim.*

trepidation because he was in disagreement with his leader'.[4] Dyer was not the only notable to defy the whip. Herbert Bowles spoke vociferously against moves to restrict committee independence. Then, in a ploy more commonly employed by dissenting Conservatives, he left the chamber before the vote was cast. George Wigman, who had replaced Bowles as leader, and was currently the Lord Mayor, also abstained. These two lost votes were sufficient narrowly to defeat Labour's initiative, a point not lost on the group. However, calls to reduce committee delegatory powers continued to be heard intermittently within the Labour group and party. With Owen pressing behind the scenes for its abandonment, with many Labour members less than firm advocates and amid bitter Conservative complaints of a lack of inter-party consultation, the move to restructure committee autonomy was eventually passed along party lines in November 1954.

This somewhat lacklustre offensive to restrict committee independence ran parallel to a general strengthening of overall inter-group disciplinary voting practice. Yet as both main parties already operated an effective formal or informal whipping system anyway, a tightening of discipline recorded only a marginal change in voting behaviour. This was not as it was presented politically. Conservatives mounted successive post-war election propaganda campaigns wholly critical of Labour's disciplinary system. Underpinned by a strategy of misinformation, it was designed to create the illusion that Tory members acted independently of group or peer pressure. As the party proclaimed prior to the 1949 election: 'Not one of us is pledged to vote other than by the dictates of his or her conscience'. Simultaneously they stigmatised their opponents as being bound rigidly not only to follow group policy, but also mandatory instructions issued by party activists:

> The Socialists have the right to enforce such discipline as they think fit upon their members, but it is a travesty of local government when members have to submit themselves to 'group meetings' of unknown persons, and to accept decisions from outside on even trifling matters.[5]

---

4 *NJ*, 3 July 1951; NAO LPC Box 10, Lab. Group mins, 27 June 1951, 27 July 1951; LPC Box 10, letter from Coffey to Phillips, 25 June 1951.

5 NLSL L.34.32, *Joint Statement from Conservative Candidates*, 1949 Municipal Election; Nott'm Conservative Ass., *Nottingham Citizen*, 1950 Municipal Election edn.

The reality was somewhat different. Shared political beliefs within both groups meant that, commonly, no dichotomy existed between individual conscience and the aggregate view. Here, in practice, a sense of collective discipline meant that public dissension from the majority line by members of either group was notably rare, the more so the farther one moved from 1945. The suggestion that the Labour group was bound by external diktats was wholly unfounded. The group's standing orders, mimicking closely the national 'model', laid down that 'three [constituency] representatives may attend Group meetings in a consultative capacity and without voting power'. In fact, in a continuingly terse internal debate occupying much of the post-war period, Nottingham's Labour group fiercely resisted any external incursion into its policy-making remit. At times, so strong was this resistance to outside influence that these 'Liaison' representatives were forbidden even to question group members, let alone act as arbiters of imposition.[6]

Nevertheless, the middle years of the first post-war decade did witness further, if pedestrian, attempts within the group to strengthen collective discipline. This was notably stimulated by a narrowing of party majorities on the council. It was a policy contested by certain elder senior aldermen, who opposed any loss of their pre-war independence in standing committees. Halls's actions as Chair of the Education Committee provide noteworthy examples, although his resistance to this 'new order' was, as we have seen, relatively short lived. It was Bowles who proved to be the most persistent rebel; his erratic disregard for group policy both pre- and post-dated the 1951 debate on curbing committee autonomy. These earlier transgressions, although reported to the group for disciplinary action, were largely ignored. However, 1951 proved to be a pivotal year in determining Labour's disciplinary stance, when on several occasions members sought to affirm a right to oppose publicly group policy. Apart from Bowles's posturing within and on committees, there was also a divisive split prompted by the renewed call to complete the city's inner ring road. Here a vocal minority strongly supported the dictates of the 'Houses First' lobby. In what amounted to a local test case, dissenters maintained that under the group's standing orders their right to an alternative public line was guaranteed on matters of conscience. The

6 Nott'm City Labour Party, *Constitution, Rules and Standing Orders* (1956), p. 21; NAO LPC Box 10, Lab. Group mins, 4 March 1949; LPC Box 10, Letter from G. Dutton to T. Ives, 11 Dec. 1956.

group hesitated before issuing a firm edict, unsure whether strength of commitment to a particular issue could rightly be defined as a moral stance. It was Transport House which finally confirmed that such group decisions were binding on all members. Meanwhile Bowles, who had already been warned verbally, was now formally censured for yet again ignoring group mandates.[7] Yet although his voting behaviour continued to be somewhat erratic, this now elderly maverick was never finally expelled. In this, the group undoubtedly showed a greater tolerance towards Bowles than he himself had shown to former Labour dissidents.

Yet on balance it was the 1951 and 1952 municipal election results, rather than individual or group predilections, which provided the greatest stimulus for increasing group authority. Here the Conservatives' operating majority (with Liberal support) was first cut to two and then wholly abrogated (Table 3.1). Eager to maximise their voting potential, both groups subsequently moved to exercise control in areas that, traditionally, had been considered outside the jurisdiction of party activity. Thus, paradoxically, at the very time when the electorate was exhibiting fickle and equally divided loyalties in offering no overall mandate to either party, local politicians themselves retreated to a position where past consensual policies and practices were set to one side in favour of enforced, often doctrinaire, hegemonic party rule.

Past inter-party agreements had acknowledged the publicly apolitical stance adopted by successive Lord Mayors and Sheriffs by offering each an unopposed return at municipal elections (see Appendix). In accepting that the Lord Mayor, acting as the impartial chair of council meetings, should abstain from voting, etiquette stipulated that the city's Sheriff (now a purely ceremonial office) should also not vote. As each office-holder was appointed by the opposing groups, the political balance remained unaffected. In 1951 this changed. In several highly charged debates, the Conservative Sheriff broke with custom by repeatedly exercising his right to vote–his intervention proving decisive on several occasions. The Labour group, after some delay, then instructed George Wigman as mayor to redress this imbalance by exercising his own and casting votes. This was an instruction which he resolutely resisted.[8] Wigman was to pay a heavy price for his stance. The following year he

7 NAO LPC Box 10, Lab. Group mins, *passim*, 1949–1952.
8 NCC, Council mins, 2 July 1951, 4 Feb. 1952, 3 March 1952; NAO LPC Box 10, letter from Coffey to Wigman, 1 Feb. 1952; LPC Box 10, Lab. Group mins, 12 May 1952.

was overwhelmingly defeated in Labour's leadership elections, an office he had held since 1947 and from which he had only temporarily resigned on the strict understanding that he would be re-elected after his year as Lord Mayor.

The consequence of Wigman's refusal, however, was to remove the very pragmatism that had underpinned the group's initial response; for all future prospective holders of civic office were required, before their nomination, to affirm their preparedness to vote by instruction. Moves twelve months later to rescind this directive were heavily defeated. However, like much in Labour group politics at this time, formal instruction still carried less than absolute weight. When once installed in office, there remained a strong resistance to this new code. John Kenyon, elected Sheriff the following year, consistently refused to yield to the group's mandate and repeated censure, partly because 'he thought it in the interests of the Labour Party for him not to vote while the [Conservative] Lord Mayor refrained'.[9] It was a decision that, arithmetically at least, made sense. Kenyon held only one vote to the Lord Mayor's two. The following year the Conservative Sheriff, William Cox, likewise opted for non-partisanship. However, in 1954 Labour's nominee, Len Mitson, took the whip and as instructed voted consistently with his colleagues.

Mitson was also to be appointed Lord Mayor in 1955. A former Tory who had crossed the floor in 1946, Mitson was certainly not of a radical vein ready to cast totally aside mayoral independence. Labour's leadership, Ernest Purser and Tommy Ives (the newly appointed group secretary), were also now adopting a more traditionalist stance in advocating 'strict impartiality' for the mayoralty. Yet it was Mitson who felt the need to qualify this reversal. Adopting a stance taken by several Tory Lord Mayors during the inter-war period, there were, he said, certain personally held priorities over which he was not prepared to disenfranchise himself; here he would follow the 'dictates of [his] conscience' and vote, if required, to defeat the then small Conservative majority.[10] Such vacillation, overall, on the part of leadership, office holders and party alike towards this one aspect of party hegemony is wholly indicative of this period of transition towards single party

9 NAO LPC Box 10, Lab. Group mins, 25 Aug. 1952.

10 NAO LPC Box 10, letter from Mitson to Lab. Group, 15 July 1955. He had in mind the closure of civic restaurants, opposed by Conservatives on doctrinal grounds, but which he equally regarded as part of the local Welfare State.

government where the 'rules of the game', so to speak, remained in a state of flux.

In breaking the equilibrium of civic abstention, Conservatives bear more than passing responsibility for this potential instability. Nevertheless, they were unwilling to extend party partisanship to the institution of the mayoralty and government itself. This is clearly illustrated by the events of 1952. Here Labour gains meant both sides were equally represented in the chamber. As the Editor of the *Nottingham Guardian* quickly explained, the Conservatives could retain control under the terms of the inter-party agreement:

> The new Lord Mayor, in due order of sequence, has been chosen from the Conservative ranks, and ... he could give his party a majority by using his extra, or casting vote. In other towns where a similar situation has arisen this has in fact been done ... Apart from the wider aspects of this sort of behaviour, which might well be thought to reduce the process of democratic local government to a farce, to act in this manner here would be an absolute negation of the long and highly valued tradition in this city of co-operation with and tolerance towards opponents on this council ... Here the tradition is that the Lord Mayor does not vote. And yet if he declines to vote he not only deprives his party of a majority, but puts it in a minority for his personal vote is lost as well ... No party, no member—no Lord Mayor—holds a monopoly in wise government. If members remember always that they have been elected to further the interests, not of their own parties, but of the city and the people who live in it, there is no reason why we should not see a continuation of the harmonious and progressive administration for which Nottingham is renowned ... What must not be allowed is a resort to the vote. The operation of the Lord Mayor's casting vote at any time during the next twelve months would [be] ... a defeat for each and every member of the Council.[11]

It was a protocol, as Kenyon recognised, to which the party adhered throughout the year. Yet the complementary calls for the adoption of an enhanced governing ethos equally representative of past consensual values were to be largely ignored. Two broad options lay before the groups to

11 *NG*, 10 May 1952.

break the political stalemate of 1952: either to formulate joint policy through 'agreement and compromise' or to reject a consensual emphasis in favour of an intensification of disciplined party politics.[12] Both opted for the latter course and the ensuing year saw local political disharmony touch areas even where previously there had been overriding agreement.

The party leaders had first to agree which group was to be considered nominally predominant: council leadership brought with it a majority on and greater sway over the selection of each committee, control of the F&GP Committee, and with it the city's finances. Littlefair from the start insisted that the Conservatives retain control, albeit at the acknowledged cost of tightening internal party discipline. Nevertheless, at his initiative, senior members of both groups met to see if a 'reasonable solution by negotiation' could be reached. Labour, too, opted initially to take a hard line, demanding a voting majority on each committee and in the council (through the forced retirement of a Tory alderman). Not surprisingly, Conservatives rejected these claims as being particularly unreasonable. Offering only minor concessions, they now invoked the inter-party agreement's arbitration clause.[13] Publicly this was a move welcomed by Labour; privately they doubted the justice of their claim. Certainly an 'overwhelming majority' of electors had voted Labour in recent city and general elections, but the Conservative counter—that they still retained marginally a greater number of elected, as opposed to aldermanic seats—was thought to be more persuasive. In what amounted to a volte-face, the group now conceded temporary leadership. In return it demanded equality of representation on all committees and the chair of the Fire Brigades Committee (FBC), normally considered a minor patronage post but which was then at the centre of an extended and deeply divisive inter-party dispute. Indeed, it was a measure of the division over the FBC that Labour offered and Conservatives rejected this solution. But it is equally significant that Labour's consensually bound overtures advocating numerical equality, and a Conservative counter-proposal likewise to share control of the F&GP Committee, were eventually to be rejected by both sides in favour of a clearly determined

12 *Ibid.*
13 *NG*, 9 May 1952; letters from Littlefair to Purser, 9 May 1952 and 14 May 1952, IAP.

party led regime.[14] After some initial resistance, therefore, Labour acceded to Conservative requests to appoint an external arbitrator.

According to the local press, such behaviour was the personification of consensual civic practice:

> Nottingham, where the parties have always scrupulously honoured agreements governing a number of matters that might otherwise give rise to endless bitterness and bickering, could well act as a role model to the country. The latest example of the way Nottingham deals with these ticklish situations is a triumph for reasonableness and decency in local government ... an attitude of 'city before party' amongst the members on all occasions, and, in particular, of a readiness to compromise when party lines really clash.[15]

Indeed, in resolving a tricky dispute the inter-party concordat did function according to its historic design, settling a controversy not only over patronage but the very control of the Corporation. Nevertheless, this vote of confidence requires qualification. While both party leaders had acknowledged the need for an early settlement, a solution placing 'city before party' failed to materialise without recourse to formal arbitration. This failure is only partly explained by the existence of, and therefore reliance on, that particular external mechanism. Both had also rejected coalition leadership in favour of party-determined control. If the practice of 'reasonableness' was the cornerstone upon which the agreements—and indeed consensus itself—was based, then the omens were less than wholly favourable.

The arbitration award was to be made in Labour's favour. Littlefair, attempting to repudiate the significance of the judgement, immediately went on record to suggest that leadership of the council meant little more than chairmanship of the F&GP Committee. Yet both parties were aware it meant significantly more, as Conservatives later acknowledged in agreeing to Labour demands for a majority on all committees. Thus at all stages of the negotiations, there was apparent resistance to resolving

14 NAO LPC Box 10, letter from Purser to P. D. Cotes-Preedy (Barrister), 19 May 1952; LPC Box 10, Lab Group mins, 11 May 1952; letters from Purser to Littlefair and Littlefair to Purser, 15 May 1952, IAP.

15 *NG*, 30 May 1952.

differences amicably. It was, however, only a symptom of a wider malaise.

*

In early 1954, Conservatives placed the breakdown of local political consensus squarely on the shoulders of an increasingly dominant left-wing element in the Labour group, 'who made co-operation between the two main political parties well nigh impossible'.[16] In fact the inherited post-war propensity for political compromise, so important to the quick resolution of disputes, had been under threat for several years. The first sustained schism had occurred in late 1951, during a period of Conservative rule and at a time of supposed local consensus. Here a lack of reasonableness found expression when the Conservative-controlled FBC opted to take a persistently authoritarian line in the aftermath of a national fireman's dispute. It was the need for a vindicatory political triumph that provided one essential element in the subsequent failure to unlock a political settlement over the council leadership in May 1952, and to degrees soured inter-party relations for some two years.

While the major terms and conditions of service of firemen were negotiated nationally, provision and control—which included a devolved power to interpret locally the disciplinary code to which all fire-fighters were subject—remained vested in local authorities. City firemen had responded to two calls for industrial action. The first, initially unofficial, was in October; the second in November 1951, where members boycotted station drills, the testing of equipment and non-emergency calls, was equally brief in lasting only two days. The FBC warned after the first action that future disruption would be countered by 'the severest measures open to them'. And true to these words, the 64 firemen—some 55 per cent of the force—who responded to the second call were immediately suspended on half-pay and charged. All but two were found guilty, five being reduced in rank and the remainder fined, with particularly heavy penalties being reserved for union organisers.[17]

Nottingham set an example in being the first authority to impose sanctions. The Home Office, for its part, repeatedly urged authorities to 'exercise wise discretion' and 'avoid any action that would exacerbate

16 *GJ*, 30 March 1954.
17 *NJ*, 8 Jan. 1952; NCC, FBC mins, Nov. 1951, *passim*.

existing difficulties'. Most employers followed this advice.[18] Nottingham's Labour group, if harbouring misgivings over the union's rejection of the Corporation's disciplinary function, also favoured a placatory approach and called for 'the easement of the [excessive] penalties so far inflicted'. Conservatives, however, viewed past events differently; it was, they maintained a 'struggle between authority and discipline on the one hand and utter disregard for law and order on the other. The men ... had to be punished so that they would think twice before they struck again.'[19] This political gulf broadened with Nottingham's growing isolation, as other authorities revoked past penalties. Consensual accommodation, however, was temporarily yet wholly absent from the local political agenda. Here polarised attempts to impose disciplinary punishments rebounded to and from committee, blocked (because of persistent Conservative absenteeism) by a temporary Labour majority in full council. Tactics, however, were transparently obvious: repeatedly to resubmit the disciplinary edicts until a mobilised Conservative majority ratified the sanctions. As tempers frayed, Conservatives became the butt of increasingly vociferous taunts of and from being 'very ardent' to outright 'fascist'. Any *rapprochement* was not aided by the FBC's 'operational' decision to fill the vacancies caused by the demotions, and to recognise a rival and blacked 'bosses' trade union, the political child of Tory MP, Reader Harris. For its part, the Fire Brigades Union (FBU) took its case to a wider audience, organising massed national protests through the city's streets and providing substantial aid for Labour candidates during the 1952 May elections.[20] In fact, any resolution to the impasse was going to be determined at the polls, for under the existing circumstances neither side was prepared to give ground. And when the election results themselves proved indecisive, not surprisingly control of the FBC became a key bargaining counter in the subsequent controversy over Corporation leadership.

Labour's arbitrated nomination to power did little immediately to facilitate reconciliation. In insisting that sole local negotiating rights be reserved for the FBU, then recompensing those fined from the rates fund

---

18 *Local Government Chronicle*, 24 Nov. 1951; *H.C. Debates*, 3 Dec. 1951, Vol. 494, col. 2029-31, also 15 Nov. 1951, Vol. 494, cols 226–28.

19 NAO LPC Box 10, Lab. Group mins, 20 Dec. 1951; *NJ*, 8 Jan. 1951.

20 *NJ*, 5 Feb. 1952, 4 March 1952; NUMD TrM Box 2, Nott'm Trades Council mins, March–April 1952, *passim*; MRC MSS 9/3/14/91, Labour Party Regional Organiser's Report (hereafter only MSS 9 ref. given), 8 May 1952.

and reinstating those demoted, the political lesions remained uncauterised. Nonetheless, the more radical demands from the Communist-dominated Trades Council and FBU (aimed primarily against the breakaway union) were, after legal and central counsel, rejected. Establishing joint consultative machinery to regulate fire brigade practices was, however, deemed acceptable, although this essentially temperate suggestion was initially rejected by Conservatives on the FBC and opposed by its newly appointed Labour chair. Tommy Scott was a moderate who stood by the pre-war tradition of committee independence. Such sentiment was currently out of place and the group dismissed him from office. This left void a politically sensitive patronage position which neither the Conservative nor Labour leaderships were prepared to countenance the other securing. With the former again requesting recourse to arbitration (finally rejected by Labour because of its cost) renewed controversy again appeared likely. Only circumstance intervened. The untimely death of Walter Halls left the chair of the Education Committee vacant. At an inter-party conference in December 1953, Labour finally ceded the FBC chair rather than have Conservatives claim the strategically more important education post under the inter-party agreement.

Industrial relations might be thought a natural arena for historic doctrinaire disagreement; indeed the propagation and protection of trades union rights remained a central and founding principle underpinning Labour's rationale in local politics. Nevertheless, this has to be set against a reputed *rapprochement*, ending inter-war hostilities, between Conservative politicians and the trades union movement nationally which reputedly served as a founding tenet of the broader post-war consensus.[21] Such a new understanding was less than obvious in Nottingham. Yet arguably the contribution of the Fire Brigade's dispute to the demise of city consensus lay primarily not in this keenly felt underlying ideological disagreement; fundamentally it rested on an all too apparent determination by each group repeatedly to impose doctrinaire solutions on its political opponents. Of course, in isolation labour issues never formed a central component of the joint civic reconstruction objectives upon which the post-war consensus was built. Yet this consensus was not based solely on an ethos of shared material objectives. Its foundation, in which local

---

21 J. Gyford and M. James, *National Parties and Local Politics* (1983), pp. 44–47; M. Savage and A. Miles, *The Remaking of the British Working Class 1840–1940* (1994), p. 78; Kavanagh and Morris, *Consensus Politics*, pp. 51–57.

senior politicians took pride, was a willingness within prescribed parameters to place city before party; a euphemism for emphasising political compromise not conflict. As several commentators have rightly emphasised, post-war British political consensus was unwritten by a 'tacit understanding' that neither party when in government would 'strain the tolerance of the other side too violently'.[22] By 1952 this governing ethic was clearly under threat in Nottingham.

Amongst the majority advocating an enhanced role for the Corporation in post-war reconstruction, it was always the city Labour group collectively that proffered the greater unquestioning support and indeed was the primary electoral beneficiary. In this sense, direct parallels can be drawn tentatively between the national and local experience. As we have established, a pragmatic commonalty of purpose existed in the immediate post-war years in Nottingham on central issues, particularly over municipal housing provision and, to a lesser extent, education and other services. Clearly, this was not wholly rooted in the wartime experience or post-war expectation; indeed it had been supported by pre-war paternalistic strands in city governance. Thus influential local Conservatives, notably Armitage and Crane, readily accepted the role of the local authority as an enthusiastic enabler after 1945, even as a minority of their colleagues remained fundamentally wedded to a private enterprise solution to local ills. The Conservative group on balance, therefore, was not a reluctant conscript to the priorities of a 'new' local welfare consensus. Nor did it totally abandon this commitment once the more immediate objectives of post-war reconstruction were in place.

Yet in terms of emphasis, the groups were to drift apart. Labour stoically defended the status quo–the solutions adopted in 1945–while Conservatives increasingly advocated an enhanced role for private provision and personal responsibility. Again the local Conservative rationale exhibited distinctive strands of national thinking in the late 1940s and early 1950s. It was a mood ably summarised under the policy heading 'set the people free', a blunt political reaction to the privations of state administered austerity. Yet, as nationally, any determined attempt to implement deep cuts in civic responsibility was tempered by a pragmatic attachment to the welfare state itself, and the partial fusion

22 P. M. Williams, *Hugh Gaitskell: A Political Biography* (1979), p. 779; I. Wilton, 'Postwar Consensus: Some Issues Re-examined', *Contemporary Record* 3/4 (1990), pp. 27–28.

within this of past paternalistic provision.[23] Yet the disagreement that did arise attracted singular attention. Partially, this can be explained by comparative reference to the contrasting harmony of the immediate post-war years. But, as with the Fire Brigade's dispute, vociferous disagreement was also a product of the fine political balance within the council chamber. The years 1951 and 1952 saw several key reports bouncing repeatedly between drafting committee and full council as both groups sought to flex their political and ideological muscles in whatever sphere they could summon a spontaneous majority. Such actions precipitated extended conflict in areas where, only a few years before, a broad consensus had prevailed.

Nowhere was this abrupt reversal better illustrated than in housing. First the parties disagreed over rents, with Labour perhaps surprisingly advocating a differential policy—or as Crane preferred to call it, 'means testing'—in response to proposed universalist increases. More fundamental disagreements were to follow quickly. Post-war consensus had essentially been re-forged in the primacy afforded municipal provision. Material and labour shortages meant that the total number of building starts each year was governed centrally, then rationed by region and subsequently divided between individual local authorities. Of these, councils were empowered to allocate a maximum percentage (normally one-fifth) to private enterprise to construct houses for sale. Unlike many other local authorities in the Midlands, and largely at Crane's initiative, Nottingham consistently issued the maximum number of private licences allowed under government regulations.[24] Despite its at times obsessive fetish with public housing provision, Labour's response—whether in power or opposition—was largely pragmatic and consensual; isolated plots were more readily developed by speculative builders whose prospective clients (to whom the licences were issued) were anyway subject to the same hardship criteria as those seeking Corporation housing. Nevertheless, a marked disparity between the two sectors did exist; comparatively waiting lists and times for private licences remained consistently and

23 I. Zweiniger-Bargielowska, 'Rationing, Austerity and the Conservative Party Recovery after 1945', *Historical Journal* 37/1 (1994), pp. 173–97; R. Lowe, 'Welfare Policy in Britain 1943–1970', *Contemporary Record* 4/2 (1990), pp. 29–32; Gyford, 'Politicization', pp. 89–90.

24 Merrett, *Owner Occupation*, pp. 17–26; Johnson, 'Regional Housing Organisation', p. 243.

notably shorter than for public housing, even after account is taken of the greater number of building starts in the latter sector.

This indulgence towards private building quotas was soon to be stretched to breaking point. The increased role envisaged by the incoming Conservative government for speculative building—readily accepted by Conservatives on the Housing Committee—to Labour eyes went beyond pragmatic accommodation; issuing licences ad hoc was not a step they contemplated with over 11,000 names on the housing waiting list. It was in fact a local example, magnified by its parochial importance, of the broader dichotomy which separated the parties' economic and social approaches nationally, namely Labour's predilection for retaining direct controls against the Conservative's strong liberalising preference for their abolition.[25] In fact, local Labour fears that increased speculative activity would undermine the Corporation's own continuing housing drive, notably after Whitehall's initial refusal to raise compensatingly public sector quotas, proved unfounded. Indeed 1952—thanks primarily to the greater efficiencies and speed of construction from employing 'no-fines' technology—saw the rapid expansion of building starts in the public sector, to accompany private growth.[26] Labour's unrest, however, was not solely altruistic. It also perceived a political motivation behind Conservative actions in encouraging private ownership among working-class families estranged by lengthy housing waiting lists. As one Labour spokesman remarked caustically: 'Any Tory who induces working class people ... to buy a house on the "glad and sorry" ought to be locked up as a permanent danger.'[27]

Indeed, the effective end of quantitative building controls quickly highlighted other disparities previously minimised while local authorities retained their primal role in housing construction. In 1951 the Housing Committee, prompted by the acute shortage of building land, acquired a 300 plot site from the city's Education Department in the prosperous suburb of Wollaton. In a debate repetitious of that over Clifton, this time the Conservative majority temporarily blocked public development, complaining not only that the needs of the private sector were being ignored but that the middle classes 'with houses in that area were entitled

25 Rollings, 'Poor Mr Butskell', pp. 192, 198, 203.
26 NCC, Housing Comm. mins, 23 Jan. 1952; Min. of Housing and Local Gov't, *Housing Returns: Appendix B.*
27 *NJ*, 5 Feb. 1952.

to some measure of protection' from municipal encroachment.[28] Disagreement was again exacerbated by fluctuating majorities in the council chamber. Here the report in amended form rebounded to and from committee, delaying development of the site for over twelve months. No sooner had Labour agreed to the sale of a parcel of this land for speculative development than Conservatives demanded that likewise part of the Corporation-owned Glapton site also be reserved for owner occupation. With Damascene pace, a philosophy that had espoused spatial class segregation now advocated the benefits of socially balanced neighbourhoods, necessary, it was argued, to attract the professional middle classes required to service the surrounding new Clifton estate. Again the controversy reverberated between committee and full council until, after a year's delay, Labour used its voting strength to force the issue.

Clearly, inter-party unanimity on housing could no longer be guaranteed. Indeed, the parties were again to split openly over the city's first major post-war slum clearance project (Denman Street), part of a larger, although by national benchmarks modest, five-year programme covering some 2,650 houses. In terms reminiscent of objections raised immediately before the war (also at a time of heightened inter-party tension), a Conservative majority rejected the recommendations of the city's Medical Officer of Health for wholesale demolition. Instead they opted both to clear but also to improve many of the properties which, although at present neglected, they considered 'basically sound'—a policy of deferred demolition recently advocated by central government. Modernisation, which Crane considered 'the brightest hope for the future', Labour argued, meant only 'the perpetuation of slum conditions at the expense of the City and to the advantage of those landlords who will benefit by the Corporation acquiring their houses at market value'. A public enquiry was later essentially to endorse the latter interpretation, concluding that the houses were 'unsuitable' on economic grounds for improvement, which anyway would 'gravely prejudice the satisfactory redevelopment of the area as a whole'.[29]

It was perhaps a measure of the steadily rising political tension that in late 1953 Conservatives, when in opposition, chose to re-open the public

28 *NJ*, 31 July 1951.
29 *GJ*, 4 Sept. 1954; NAO LPC Box 7, Nott'm Lab. Group, Report on Housing in the Denman St. Areas, Sept. 1954; NCC, Housing Comm. mins, 8 Sept. 1957.

debate on the caucus block vote. Undoubtedly the fine political balance operating since 1951 had resulted in a tightening of discipline in both parties. Thus, in censuring Labour's stricter predilections, Littlefair adduced:

> I am not criticising the procedure [the group vote] for strictly political issues. What I am protesting against is the use of the weapon for non-political issues where, as the Press so rightly put it, the tail wags the dog.[30]

Cross-party voting in full council, although never a prominent feature of post-war politics in Nottingham, had further declined in recent years. Strictly, however, this was not a product of fewer free votes; it was the result, amongst all members, of a greater conformity to their respective party lines. Indeed, in other ways, little had changed since 1945. The majority of reports still received bilateral group support and thus arguably a broad consensus still existed over a wide range of functions concerned with the efficient, technical administration of public services. Parallel to this, committee work itself was rarely subject to a formal group mandate, even if here political allegiance increasingly overshadowed the previous guiding ethic of autonomy.[31] Yet, judged contemporaneously, Littlefair's identification of the apolitical, of which he gave several recent examples, was in itself partially flawed. Attempts to force the sale of scarce Corporation land to speculative builders, for example, hardly qualified for apolitical status; clearly it reversed and broke past consensually agreed reconstruction policy. Indeed, Conservatives were soon openly campaigning for the substitution of private for municipal development at Glapton in the interests of municipal economy.[32]

In citing the municipal purchase of the city's castle, Littlefair was on safer ground. Here disagreement arose over the method of payment, as the Labour group stymied the preferred method advocated by F&GP Committee, its own senior aldermen and the Conservative group en bloc. In itself this was indicative of an erosion, albeit gradual, of patriarchal

30 *GJ*, 3 Nov. 1953.
31 P. Durrant, 'The Party Caucus in Action', *GJ*, 6 Nov. 1953; L. J. Sharpe, 'The Politics of Local Government in Greater London', *Public Administration* 38 (1960), pp. 170–72; J. G. Bulpitt, 'Party Systems in Local Government', *Political Studies* 11/1 (1963), pp. 11–35.
32 NLSL L34.32, Mrs May Holland, *Election Address*, May 1954.

power. The Conservative disciplinary machine still depended heavily on the deferential acceptance of hierarchical authority. This was always less true of Labour, but particularly since Bowles's departure. Here all members, theoretically at least, were subject to a collective disciplinary code, undoubtedly more formal and rigid but also in many ways more internally democratic. Yet the F&GP Committee remained the council's most potent and prestigious body. As the local press commented, a dilemma existed for those Labour members who had as yet not wholly come to terms with the revised order of party primacy; for it was obvious that 'some senior members of the Labour benches were embarrassed by the prospect of an instruction being given to the Finance Committee'. In fact, many refused so to do and sided with the Conservatives. It was to be the last significant example of such behaviour in the council chamber. When the council again met, Labour members without dissension endorsed the group's majority decision to overrule the committee's recommendations. Behind this arithmetic lay the nexus of Littlefair's complaint—that policy had been passed against the expressed wishes of a majority of council members.[33]

*

Despite the deterioration in bi-party relations by 1953, there were as yet no formal moves to dissolve the existing inter-party concordats. Opinions were, however, to change. This was visibly promoted by a groundswell response to two key issues: the extended failure of the two parties to agree ward boundary revisions and a separate and intemperate dispute over civic patronage. Each moved activists in both parties to question the rationale of formal power sharing, although it was to be Labour who, in contrast to 1938, led the pace in finally severing the links binding the two groups.

When in 1935 the question of new ward boundaries had previously arisen, both parties had left the drafting of proposals to Corporation officials, whose judgement they later endorsed. Such procedures were again finally adopted in 1953, but only after earlier inter-party attempts to reach a consensus had repeatedly failed. Tom Owen then prepared two

33 The group was heavily divided regarding the castle finances, 14–11 votes. Over Glapton, 20–6 favoured municipal exclusivity, Lab. Group mins (dated hereafter being in the author's possession), 24 July 1953, 2 Oct. 1953.

alternatives. Both were acceptable to Labour, as each was thought to enhance the party's electoral prospects. For the same reason, each of the Town Clerk's proposals was unequivocally rejected by Conservatives. They then submitted their own outline, dismissed by Labour as 'so obviously politically biased' as to be 'hardly worth considering'. Equally, city Tories regarded Owen's proposals as 'dead and buried'. Yet that which Littlefair referred to consistently as 'an ugly brat', Labour consistently sought to resurrect and officially consecrate.[34] For Owen, who acted as mediator, the failure to reach agreement reflected the prevailing political malaise then afflicting the city:

> I express my regret that the Parties have not been able to agree a scheme. I can well understand that there are many matters of policy upon which the two Parties are so opposed that they cannot reach agreement, but I should have thought that more effort could have been made on this issue. The Parties have unfortunately been at arms [sic] length.[35]

Independently, however, Labour had already prepared new proposals of which Conservatives intentionally received scant notice, and which anyway they later rejected as being of the same bastard lineage. Rubber stamped by the Labour-controlled F&GP Committee, this revision then went forward to full council for ratification.

As the local press recorded, the ensuing debate publicly registered a turning point in inter-party relations:

> It was impossible to escape a feeling that this [special] meeting [on boundaries] might mark the end of an epoch in the Council's history and the beginning of a new phase in which political conflict becomes more acidulated and corrosive. Hitherto there has been, in spite of warm argument at times, a sense of underlying unity and a willingness to subordinate political considerations for the City's good. None of this was discernible yesterday. There was more cold distance than hot temper about the debate, with each side accusing the other of being unco-operative.[36]

34 MRC MSS 9/3/15/204, 8 and 9 Dec. 1953; letter from Littlefair to Purser, 31 Dec. 1953, IAP; *GJ*, 10 June 1954.
35 Letter from Owen to Purser, 4 Feb. 1954, IAP.
36 *GJ*, 10 June 1954.

Ill feeling extended beyond hostile exchanges between members. Owen also was the butt of repeated allegations that he had tried to sabotage Labour's objectives. Refuting these charges, the Town Clerk in turn revealed that he had been abused by Labour members for not actively prosecuting his own original proposals—or in effect for not taking a partisan line. Tolerance and compromise, apparently, had been wholly subsumed by political vexations and objectives.

The acrid atmosphere of June 1954 was not solely attributable to animosities over electoral reforms; it was also rooted in the very operation of the inter-party agreement. Earlier that year, the City Labour Party had broken tradition in opting to oppose Bill Cox, the retiring Tory Sheriff, at the forthcoming municipal elections. Neither Ernest Purser, nor a majority of the Labour group he led, approved the decision. Indeed, they had argued and voted against this at the requisite joint constituency meeting. In so doing, the group leadership upheld and conformed to the letter of the inter-party concordat, which stipulated unopposed returns for civic office holders but acknowledged that on occasion group leaders might fail to impose their views on independently minded local party organisations. Conservatives, not unrealistically, and particularly so at a time of rising political tension, were less concerned with the finer procedural points; they judged the outcome, not the intent. Purser's plea had been rejected ostensibly on two counts: that it deprived the electorate of their right to vote and party activists of the opportunity to hone their campaigning skills in a key ward. There was, however, a compelling and unconnected third reason: Cox's deep unpopularity with Labour members as one of the former wartime rebels.

Notably it was the decision to oppose Cox—that is, the breaking of tradition—which provoked Tory claims of 'Bevanite' or 'Semi-Communist' domination; thus a contrast was drawn between those now exercising a dominating 'evil influence on the affairs of the city' and Labour members of the old school of 'honour and integrity'.[37] Such disparate labelling was largely rhetorical. As the next chapter shows, although now tolerated (which was not the case in the late 1940s and early 1950s), the left were still excluded from that circle holding the civic levers of power. The exception, perhaps, was Tommy Ives. A professional organiser of national repute, he was appointed secretary to the city party, and later to the group, at the end of 1953. Again Ives was certainly no

37 *GJ*, 30 March 1954, 31 March 1954, 30 April 1954.

extremist, in Labour party terms anyway. He was, however, a constant irritant to Conservative hackles, partly because of his undoubted organisational dynamism, but also because his full-time paid status infringed the Tory amateur ideal of local government.[38]

The 1954 municipal election was an acrimonious affair where the press reported 'the gloves have been off and the punches have not been pulled'—a combat largely governed by the disputes over Cox and boundaries' redistribution.[39] In fact, the intransigence and antagonism generated both epitomised, and further exacerbated, the existing degeneration of inter-party co-operative spirit. Thus Nottingham's politics, regulated previously by the continuities imposed by reconstruction, now had new, if less guided, objectives which reaffirmed and expanded the party political imperative to the detriment of certain older cohesive civic values. During this friction-generating transition, a premium was placed on party advantage, no matter how temporary. The Conservatives' charge, set against the underpinning realities, that their opponents abused their status as the majority party to redraw electoral boundaries to ensure that Nottingham was 'Labour for good and all', serves to illustrate. Undoubtedly that was Labour's underlying intention. Yet the advantage gained was minimal. For it was widely appreciated by city politicians that all boundary proposals were automatically subject to a public enquiry. Here both sides submitted their own partisan outlines. Both were rejected. Only then did the two parties—in collusion with the Commissioner—draft fresh proposals that, with minor amendments, formed the basis for a compromise solution. Less than a year later, Conservatives (now the majority party) themselves sought to re-open the dispute by amending this negotiated settlement; here attempting, unsuccessfully, to reintroduce a business-weighted city vote.[40] Once exposed, it seemed, political lesions fermented and flourished.

The questions raised by Labour's decision to oppose Cox had perhaps greater immediate significance for the subsequent dismantling of formalised inter-party co-operation. Viewed dispassionately, the clauses relating to civic electoral protection were never a major component of the inter-party power-sharing agreements. Civic honours, however, held a

38 NCC, Council mins, 9 June 1954, 19 July 1954; *The Economist*, 22 Aug. 1959; *The Times*, 2 May 1960; interview with Oscar Watkinson, 6 Feb. 1989.

39 *GJ*, 13 May 1954.

40 *GJ*, 30 April 1954; NAO DDPP 2, Nott'm South Con. Ass., Annual Report 1955; NCC, Council mins, 3 Oct. 1955.

central place in the hearts of many councillors. Yet the exact terms of the protocols were never widely publicised even within the ranks of the parties themselves. Thus there was more than a touch of irony in both party leaderships subsequently demanding of the electorate during the 1954 municipal campaign that they pass judgement on the parties' broader conduct in interpreting what remained a confidential agreement. Moreover, the hierarchically imposed truces—the most visible aspect here in that it directly affected local campaigning—irritated branches. Thus it was that activists in both parties, in mimicking civic antagonisms, first sought to nullify formal co-operative practices in favour of unregulated, open competition. At the same time, the fundamentals—those clauses covering committee appointments—were also not functioning correctly. The death of a number of long-standing committee chairs generated considerable friction over replacements in the years following, to a degree that in May 1955 Labour threatened to resign all committee posts.[41] Thus the old adage of filling places according to seniority and custom fell victim to increased party tensions. Put simply, this most comprehensive of agreements no longer brokered consensual objectives.

It was, however, further discontent at grass roots level—once more against imposed controls negating party contests—which provided the immediate impetus for change. In June 1955 both party leaders agreed that because of pending boundary changes, no by-elections would be held that year, the incumbent party automatically taking any vacancy. This temporary addendum was later ratified by Labour delegates, but its content was not revealed to local Tories. Radford Conservatives were, therefore, a little surprised when instructed by Littlefair not to contest their ward following the death of the sitting Labour member. The hierarchical ratification of yet another 'secret agreement' caused considerable unease in Tory ranks, particularly amongst younger members, and Littlefair unusually faced a series of challenges to limit his future independent authority. In Labour ranks also there was growing disquiet centring on the individual freedom to contest seats, which was largely a short form for the recognition and expression of placing party first. Earlier calls in January 1955 to terminate immediately all existing arrangements were, however, instantly rejected by the Labour group.

41 NAO LPC Box 10, Letter from Purser to Littlefair, 17 May 1955; *ibid*, Box 12, letter from Littlefair to Wigman, 23 May 1956; Lab. Group mins, Jan. 1955–June 1956, *passim*.

Although now deeply divided themselves, they also insisted that local activists had no direct role to play in this arena. However, the seemingly perennial disputes over committee allocations took a hand and in March 1956 both party and group announced their intention to renegotiate fundamentally the agreements.[42] This accurately reflected the recently expressed mood both of party members and councillors, more particularly as the life-span of the existing concordat drew to a close. Yet with a renewed sense of irony, the one aspect of the agreement which Labour promised not to alter radically was that covering the automatic re-election of members holding civic office. Thus at the end of this political era, the most contentious and publicly aired component of the agreement was retained, not in the interests of local democracy, but of those many council members who saw a potential appointment to the mayoralty or shrievalty as a fitting pinnacle to their political career.

*

The two group leaders finally met in January 1957, each with their own reconstituted draft agreements. In certain areas, Labour offered flexibility in its approach—retaining largely intact, for example, the annual rotation of civic offices instead of its preferred option of allocation according to party strength. Agreement was also reached on the future assignment of aldermanic places. The weighting system accorded to length of service was abandoned, as was the protection previously afforded serving aldermen. In future a party's entitlement was to be recalculated triennially on a ratio (1:3) directly proportional to the number of elected councillors each had at that time. The significance of these changes should not be overlooked. Aldermanic protection had been a past bulwark of the apolitical code. Now nominations were wholly dependent on electoral success; 1958, for example, saw the automatic and forced retirement of three Conservative elders who had 70 years' service collectively. It was the final acknowledgement of local party primacy over aldermanic individualism, at a time when the aldermanic system as a whole was

---

42 *GJ*, 8 March 1956, 10 March 1956, 19 March 1956; NAO DDPP2, Nott'm South Con. Ass. mins, 1956 AGM.

being increasingly questioned as an institution incompatible with democratic principles (although it was not finally abolished until 1974).[43]

The Labour and Conservative drafts did, however, differ substantially in two respects. Under Labour's constitution, responsibility for candidature selection was vested in the City Labour Party, a delegatory body drawn from the city's four constituencies and affiliated bodies. Conservatives repeated past demands that the group retain a veto to protect nominees to civic office from a forced election after their year of office. It was a request with which Wigman (now re-elected leader) simply could not comply, for it required a change to local and national party rules. More particularly, the two parties differed substantially on Labour's central thesis that 'the majority party decide the Chairmanships and Vice-Chairmanships' of all council committees.[44] No matter that it shared responsibility for escalating inter-party tensions in preceding years, nor that there was activist dissatisfaction with the protective nature of the protocols, the Tory group had no desire to abolish power-sharing at this juncture. Littlefair's 'outrage' was clearly expressed:

> The very first opportunity that a slender Labour majority had power, they seized that opportunity to take what I cannot but regard as a scandalous, unscrupulous dictatorial seizure of power. It is a flagrant refusal of the treatment they have received in the past and which we hoped and expected would be carried out in the future ... I am sure that some of the [Labour] members' sense of decency and their idea of sportsmanship is such that this must be as revolting a move to them as it is to us on this side.[45]

Particularly insidious to Conservative minds was the dismissal of Crane as Chair of Housing, a post he had occupied with joint support since 1919.

Clearly Littlefair's assertion requires qualification, not least in its failure to acknowledge Conservative abolitionism in 1938, the subsequent joint party adherence to the protocols since 1945 or the recent growing

43 P. W. Jackson, *Local Government* (1967), pp. 85–86; Jones, *Borough Politics*, pp. 265–67, 325–45; *Royal Commission on Local Government in England: Minutes of Evidence* (1967), Vol. 12, pp. 298, 330–31.

44 Draft Proposals on Majority Responsibilities [taken from election policy 1956], IAP; Lab. Group mins, 17 Dec. 1956, 22 Feb. 1957, 28 Feb. 1957.

45 *GJ*, 4 June 1957.

disquiet in both parties. Yet if Labour's *raison d'être* for change was now based solely on the 'seizure of power', then its goals were indeed short-term: or as likely, that is, to be as detrimental to Labour civic careers as, more immediately, to those of their Conservative counterparts. Nevertheless, the press followed Littlefair's lead in suggesting that Labour had 'pulled a fast one', gambling that Conservatives, when re-elected, would not retaliate. Littlefair did immediately guarantee that when returned to power he would re-introduce joint rule. In practice, this exercise in 'placing city before party' was to be limited to one chair, which Labour anyway rejected.[46] In fact, the tenets of single party rule, once introduced, quickly became an integral part of Nottingham's political government. When the protocol was renewed in 1962, the ruling Conservative group formally abandoned its previous hostility and underwrote this principle into the fourth post-war agreement. They were to repeat this endorsement in 1968, when again they were the majority group (see Appendix).

Short-term, however, in acknowledging that Conservatives remained opposed implacably to changes in committee patronage, the Labour group dispensed with consensus in favour of unilateral imposition. The new agreement was eventually signed in April 1957. At the same time, Conservatives were offered, by way of compensation, all the committee vice-chairs—a not uncommon practice elsewhere. It was a compromise that later formed the basis of much criticism from within the party, where the group's participation in even this modified system of joint rule allegedly promoted an unacceptably 'comfortable atmosphere' of inter-party co-operation. Yet in the insular world of local government, fundamental changes concerning patronage almost automatically courted controversy from all quarters. That this occurred in Nottingham merits no great surprise; it too was common elsewhere.[47] Ultimately the proposals eventually implemented by Nottingham's Labour group were only radical when measured against the city's own past; that is why they attracted criticism from both left and right.

In other ways, however, 1957 marked a notable change. The 1945 and 1951 agreements embodied a continuance of the pre-war model of

46 *GJ*, 4 June, 13-15 May 1961.
47 Howard, *New Statesman*, 21 Aug. 1964, p. 234; Lab. Group mins, 14 May 1961, 18 July 1961, 27 July 1961; Bulpitt, *Party Politics*, pp. 64–65; Jones, *Borough Politics*, p. 67; Bealey et al., *Constituency Politics*, p. 345.

oligarchic paternalism in city governance. The concordats simply confirmed the practice of insular, self-perpetuating decision-making within the bi-modular political circumstances of post-war Nottingham. They did this by drawing on a formula geared to perpetuating the guiding authority, 'wisdom' and 'benevolence' of an established ruling political leadership–Nottingham's own civic 'Great and the Good'. Elsewhere, Peter Hennessy suggests the phrase conveys an 'apolitical, high-minded, non-partisan' approach to public administration.[48] Undoubtedly this would have been an epithet of which the city's post-war leadership would have privately approved, just as it was an approach which they espoused publicly during Nottingham's reconstruction phase.

48 P. Hennessy, *The Great and the Good: An Inquiry into the British Establishment* (1986), p. 11.

CHAPTER 5
Militants, Reactionaries and Expulsions 1945–60

Analysis so far has stressed the commonalty of cause which encompassed both groups immediately during city reconstruction, and suggested, moreover, that a close correlation existed chronologically between this reconstruction process and the fluctuating fortunes of post-war local political consensus. The acts of placing 'city before party' and accepting historically engineered limits to disagreement over patronage distribution, fixed within an inherited—indeed, a re-invigorated—framework of tolerance and compromise, represented an overarching ethos which pragmatically set aside ideological divisions (that is, those forces which represent the antithesis of consensual practice). Nevertheless much recent criticism of the consensus theory has focused heavily on the centrality of the ideological cleavages that separated the two parties nationally at the war's end, and which impinged significantly upon the post-war political settlement.[1] We need, therefore, to explore this aspect of political life as it existed locally, going beyond questioning oft-repeated Conservative opinion that Labour was both intemperate in its disciplinary practice and increasingly radical in its politics.

At first glance there does appear to be a parallel inversion in the consensus chronologies operating locally and nationally, where in each ideology and pragmatism are reciprocally transposed as key determinants, albeit in the context of the broader trend to cultural diversity and greater freedoms which gradually broke open British society through the 1950s from its restrictive, if more socially cohesive, past.[2] Nationally, as noted in the introduction, the literature places a particular emphasis on the growing commitment by Conservatives, in part for electoral reasons, to the social democratic agenda. In contrast, the general trend in Nottingham

1 Morgan, *People's Peace*, ch. 1; Harris, 'Political Ideas'; S. Brooke, 'The Labour Party and the Second World War', in A. Gorst, L. Johnman and W. S. Lucas (eds.), *Contemporary British History 1931-1961: Politics and the Limits of Policy* (1991), pp. 1–16.
2 Marwick, *British Society, Part II: Roads to Freedom 1957–72*, pp. 114 ff.

was one of party divergence not congruity. Thus the early 1950s was marked by the reassertion of overtly stated ideological rivalries which impinged on policy formation. That this was a key factor in deteriorating inter-party cooperation in the council chamber and committee room is obvious. But, as noted, it was not the only reason or root determinant. Party rivalry, of which dogmatic advocacy was an expression, was also the product of fine party balances, which in turn saw a circular extension of party discipline and a lessening of political accommodation and compromise. Increased party discipline, particularly in the Labour camp, was not wholly a product of political stalemate. It did, however, form the foundation for what might loosely be seen as the progressive and pervasive politicisation of new and important areas of inter-party activity, initially and most noticeably within the committee structure but also expressed through the rigidity of the caucusing process itself.

It would be a mistake to confuse increasing politicisation (given both its national origins and bi-party local characteristics), or indeed the Labour group's increasing propensity to pursue a controversial line, with local political extremism. In fact, Conservatives only too readily conflated the two. Here Tory hyperbole generally accompanied any break with, or change to, the existing structural status quo: thus Purser's failure to enforce the electoral truce for Cox's return provoked claims of Bevanite domination; the abolition of single party rule was portrayed as the end to local democracy. Of course, it must be remembered that the use of militant terminology to caricature their Labour opponents was a well-used tactic employed by Conservatives and the local press (mimicking in this respect nationally established precedents).[3] Its most basic form found expression in the constant reference to Labour members as 'the Socialists'. Local election coverage saw newspapers refer collectively to an 'anti-Socialist' vote, or present Conservative and Liberal candidates as representative of a hypothetical anti-Labour bloc. Unity, however, was not identified as a characteristic of the Labour group or party; here an honourable 'old guard', protective of past consensual practices and values, fought a valiant rearguard action against an increasingly pervasive militancy. In part, this mythology was nurtured by continuing reference to the chasm that existed between the disciplinary practices of each group. While Labour, allegedly, was held moribund by its collective and rigidly enforced disciplinary codes, Conservatives stressed (as they had since

3 *Ibid*, pp. 103–04.

1945) that their own members were 'free to act on [their] own initiative in whatever way' each considered 'served the best interests of his electors'. Common sense, of course, dictated that this meant accepting and complying with the Conservative whip; again it was not unknown, as was the case with Joseph Gregg-Herriot, for its members to be subsequently de-selected if their views ran counter to group policy.[4]

However, the call promoting individual freedoms had always extended beyond local Conservative concerns over members' voting behaviour. Certainly, the mid-1950s saw a dampening of the Tory preoccupation with individualism as a major campaigning issue. Conservative candidates in Nottingham no longer conjured up the vivid metaphoric images of enslavement–of 'chains' and 'shackles'–employed in 1945 when describing Labour's proposed regulatory approach to economic and social policy.[5] While the Conservatives continued in the early 1950s to 'set the people free' of the remnants of wartime controls, nevertheless, in embracing the broad tenets of the post-war Keynesian settlement, they repudiated, amongst other things, 'the dichotomies of ... personal freedom versus social justice'. Thus, by the time of the 1955 general election, this once ebullient battle-cry no longer held pride of place in the party's national armoury.[6] Parliamentary revisionism, however, was not necessarily mirrored at a local level. Indeed, Conservative constituency activists nationally acquired, perhaps unjustly, a reputation for reactionary vigour more in keeping with the party's ideological past.[7]

To degrees, such generalisations are applicable to Nottingham's local party hierarchy. The inter-party power-sharing agreements themselves, in emphasising a pragmatic co-operative spirit, broadly represented a local consensual tradition which was re-invigorated by the joint agreement over the social priorities allied to reconstruction. Beside this agreement,

---

4 NLSL L34.32 S. Pearson, *Election Address,* May 1957; NAO LPC Box 10, letters from A. J. Rowlands (Abbey Ward Con. Ass.) to J. Gregg-Herriot, 21 Feb. 1956 and J. Gregg-Herriot to Purser, 29 Feb. 1956.

5 *NJ,* 8 June 1945, 13 June 1945; Addison, *Road to 1945,* p. 265.

6 Marquand, *Unprincipled Society,* p. 19; D. E. Butler, *The British General Election of 1955* (1955), pp. 33–35; for a different emphasis, see Rollings, 'Poor Mr Butskell', pp. 183–205.

7 L. Epenstien, 'British MP's and their Local Parties: The Suez Case', *American Political Science Review* 54 (1960), pp. 374–90; R. T. McKenzie, *British Political Parties* (1964 edn.), pp. 631–34. For a rebuttal, see R. Rose, 'The Political Ideas of English Party Activists', *The American Political Science Review* 56 (1962), pp. 360–71; also J. Biffen, 'The Constituency Leaders', *Crossbow* 4/13 (Aut. 1960), pp. 27–32.

however, sat two other distinctive strands of thought. The first, best identified as city paternalism, emphasised the Corporation's traditional responsibility for welfare provision. Here, force of circumstance—particularly post-war shortages and government policy—only served to reinforce earlier concerns over, for example, poor working-class housing. It was a cause pressed vigorously by its Tory proponents, to a degree that in intent it merged successfully with post-war expectations re-defined under the auspices of Welfare State rights. Thus, publicly funded intervention as an extension of civic responsibility was an already developed and central trait within the city's municipal ethos. However, Conservative commitment was also marked by its sometimes attenuated nature: here (although to a lesser degree than in the 1930s) continual justification, as opposed to an ethically compulsory obligation, was still necessary. The criteria employed to justify intervention also indicated a less than wholesale change in attitude. Littlefair's commentary that city bus subsidies for the elderly could be viewed as a matter of 'local charity' serves to illustrate the latter point. Moreover, in the field of housing, the party's paternalistic attitudes could, at times, be archaic: for example, it refused, until forced by central government, to adopt even inter-war specifications when providing additional working-men's hostel accommodation in the mid-1950s.

Paternalism also rarely extended beyond those areas covered by statutory responsibility. In that sense, it retained a strong minimalist characteristic, reflective of the other harsher, dogmatic tract to local Conservative hierarchical philosophy which was solidly rooted in the individualist tradition. At its most extreme, this saw British post-war society in 'crisis'. In a brief exposition against Keynesian economics and living beyond one's means, Sir Charles Pain (President of the City Conservative Party) explained that this ferment would

> exhaust itself only when the masses of the people have cast from their lips the cups which contain the poisonous and enervating potions of Marx and his modern disciples [Keynes] ... We want to get back to that grand old philosopher of Victorian times, Samuel Smiles, who preached the nobility of labour, the sanctity and the importance of the soul of the individual as against the state, the

nobility of work and the virtue of thrift in the individual, the municipality and in the state.[8]

Advocacy of a blanket minimalist approach, particularly by prominent Conservative businessmen, remained a potent force in post-war local party thinking which sat uneasily with an opposing paternalist rationale. Compensatory minimalism was most ardent in the years immediately after 1945; a reaction against what in industrial and political terms was perceived to be a loss of influence in the community in which traditionally they had held dominant sway as natural, if self-selected, leaders. Tory electoral rejection, moreover, precipitated self-doubt; measured in the repeated demands that Labour acknowledge deferentially that 'the place this country had gained prior to the war was due entirely to the enterprise, skill, hard work and ability displayed ... by employers' for, as a party, Labour lacked those 'able to assume the leadership of industry'.[9]

The dilemma, for such it was, which faced Nottingham's Conservative party in 1945 was in matching the obvious and pressing need for reconstruction (or put another way, honouring its paternalistic obligation) against a then enlivened minimalist reaction. In fact, the internal arguments, although heated, proved short-lived; Labour's wholehearted support for public regeneration, when coupled with Tory progressivism, quickly outflanked minimalist objections. However, the Conservative right was reinforced in 1949 with the election of textile manufacturer Joseph Littlefair as party leader. He replaced Cecil Armitage, a founding architect in renewing the inter-party agreements post-war. Armitage had already once threatened resignation because senior, influential sections of the party expressed dissatisfaction with his consensual approach. Littlefair's appointment now brought a more abrasive tone to the party at a time when Conservative confidence and organisation were recovering from its earlier heavy electoral defeats. As local Conservatives proclaimed boldly in 1950: 'There is no middle way', for 'Socialism is the bridge across which Communism advances'.[10]

8 Nott'm Chamber of Commerce, mins, AGM, 1947.

9 *Ibid.*, Ald. Sir Albert Atkey, Counc. Littlefair, 30 June 1947.

10 *NJ*, 21 Jan. 1947, 1 March 1947; letter from Tom Baxter to Norman Smith, 3 Dec. 1947, IAP; NAO DDPP2/2, Nott'm South Con. Ass., Annual Reports, 1948–50; Nott'm City Con. Party, *Nottingham Citizen 1950 Election Edn.*; Littlefair, *Guardian Journal Evening Post News Emergency Edition*, 28 July 1959.

Other circumstances also came to favour a more hawkish Tory approach to city politics. The initial euphoria for reconstruction was to be tempered by the realities of limited resources and, short-term and to a lesser degree, competing political priorities. Labour's advocacy of a more overtly party-based discipline also nurtured the growth of ideological partisanship in which minimalism, through its corollary individualism, provided a natural focus for Conservative opposition. The major controversies of the period, with a few notable exceptions, were all weighted on one side by minimalist or libertarian pre-occupations: members' voting freedoms, trade union rights, Conservative opposition to committee changes, and later in the 1950s, support for the city's Chief Constable (after his suspension), the construction of a civic theatre and press freedom.

The Conservative perspective, in seeing a central relationship between alleged Labour extremism and the rigidity of its group system, believed tacitly that greater individual expression from the Labour benches would moderate the pace of change. There was some truth in this assertion. The strength of the caucus lay in its mandatory imposition, which both stifled internal dissent and added momentum to decision making and implementation. Conservative minimalist instincts, in a local context, extended naturally from their equally strong reserve against 'radical' change. It was Labour that provided the impetus for reform to the city's post-war political structure and for any extension of its responsibilities. Conservatives, comparatively, defended the status quo. Such a passive stance was less reliant on an empowering disciplinary caucus. Pragmatically, therefore, Conservatives could afford a greater tolerance towards individual expression. Yet in one major respect, the association of caucus rigidity with latent militancy was completely misplaced. Throughout the post-war period, an essentially right-of-centre Labour hierarchy used this power, in conjunction with the authority of the City Party's executive, to silence left-wing criticism. Far from being a purveyor of radicalism, Labour's stricter disciplinary codes in fact promoted an inner conservatism which successive waves of left-wing activists failed to breach.

Of course, factionalism—and particularly militancy—in Labour ranks gained a high profile during the 1950s because of the ideological schisms in the Parliamentary Party, and later with the internecine battles over Clause Four and unilateralism. Here, for example, Edward Janosik's authoritative survey found that either 'moderate or left-wing opinion so completely dominated some constituency parties that opposition to the prevailing view was abortive'.[11] City Conservatives were equally happy to brand its opponents 'Bevanite' or 'semi-Communist' led, the two epithets being interchangeable. This was symptomatic of much of the ambiguity underpinning local accusations; but then it was also apparent nationally, given the doubts over even Bevan's status for membership of the disaffected parliamentary grouping bearing his name.[12] Certainly in Nottingham there were few signs that the Labour group itself was swayed by the doctrinal diatribes emanating from London. Only in the late 1950s did council members become noticeably tied to a broader agenda encompassing contentious issues (nuclear disarmament, South Africa, détente) outside a parochial remit, and then such flirtations remained essentially the tip of a dominant, local policy remit orchestrated by an essentially centrist group leadership.

Yet it would be misleading to suggest that, at times, Nottingham's constituency parties did not offer a leftist perspective—they did. Indeed, left-wing activists rose to prominence in the party and, especially, the broader Labour movement. This was particularly true of Nottingham's Trades Council, under left-wing stewardship throughout the post-war period—notably that of Jack Charlesworth, its Communist secretary. In language it espoused the values, not of consensus but of class war: for 'The Tories are the traditional enemies of the Working Class' and Labour 'has nothing in common with a Party guilty of persecuting the early pioneers of the Trade Union Movement, and which banished our forefathers from these shores'.[13] Equally, it opposed national guidelines restricting contact with proscribed left-wing organisations; here only the outbreak of the Korean War predicated a notable reversal in easily overturning past decisions to affiliate to the British-Soviet Friendship Society. Yet there was always a sizeable minority who, with close TUC support and liaison, actively opposed overtly leftist fraternisation and who vied for the support—with the left—of those delegates who held centre ground. Only by the narrowest of margins, and amid acrimonious debate, did the Executive and full council agree association to, and to campaign with, such groupings as the British Peace Council in 1950. Yet parallel

11 E. G. Janosik, *Constituency Labour Parties in Britain* (1968), p. 103. His survey was conducted during 1962–63.

12 Morgan, *People's Peace*, pp. 103–4; for Bevanism (and also leftist splinter groups) see M. Jenkins, *Bevanism: Labour's High Tide. The Cold War and the Democratic Mass Movement* (1979).

13 NUMD TrM Box 2, 1951 Manifesto, Trades Council mins, 17 Oct. 1951.

plans to organise a local 'Peace Conference' were defeated. Thus, despite its pronouncements, the Trades Council was far from being monolithic in political outlook. Indeed, it had a strong pragmatic core: ironically, it was, for example, by its own admission on 'excellent terms' with Nottingham's Chamber of Commerce.[14]

Particularly in the early post-war years (as in the 1930s and early 1940s), group and City Party relations with the Trades Council were permanently strained. A Joint Consultative Committee (JCC), re-established in 1944 and again in 1950, failed to fulfil its mediatory function. Thus, despite an early optimism, Trades delegates were soon again bemoaning a lack of response by councillors to matters raised at the forum. For their part, the City Party and group resented any interference in local affairs unconnected directly with trades union matters; being particularly annoyed, for example, by criticism of the lack of medical facilities in parts of Nottingham. Chris Coffey, a National Union of Railmen delegate, expressed this displeasure at what again was perceived as another attempt to 'belittle the local Labour Party':

> You will appreciate the Trades Council meetings are really public, as both local newspapers are in attendance to report, and they do report, but only the spicy bits that attack the Labour Party. We have a Joint Consultative Committee in being—The Trades Council, The Co-op, and ourselves, [sic] at no time have the Trades Council referred any Political matters [directly] to us, but they refer plenty of TU matters [sic] in fact if you see the minutes of the TC you will observe it is nearly a political meeting—of course it is run by Comms [sic], so what can you expect.[15]

Coffey was firmly to the right of Nottingham's Labour group. As City Party secretary, he used his office to squash any contact with left-wing groupings, even insisting that police physically intervene to prevent the local Communist party's traditional participation during the 1952 May Day parade.

---

14 *Ibid.*, Box 3, letter from Charlesworth to R. Boyfield (TUC), 23 Oct. 1950; MRC MSS 292/79N/22, letter from C. P. Callinan to R. Boyfield, 5 Sept. 1950; see also R. Stevens, '"Disruptive Elements"? The Influence of the Communist Party in Nottingham and District Trades Council, 1929–1951', *Labour History Review* 58/3 (1993), pp. 22–37.
15 Letter from Coffey to Tom O'Brien, MP, 28 Nov. 1952, IAP.

Nevertheless, Coffey's responses were not wholly inconsistent with those of the group and City Party hierarchy generally. Here, conspicuous efforts were made to distance themselves from Trades Council campaigning activities and negate their political legitimacy. The rigour with which this self-imposed code of centrist isolation was enforced led to decisions which, when viewed from outside this rationale, appear extraordinary—even irritating those on the Trades Council who vigorously opposed Communist influence.[16] In 1950, the TUC and Labour Government instigated a national campaign to improve food hygiene standards. By way of reply, the Trades Council unanimously called for Labour party participation in a vigorous joint campaign, coordinated by the JCC, to promote politically 'a code of rules for the handling and distribution of food in the interests of public health'. The Chamber of Commerce, however, which co-ordinated the business community's response and had always opposed controls, wanted voluntary self-regulation. This in turn provoked a suspicion amongst small shop-keepers that the issuing of complying certificates would be manipulated by the larger and wealthier concerns to their own advantage. Given the Conservative presence in the Chamber, it was, according to Charlesworth, political 'dynamite'.[17] Either way, however, it was a campaign in which the City Party refused to participate. The underlying reason for this and other parallel decisions is not hard to discern. Notwithstanding national prejudices, the sympathies of leading local Trades Council members were incompatible with the conciliatory rationale adopted by the city's Labour hierarchy; it followed that all Trades Council initiatives, irrespective of merit, were politically tainted.

Explaining the City Party's decision to sever relations in 1953, Jim Cattermole (Labour's East Midlands Regional Organiser) noted simply that 'the Trades Council have been dealing with political matters which ought to be outside their [sic] responsibility.'[18] Yet the ready

16 Stevens, '"Disruptive Elements"?', p. 30; MRC MSS 292/79N/22, letters from J. P. Callinan to R. Boyfield, 12 June 1950 and 5 Sept. 1950.

17 *NEP*, 14 Nov. 1950; *NJ*, 16 Nov. 1950; *NG*, 16 Nov. 1950; NUMD TrM Box 17, hand-written note on 'Clean Food Campaign file'; ibid., JCC mins, 5 March 1951; *ibid.*, Box 2, Trades Council mins, 17 Jan. 1951.

18 MRC MSS 9/3/15/60, 26 March 1953. Cattermole later became a prominent organiser for the Campaign for Democratic Socialism, the pro-Gaitskellite group established to counter left-wing influence in the party; B. Brivati, 'Campaign for Democratic Socialism', *Contemporary Record* 4/1 (1990), pp. 11–12.

compartmentalisation of the political and industrial in the manner prescribed by local councillors and Labour officials was misleading, even artificial. Consider, for example, the Trades Council's enthusiastic support of the National League for the Blind in its battle for trades union representation. Pre-war in origin, the campaign for 'adequate local negotiating machinery' was instrumental in the Trades Council's decision, in a bid to re-open local channels of political influence, to press for the reformation of the JCC in 1950. Attempts to establish trades union bargaining rights nationally had been repeatedly blocked by local authority organisations (which subsidised blind workers' wage levels but delegated managerial responsibility of local workshops to the voluntary sector) and the National Association for Blind Workshops. The League then sought separate local agreements. Nottingham's Labour group was less than enthusiastic, but finally agreed in October 1950 to support the establishment of a local Joint Industrial Council. By the following September—in what the Trades Council took to be the expression of 'an apparent indifferent attitude'—no advance had been made.[19]

Although later granted negotiating rights nationally, the League still favoured the creation of formalised local consultation with employing authorities, integral to the union's strategy to transfer jurisdiction for blind education and employment provision from the voluntary to the public sector. It too remained 'very disappointed with some of our Nottingham Labour colleagues'. Indeed, the Trades Council's support for the League's aims—the ending of charitable status and control, and for full negotiating rights—formed an unlikely but nevertheless central hinge in the deteriorating relations between group, party and the Trades Council. As Charlesworth noted in 1953:

> It is with intense regret that we have not achieved the fullest co-operation with the J.C.C.. The outstanding subject that has continued to engage the attention of the Committee during 1952 has been the position of blind workers and their struggle for the establishment of joint consultation with their employers.[20]

19 NUMD TrM Box 3, letter from Charlesworth to Coffey, 8 Sept. 1951; letter from G. L. Ball (Nat. League Blind) to Charlesworth, 14 Aug. 1950.
20 NUMD TrM Box 3, letter from J. Perry (NLB) to R. S. Barnes (Nott'm TWU), 25 Sept. 1951; Charlesworth, Nott'm Trades Council, *Annual Report and Directory 1953.*

Such a 'struggle' defies easy categorisation, although certainly its local component—with the city as an employing authority—made it contentious politically. That said, there are good grounds for viewing the initial campaign at least as a wholly industrial concern: one of union recognition, backed by the TUC, on behalf of an affiliated body. Shortly after, the JCC was abolished.

Yet by the mid-1950s, there was a dramatic improvement in relations between the Trades Council, City Party and even the group. According to Charlesworth, much of the credit for this *rapprochement* went to Tommy Ives, who was 'ever ready to confer with us on any matter of mutual concern'. Undoubtedly there was a strong element of truth in this assertion. Cattermole, since his arrival in Nottingham, had consistently drawn attention to the acrimonious and personalised tenor of city Labour politics. His solution was to import an outside professional organiser to replace Coffey, who had stepped down as group secretary during his year as Lord Mayor. Ives's appointment did much to ease existing tensions; for he, unlike his predecessor, was tolerant of, and never automatically hostile to, the purveyors of left-wing opinion. The reformation of the JCC shortly after Ives's arrival also did much to improve this reconciliation. By 1956, the Trades Council was speaking of a city Labour movement with a 'unity of purpose that even four years ago was not thought possible; now no irritating differences exist'.[21] Greater harmony, however, was not necessarily a product of a corresponding group radicalisation. Ives's tenure did correspond with a period of major structural change in the city's political history, when group and party opted to take a more adversarial stance—an approach long favoured by the Trades Council—by ending bi-party rule. Yet it was also a period when the Trades Council itself took a step to the right in electing for the first time a majority of 'known moderates' to its ruling Executive. More importantly, the Trades Council reciprocally exercised restraint in its public condemnation of local Labour policy, referring disagreement to the JCC or debating sensitive issues in camera to avoid the attentions of an unsympathetic press and what was now deemed to be 'undesirable publicity'.[22] It was an

21 Charlesworth, Nott'm Trades Council, *Annual Report 1954*; *ibid.*, 1956; see also MRC MSS 9/3/14/122, 26 June 1952, MSS 9/3/15/66, undated (approx. March 1953).

22 *NEP*, 21 March 1957; NUMD TrM Box 2, Trades Council mins, 17 April 1957, 17 July 1957; Charlesworth, Nott'm Trades Council, *Annual Report 1959*.

expression of mutual sensitivity that would have been unthinkable in the immediate post-war years.

It was, however, a relatively short-lived respite. Concurrent with Ives's departure in 1960, Labour's heavy electoral defeat following their suspension of the city's Chief Constable (Athelstan Popkess), and the consequential impulse towards inter-group consensual realignment that this produced, the Trades Council also once again went its own way at a time nationally when relations between left and right were growing ever more hostile. Ives's parting plea was against those again seeking to ostracise the left: this, he argued, 'could only assist the Tories and not the Labour Party'. Shortly after the Trades Council broke its now customary silence publicly to condemn group policy over increased housing rents, calling on it 'to adopt Socialism to win working class support and not to implement Tory policy'.[23] It was wholly reminiscent of earlier disputes.

*

If relations within the Labour movement were of a somewhat variable nature, the dominant political tone was always set by those seeking and exercising an electoral mandate—the City Labour Party and group. Those who controlled this machinery exercised considerable sway: witness Ives's moderating role in easing internal tensions. Nevertheless, those prominent in city Labour politics identified more frequently with the party's right, or adopted a broadly reactionary stance specifically to contain leftist opposition to the status quo. This is not to suggest that Nottingham remained cocooned from national factionalism. It did not. In fact, national divisions helped foster existing local antagonisms—in extreme cases provoking expulsions. Yet, interestingly, marked contrasts existed between the support proffered by city constituency parties to left-wing parliamentarians facing expulsion and the, at times, fickle assistance afforded local members facing disciplinary action. Aside from a detached idealism lacking when the 'miscreant' was known, again this reflected the perfunctory authority exercised by the City Party Executive when presiding over local affairs, and its not infrequent aim (shared by the group) of excluding radical influence from Nottingham's political

23 NUMD Box 2, Nott'm Trades Council mins, 15 March 1960, 17 Aug. 1960.

structures.[24] In the early 1960s, when this 'old guard' lost control of the executive to the new radical left, it was the group and its supporters in the City Labour Parties who intervened promptly to enforce again the established local orthodoxy.

Major players in this left-right conflict were Labour's full-time staff. Ives's left-of-centre credentials have already been noted. Those, however, responsible directly to Transport House—Tom Baxter, who died in 1952, and particularly his successor as Regional Organiser, Jim Cattermole—actively sought to counter radical influence. Of course, Labour historically always entertained fears of entryism and Nottingham's officials actively encouraged adherence to a national policy of excluding, for example, Communist affiliation and influence generally. It was not always successful in this latter aim. Constance Kay, the Region's Women's Organiser, when reporting on the 1945 general election, openly admitted that not only had Communists actively participated in Labour's campaign, but that its party organiser had been a key worker in Labour's central committee rooms. Similarly, Baxter and James Harrison MP, when attending a reception for a visiting delegation of Chinese delegates, instead found themselves unwittingly promoting a 'propaganda stunt for the benefit of the Communist Party'.[25]

In fact, there was fairly close liaison between Transport House and the regions to control extremist influence, not just in the Labour Party itself but also in the trade unions—a particular concern during the Attlee administration. In 1949 Baxter, for example, on learning that three of the six nominees seeking election as organisers for Association of Locomotive Engineers and Firemen (ASLEF) were Communist party members, contacted Morgan Phillips (the national Party Secretary) so that something might be done 'through the *Daily Herald* and in other ways to spoil C.P. tactics'. Phillips adopted a twin strategy here as elsewhere, urging his network of regional organisers not only to 'whip up support for "moderate" candidates', but also to subvert Communist nominations. Such initiatives mirrored closely the very political interference in the internal

24 NMLH (Nott'm West CLP file), letter from T. Roper to J. Griffin, MP, 28 May 1949; NAO LPC Box 7, letter from R. T. Sloman to M. Phillips, 27 Dec. 1952; MRC MSS 9/3/14/122 and 219, 26 June 1952 and 20 Nov. 1952; MSS 9/3/15/117, 18 June 1953.
25 NAO LPC Box 7, Kay, Report on Gen. Election, 3 July 1945; ibid., letter from Baxter to Div. & local Lab. Parties, 13 April 1946; NMLH GS/EMRLP/45, letter from Baxter to Phillips, 17 Oct. 1950.

affairs of autonomous bodies to which Nottingham's own Labour party took great exception in its relations with the Trades Council. The operation of this double standard even at times provoked division in the local party, as Cattermole found when attending a meeting of Amalgamated Engineering Union (AEU) Labour members in Nottingham. Here the chair of Meadows Ward resolutely opposed a policy of caucusing support for candidates to union office and promptly left, declaring his intention of supporting a Communist nominee. Others at the meeting, however, adopted a wholly pragmatic tack: agreeing, not so much to support nominees, but rather to publicise the political credentials of the Communist.[26]

Not all post-war factional in-fighting centred on the stifling of radical influence. For example, Roland Green (later the influential Chair of Education) sought the de-selection of a neighbouring councillor in a safer seat, allegedly packing selection meetings with his own supporters, for no other reason than having suffered a 'smart check' to his own political ambition with his earlier electoral defeat in May 1947. Undoubtedly he would have succeeded had not the Co-operative Society intervened by threatening to withdraw financial support from the constituency, the Society taking great exception to the 'intrigues and backdoor methods' being employed against their nominee, especially by one of their own employees—Green.[27] In fact the Co-operative Society, as Labour's chief financial benefactor, through direct sponsorship, subsidised employment and interest-free loans, had the power to exert considerable influence over candidate and officer selection. In general, however, it chose not to intervene directly other than by offering its not inconsiderable support to the existing status quo.

But not all attempts at de-selection were initiated by the right. Geoffrey de Freitas, elected for Nottingham Central in 1945, split local party support for his continuing candidature when his considerable commitments as Attlee's Parliamentary Personal Secretary impinged upon his constituency duties. Even when in Nottingham, it was alleged, de Freitas was more inclined to entertain middle-class businessmen than

---

26 NMLH GS/EMRLP/7, letter from Baxter to Phillips, 13 May 1949; GS/EMRLP/10, letter from Phillips to Reg. Organisers, 25 May 1949; H. Pelling, *Labour Governments*, p. 222; MRC MSS 9/3/15/187, 31 Oct. 1953.

27 Letter from N. Smith MP to Baxter, 9 Nov. 1947, IAP; NAO LPC Box 12, NCS, Directors' mins, 13 Dec. 1949; *ibid.*, letter from C. Forsyth (Man. Sec. NCS) to J. Bailey (Sec. Nott'm Co-op. Party), 18 Dec. 1949.

speak to local activists. Further disagreement eventually saw de Freitas opting to stand in Lincoln in 1950. His successor, Ian Winterbottom, although attentive to his local responsibilities, also faced similar social resistance even in wards lacking a strong radical bias. Both men came from similar backgrounds—ex-public school and Cambridge educated. It was, however, the left which chiefly exerted leverage for their de-selection. For Winterbottom, this surfaced openly after his defeat in 1959, when motions of no confidence were submitted to prevent his re-nomination because of his 'non-Socialist' views.[28] The earlier departure of de Freitas, against the express wishes of such establishment figures as George Wigman and Borough Party Secretary Tom Roper, can be specifically connected to growing disagreements with newly elected constituency officers, the most prominent of whom was Bob Shaw, then Secretary of Nottingham Central. Shaw, a former Independent Labour Party member and Trotskyist, was currently also the local secretary of Socialist Fellowship—a derivative of the Revolutionary Communist Party—and proscribed in 1951.

Shaw was elected to constituency office in early 1949. It was a term destined to be as divisive as it was short-lived; a vote of no confidence was passed in his stewardship in June and he resigned the following September. Shaw was accused of 'smashing' both his constituency and ward organisations by Cattermole, who also thought his views wholly incompatible with Labour party membership. Not everybody in Nottingham acceded to this diagnosis. Considerable support existed within the party, although more for his right to express radical opinion, than for the opinion itself. This dissent heightened when the City Party, backed by the National Executive Committee, voted not to re-admit either him or his wife to party membership. The City Party had earlier sought to limit public expression of the Shaws' views, intervening openly to impose an approved municipal candidate and literature upon their local ward. It was, however, Coffey's intervention that was later to prove decisive. The forced abandonment of Market Ward's AGM in 1950, after bitter factional disagreement, led to an emergency meeting two weeks later. Here, Coffey, using his authority as Borough Secretary, arbitrarily allowed those lapsed branch members who had resigned with the left's

28 NAO LPC Box 10, letter from Shaw to de Freitas, 21 April 1949, letter from Roper to Windle, 7 April 1949; NMLH (Nott'm Cen. file), Tom Baxter, Organ. Report, 28 July 1948; MRC MSS 9/3/14/224, 24 Nov. 1952; LPC 3 Market Ward Lab. Party mins, 11 Nov. 1959.

take-over of the ward, not only to vote in the election of officers but also in favour of their own re-admission.[29] It was a decisive, if irregular, intervention, for as those now deposed complained:

> Despite the fact that all the positions were not filled, left wing members were deliberately excluded from all offices despite the fact that they have, over the last three years, been amongst the most active persons in the ward.[30]

And indeed, there was a prophetic truth in these parting words, for within the year, the branch collapsed. Shortly after, the Shaws left Market Ward and moved to another part of the city. It was then that, on Coffey's advice, their application for membership was rejected—as was a subsequent appeal. However, within their newly adopted constituency (Nottingham East), support for re-instatement grew steadily until finally its management committee voted overwhelming in favour of re-admittance. With Cattermole and Coffey both lobbying hard, the NEC rejected the demand. Six months later, a similar petition was also dismissed.

Not all constituencies were as supportive of local dissidence. R. T. Sloman, twelve years Secretary of Broxtowe Ward in Nottingham North-West, was suspended in perpetuity from holding office for speaking against a branch motion at a constituency meeting, and despite having voted as mandated. As Cattermole later concluded, this was merely a ploy by those on the right, fuelled by past 'problems' in the ward, to remove Sloman because of his links with 'the *Socialist Outlook* crowd in the city'. Characteristically, he concluded:

> I feel that the decision to exclude him from office for all time is a very severe one but I think we want to be careful not to discourage

29 MRC MSS 9/3/14/116, 19 June 1952; NEC mins, 23 Sept. 1953; NAO LPC 1–2, Market Ward Lab. Party mins, 1947–51, *passim*; LPC Box 10, letter from F. E. Brown to Coffey, 6 March 1950.

30 NAO LPC Box 10, letter from 12 Market Ward members to Nott'm Central CLP, 22 March 1950.

the good people in the ward by ourselves at this stage varying the decision.[31]

The constituency, although having ruled earlier that Sloman's conduct was not contrary to his imposed mandate, also opted not to intervene. Yet it happily entered pleas on behalf of left-wing parliamentarians facing expulsion, and had recently submitted a conference resolution bitterly critical of the national leadership's failure to follow a strictly pro-Bevanite line. Undoubtedly, Cattermole played a role here in moderating the constituency response in an area where, if it had so chosen, it could have exerted considerable sway. Nevertheless, the behavioural inconsistencies are clearly delineated, the more so given that the NEC later ruled that the life ban imposed on Sloman was unnecessarily harsh.[32]

Such cases well illustrate the then divided cultures of city politics. For those officially responsible for organising party activity—Coffey, Baxter and later Cattermole—the curtailing of radical tenor meant one less disruptive and pernicious influence. Yet this strategy, although effectively employed, also proved by degrees to be counter-productive, engendering a perennial atmosphere of discontent and mistrust. Indeed, support for the Shaws' re-admittance should not be viewed solely as evidence of a strong and united militant philosophical local vein. Opposition to the NEC's governances matured, rather than erupted spontaneously; it was only gradually that a broader-based majority came to lobby against what was perceived as a single-minded persecution by those above which ignored local sentiment. Commenting on his own experiences to Coffey in 1952, former councillor George Dutton complained:

I can no longer pretend to be unconcerned at the bitterness and suspicions that seem to constantly arise at the varius [sic] meetings that have been held ... What is exactly behind it all, [sic] I have never at any time been concerned with personalities or individuals but with principles and policy ... For myself I would appreciate your reasons for the attitude you take to myself, [sic] what grounds have you for the doubts and suspicions you seek to arrouse [sic] at

31 NAO LPC Box 7, letter from Cattermole to A. L. Williams (Nat. Agent), 3 July 1953; NMLH (Nott'm NW File), Report on the Appeal of R. Sloman held on 17 March 1953.

32 NMLH (Nott'm NW file), letters from Sloman to Hill, 6 Nov. 1952, Roper to Griffin, 28 May 1949, Hill to Phillips, 30 July 1952; see also NAO LPC Box 7.

the meetings towards me, [sic] if there is anything tangible I would appreciate your candidness and frank criticism, for I reiterate there has never been any personal antagonism from me to yourself [sic].[33]

Dutton's chief offence, if such it was, was to offer prominent and continuing support to protect the freedoms of those more to the left than himself. For Dutton, the fear of persecution through association lasted many years, such was the pervasive atmosphere of suspicion in Nottingham. It was a legacy which survived even the party's leftwards shift in the latter half of the 1950s.[34] Earlier in the decade, however, divisions extended beyond mere antipathy. As Jack Robbins, the Shaws' primary parochial adversary, clearly spelt out when returning to Market Ward with Coffey's support 'to rid it of these [leftist] people': 'he [Robbins] had influential friends in the city and a word from him was sufficient to get people watched'. It was not an idle boast, for Coffey (as Chair of the Watch Committee) had close ties with the city constabulary and particularly Popkess, the Chief Constable.[35]

Of the formal controls available to Nottingham's Labour hierarchy, the most ubiquitous was the power of veto over prospective municipal candidatures. Nomination rights were vested in local branches and affiliated organisations, which then submitted the names to the City Party for approval. In practice, this task was delegated to its executive, which interviewed nominees, and then rejected or confirmed their candidacy. The City party thereafter formally ratified the names submitted on this approved 'panel' list, from which wards made their selection. However, the reasons for inclusion or rejection remained confidential to the executive, and only in exceptional circumstances was a candidate's suitability debated at a full delegates' meeting. Reasons for exclusion were legion: age, lack of experience, incompetence or political inclination. Again the most vocal objectors to city selection procedures came from the party's left; it was its candidates who more frequently were either rejected or as likely offered only un-winnable seats—while the hierarchy, as one critic remarked later, kept the 'safe seats for old faithfuls and party

33 NAO LPC Box 12, letter from Dutton to Coffey, 25 July 1952.
34 NAO LPC Box 10, letters from Dutton to Ives, 22 Oct. 1957 and Ives to Dutton, 24 Oct. 1957.
35 NAO, LPC Box 10, letter from F. E. Brown to Coffey, 6 March 1950; NAO LPC 2, Market Ward Lab. mins, 6 March 1950; interview A. R. Griffin, 10 Feb. 1995.

hacks'. It was a policy which on occasion generated considerable friction between nominating bodies and the City Party executive, not least because the latter, even when pressed, frequently refused to justify its decisions.[36]

The oft-cited notion that a shortage of candidates precluded acts of restrictive practice did not apply locally, where prospective nominees for winnable seats were never in short supply.[37] Indeed, the preferred advance or curtailment of certain candidacies was an accepted feature of Nottingham's city politics, the mechanisms being by no means impartial or without prejudice. Coffey, when City Secretary, always made enquiries prior to panel meetings as to the character and political persuasion of those suspected of not showing 'the respect required': a euphemism for holding radical views. The subsequent panel interview could be extremely heated. The best documented case involved Jim Callinan. Outspoken and to the left of the party (being damned particularly for his past and continuing support for Bob Shaw), Callinan was also an extremely able and enthusiastic organiser, abilities for which he was held in high regard even by those opposed to him politically. Nevertheless, it was apparent immediately that strong opposition existed to his candidacy from leading figures on the executive, an opposition based as much on personal antipathy as on his political views. Callinan was first accused of active association with the Nottingham Peace Committee (not then a proscribed body), an accusation which he, and later its secretary, anyway denied vigorously. Alleged impropriety was not limited to charges of guilt by association. He was also arraigned—incorrectly—of deliberately falsifying his membership payment card and of misleading the executive over his past record of party stewardship. It was these later charges that provoked a local storm. The executive, split internally, and after heated exchanges with Callinan, rejected his nomination. News of the charges spread quickly. With party officers refusing to proffer even a partial apology, the subsequent internal enquiries instigated by both the City Party and Central

36 R. Gosling, *Personal Copy* (1980), p. 102; NAO LPC Box 10, letters from G. Ward to Coffey, 23 July 1952, Shaw to Coffey, 6 Aug. 1952, Coffey to Ward, 16 Sept. 1952; interview with Eric Foster, 10 March 1989. See also NMLH GS/EMRLP/83–101 when Robin Hood Ward (a safe seat) sought to de-select a 'favoured' prospective councillor against the executive's wishes. The executive, which sought to ignore local opinion, also subsequently proved to be unco-operative with the internal enquiry instigated to investigate.

37 Gyford, *Local Politics*, p. 67; J. Brand, 'Party Organisation and the Recruitment of Councillors', *British Journal of Political Science* 3 (1973), pp. 477–78.

Division Executive failed to diffuse the rising mutual antipathy which threatened to engulf completely internal Labour party relations. Regional and national officials then had to intervene to restore a semblance of stability.[38] Nevertheless, Callinan never stood for the city council.

It was into this seething cauldron that Cattermole stepped on his arrival in Nottingham in 1952. One of his first duties was to attend an executive panel selection meeting, notable, according to his account, for being 'an extremely acrimonious affair', taking far too long and lacking in policy substance. Thus his fresh eyes observed first hand the dominant and divisive role played by leading personalities in city politics but which nevertheless also built upon an overt, if less than precise, ideological divide.[39] Steck has suggested subsequently that Labour constituencies were not the power-house for Bevanite factionalism first thought, arguing that central cleavages 'failed to penetrate the rank and file so deeply nor so widely as to mobilise C.L.P.'s behind one side or the other.'[40] There is no doubting that the lesions in Nottingham were not directly attributable to a national schism; the divisions between locally competing factions pre-date any 1951 parliamentary watershed. Yet while the origins of city disputes belonged to an earlier time (as indeed, to degrees, did those at Westminster), in practice aggressive local anti-left sentiment, and the reactive antipathy this bred in certain constituencies, came of age in the early 1950s. It was not only a case of competing ideologies, of left versus right; it was more disparate factions parading behind unrepresentative but nevertheless prominent totem figures to give cohesion to a broad cause.

*

The one area largely untroubled by political schism was the Labour group itself, primarily because its officers and associates acted to curtail left-wing ingression. The arrival of Ives and other prominent members like Charlie Butler (National Organiser of the Tobacco Workers' Union) mitigated this exclusivity. However, it was not simply new personnel. Modifications in group behaviour and image also reflected the

38 NAO LPC Box 12, written statement by Dutton (circa Sept. 1952), letter from Dutton to Coffey, 25 July 1952; MRC MSS 9/3/14/177, 21 Sept. 1952.

39 MRC MSS 9/3/14/122, 26 June 1952.

40 H. J. Steck, 'Grassroots Militants and Ideology: The Bevanite Revolt', *Polity* 2 (1970), p. 441.

increasingly adversarial ethos of inter-party relations in the 1950s—particularly after the forced adoption of single party rule. This demise of secular intimacy between the two rival groups, coupled with the consecutive return of Labour administrations after 1956, opened the parochially introspective world of Labour council politics to broader political influences. Labour confidence grew apace as temporarily it became the natural party of city government. With this came a lessening, although not an abolition, of the internal party tensions which had dogged the post-1945 decade.

Perhaps the strongest indicator of this outreaching can be seen in the group's vigorous prosecution of new non-statutory areas of provisions: notably the construction of a new Playhouse (see Chapter 8). It was not a wholly endogenous reaction; it built on and absorbed external impetuses from national and local movements, just as it consolidated past initiatives from within the city's body politic. Nor did self-assertion provide, necessarily, a catalyst for radical change. Group responses were frequently cautious, retaining much of their past inner-conservatism. Indeed, critics were to argue that change promoted increased authoritarianism, not openness. Yet contrasted with its own past record (and with the more utilitarian instincts of contemporary Conservative municipalism) Nottingham's Labour group certainly exhibited signs of a greater ideological plurality—influenced by the concerns of those to the left of the party. Two examples amply illustrate this latter positive yet chequered response: support for civic contacts with the Soviet Union (later coupled with the campaign for disarmament) and the use of direct works for council house construction. Both were core ingredients of the left's agenda throughout the post-war period.

Direct contact with Communist or associated institutions had, as noted, not only been considered taboo but also rigorously penalised. This did not change overnight. The hostilities generated by local antagonisms cast shadows of suspicion and doubt well into the 1950s. Nevertheless, there were to be some startling developments when judged by local standards. In 1955, the Corporation received an invitation to visit from the Soviet Council of Minsk. Conservatives rejected the offer. However, after prolonged discussion (particularly over the bona-fides of the intermediaries involved), the Labour group agreed to support the initiative, and accepted a subsequent offer five years later when in power. In 1956, it also issued the first of several standing invitations to Russian premiers to visit Nottingham. Direct contact with local communists was, of course, still prohibited. It was, however, a notable break from the past unquestioning hostility towards any association with Eastern Bloc philosophy. It also signalled an albeit temporary reversal in the traditionally exclusive local orientation of city politics. The extent of this change was graphically illustrated when in May 1960, leading group members headed by John Kenyon, the city's Lord Mayor, delivered a 20,000 signature petition supporting unilateral British nuclear disarmament to the Paris great powers test-ban summit.[41] Here was concrete evidence of a volte-face; in one major area at least the group was now taking very much a left-of-centre stance, a transformation tempered only by the Campaign for Nuclear Disarmament's populist base when set against an earlier peace movement proscribed for its overt Communist links.

Any transformation was less apparent in those very local matters that formed the staple diet of council business. In its attitudes towards direct labour, for example, the group exercised considerably greater reserve. Early trades union pressure to reverse the policy of competitive tendering was rejected as impractical during the reconstruction period. In fact, the group and the National Federation of Building Trades Operatives (NFBTO), the most persistent of the lobbyists, took wholly different perspectives. The latter adopted a persistently anti-private enterprise stance, claiming that a directly employed Corporation workforce could build cheaper yet better properties. The group, on the other hand, pragmatically demanded empirical evidence of this cost-efficiency to a degree that it was perceived to be openly antagonistic towards the introduction of direct labour.[42] In August 1953 the two sides again met, setting in motion what proved to be a prolonged and exhaustive consultation process. By 1955, with the union complaining bitterly that past assurances had been passed over, the group agreed to establish a sub-committee of enquiry and enter into a manifesto commitment. The sub-committee met throughout 1956, taking evidence and visiting other authorities with direct labour experience. Yet it was a painfully slow process. Publicly, at least, the group appeared wedded to the principle, arguing that in areas like maintenance, direct works was now saving ratepayers 'hundreds of thousands of pounds'.[43] In practice it entertained serious doubts even here, culminating in a temporary moratorium in late

41 Labour Group mins, 3 Nov. 1955, 5 April 1956, 24 Nov. 1956, 1960 *passim*; *NEP*, 18 May 1960.

42 NUMD TrM Trades Council mins, 19 Oct. 1949; NAO LPC Box 10, letter from NFBTO to Coffey, 15 May 1952, letter from Willbery to NFBTO, 22 Oct. 1952.

43 Nott'm City Labour Party, Municipal Election Policy Statement, 1958, IAP.

1958 on all direct labour applications until yet another more thorough investigation had been completed. The results in the new housing sector were even more disappointing for the unions. In early 1957 the group finally authorised a small pilot scheme of six houses at Clifton to be built by Corporation labour. When the contract was finally completed it was both over-budget and late. Union protestations were brushed aside and no attempts were made to repeat this or larger experiments.

The poor results merely confirmed Labour members' suspicions about the inefficiency of the city's direct works enterprises, doubts that had tempered any ideological enthusiasms for a decade and beyond. Conservatives had anyway always vigorously opposed any expansion of direct works. Now one of their first acts upon being returned to power in 1961 was to wind down Estates Department activity generally and instigate their own internal enquiry into substituting private enterprise provision at the expense of directly provided services. Within four months, after having already made substantial cuts in city capital expenditure, Conservatives prohibited the Estates Department from tendering or undertaking any work other than routine maintenance. They also placed a moratorium on recruitment and on work it had historically undertaken for other committees, as well as discarding competitive tenders already submitted by other city departments. Although initially decrying this action for its ideological base, thereafter the disparities between the parties again became increasingly blurred. Indeed, later the Labour group unanimously acknowledged that departmental efficiency was 'deplorable', that there was a 'general dissatisfaction with repairs' and that an enquiry was 'long overdue'.[44] So saying, it persuaded a now hesitant building union to co-operate with an external enquiry conducted by management consultants into the running of the department. Indeed, the notoriety achieved by the city and Labour politicians alike in 1959, followed by electoral humiliation in 1960, emasculated that embryonic group radicalism which existed. In consequence, future doctrinally-based campaigns received less than enthusiastic group support.

44 Lab. Group mins, 16 July 1963.

CHAPTER 6
Labour Takes Power: Images of Crisis and Caucus Rule 1956–61

In May 1956, Labour regained control of the Corporation with a four seat majority. By 1958 this advantage had risen to twenty, shortly to become twenty-six after the aldermanic elections. This gave Labour the then largest majority ever held by one party over its rivals on the city council, a victory superseding even the party's post-war national and local triumphs.[1] Labour hegemony, however, was never simply a matter of electoral success. The 1956 election also heralded the beginning of a brief era in post-war city politics in which, more than before in modern times, the actions of a single party were held to dominate and colour local political perceptions. The images projected, however, were far from benign. Across Britain, considerable disquiet was then being expressed over the activities and apparently authoritarian behaviour of certain Labour-controlled local authorities. The Home Secretary, R. A. Butler, for example (when broadcasting to the nation immediately prior to the 1960 local government elections), felt able to pronounce that an apparent 'dictatorial mentality' was a characteristic of Labour-controlled councils over the country. Hugh Gaitskell was hardly less flattering when at the 1959 annual party conference he criticised the 'apparent arbitrary and intolerant behaviour' of certain Labour councils.[2] Nottingham was one of those authorities frequently denounced, the city having acquired a national notoriety during a prolonged dispute between Labour councillors and Nottingham's Chief Constable.

Local party officials were always quick to blame 'unfair criticism in the press' rather than their own actions for their nefarious reputation and

---

1 Labour's majorities here were later to be dwarfed by those of the Conservatives from 1967 until 1972, peaking in 1969 with a majority of 42 seats, and, of course, by Labour's majority in 1995 (taking 51 of 55 seats).

2 *The Daily Telegraph*, 12 May 1960; quoted in J. Gyford, *The Politics of Local Socialism* (1985), p. 8.

later electoral unpopularity.[3] Such a response, the perennial retort of all—and particularly Labour—politicians and their apologists, might generally be thought to evoke only limited sympathy. Once we step outside the inner world of city political circles, this was certainly true of Nottingham's electorate. In May 1959, on the eve of the crisis and in a bad year for Labour nationally, the local party lost only one seat. In 1960, however, there was a dramatic reversal. Of the seventeen seats contested that May, eleven were held by Labour. Of these, nine fell to Conservative or Liberal opponents. This marked the end of its period of dominance. Labour was left with only a single seat majority, an advantage immediately nullified in a by-election. Thereafter it was forced to rely on the casting vote of Roland Green, as Lord Mayor, to push through controversial policy. This proved a fitting climax to a dramatic period of the city's political history, but one which also perhaps exemplified broader national schisms and responses.

What, then, went wrong? In July 1959 Labour members on Nottingham's Watch Committee, in following the Town Clerk's counsel, voted to suspend the city's Chief Constable, Athelstan Popkess. The Chief Constable, it was said, had acted partially in publicly pursuing anonymous allegations into the alleged financially corrupt practices of certain Labour members; nor was he prepared to give an account of his actions to the Watch Committee, which according to the Town Clerk he was legally bound to do. It is worth noting that subsequent police investigations found that in essence there was no substance to any allegation of major financial impropriety. Indeed, it was later suggested that Popkess's actions had been dictated by malice, motivated by the council's rejection of his enthusiastically pressed requests for additional finance for police housing and for establishing a corps of traffic wardens.[4]

Popkess's controversial suspension unleashed wide-scale popular dissent, ably orchestrated by Conservative councillors and parliamentarians eager to point to yet one further example of local Socialist illiberality in Nottingham. As one Tory member of the Watch Committee declared, when speaking to a reputed crowd of some 7,000 gathered to protest the decision, 'an iron curtain has dropped between the citizens and their elected representatives'. Demonstrators held placards

3 GJ, 13 May 1960.

4 Letter from Popkess to Owen, 4 June 1959, IAP; NEP, 15 March 1960; NCC, Watch Comm. mins, 8 July 1959; report by T. Ives, 'The Suspension of Nottingham's Chief Constable', 5 Aug. 1959, IAP.

aloft demanding: 'City Big Brothers Resign' and 'Sack the Power-drunk Civic Dictators'![5] Political theatre this may well have been, but in scale alone it was a unique event in Nottingham's post-war history. However, to opponents of Nottingham's Labour group, and indeed to some of its 'friends', the 'Popkess Affair' was quite simply an outward, if dramatic, expression of a deeper structural malaise then infecting the city's political system. Labour's domination during this period, according to contemporary critics, promoted the intolerant, dictatorial rule of a conspiratorial caucus clique; in short, city government had regressed to the closed and manipulative system of the nineteenth century.

Table 6.1 *Political parties' strength on Nottingham City Council 1957–66 after annual municipal elections*

Year	Labour	Conservative	Liberal	Independent	O/A Maj
1956	36	32	-	-	4
1957	38	30	-	-	8
1958	47	21	-	-	26
1959	45	23	-	-	22
1960	34	32	1	1[a]	0[b]
1961	29	38	1	-	8
1962	28	39	1	-	10
1963	38	30	-	-	8
1964	43	25	-	-	18
1965	38	30	-	-	8
1966	35	33	-	-	2

Notes: [a] The Independent was Coffey, expelled from the Lab. group in April 1959. He accepted the Conservative whip in May 1960 and was subsequently re-elected as a Conservative alderman in May 1961.
[b] Lab. initially held a majority of one, but lost this at a by-election in June. Thereafter they governed, on occasion, by using the casting vote of Green (Lab. Lord Mayor).

More recently, John Gyford has also argued that the real problem for Labour councils was 'more than one of image or publicity': 'that in an attempt to maintain discipline and solidarity in a potentially hostile world' Labour groups at this time became 'not merely secretive but also

5 *Guardian Journal Evening Post News Emergency Edition* (hereafter *GJ Emerg.*), 21 July 1959. The public meeting in the market square, however, was cleverly timed to correspond with the local rush hour.

increasingly remote from those whom they sought to serve'.[6] Gyford's comments are apposite in seeking to place group responses within a broader political and social context, while the 1960 election results certainly suggest wide degrees of voter alienation. The late 1950s in Nottingham, however, was also notable as a period of transition: first with the friction creating imposition of single party rule, which although arguably democratic in intent also attracted the attributes of dictatorial rigidity associated with the party's caucusing practices; secondly, as already noted, as a time when Labour sought to broaden its own horizons and the responsibilities of the Corporation it governed. The juxtaposition of a 'visionary' ethos against a governing and inward-looking disciplinary ethic made uneasy bedfellows. The following chapters explore that relationship.

Outside the Conservative party, contemporary opinion on the successive post-1956 Labour administrations reflects this inner contradiction, being interestingly diverse yet seldom passive. Commenting on the late 1950s and early 1960s, one visiting American academic remarked on the intrinsically 'cozy [sic] atmosphere of Nottingham's council politics' which made any reference to 'party divisions often misleading and irrelevant'. This sits uneasily, chronologically, with Driberg's already cited and favourable reference to Labour's democratically oriented 'revolutionary' zeal at this time. Nor does it reflect Antony Howard's overt emphasis on Nottingham's pre-1960 Tammany phase of city boss politics, with its overtures of corrupt practice; here the group only draws praise for its enthusiastic promotion of the new Playhouse, the contract for which, in a subsequent 'decline into philistinism', the incoming Conservative administration sought to nullify.[7]

Clearly there was no great novelty to the charge of Labour's anti-libertarianism; such a hypothesis had been postulated many times before by Conservatives and Liberals, although less frequently by those, like Howard, on the left. Specifically, by the 1950s local protest sought to highlight an alleged lack of joint party consultation. Increasingly, Tory publicists argued, all council policy was pre-determined by the Labour

---

6 Gyford, *Local Socialism*, pp. 8–9.

7 I. Katznelson, 'The Politics of Racial Buffering in Nottingham, 1954–68', *Race* 11 (1970), p. 433; Driberg, *Reynolds News*, 5 July 1959; Howard, *New Statesman*, 21 Aug. 1964. See also E. Bryson, *Portrait of Nottingham* (1974), pp. 189–90.

group caucusing mechanism. Local Conservatives were quickly to dub the later 1950s the era of 'Socialist Dictatorship', an epithet born initially from Labour's abandonment of the traditional division of committee chairmanships according to party strength, but later extended to caricature the party's allegedly authoritarian approach to city government generally. Here opponents suggested that the 'real' power in Nottingham was not so much vested in the controlling Labour group, but more specifically in 'the hands of two or three individuals, who may not even be members [of the council] ... honest and capable though some councillors are they are not capable of standing up to those who hold the big stick over them'.[8] The comments were those of a former local Labour agent: the most notable and frequently targeted figure, again, was Tommy Ives. At times thought autocratic, his influence was held to be particularly formidable, or alternatively pernicious, in matters of policy formation through the group's Policy Sub-Committee (a body consisting primarily of the group's officers, committee chairs and later vice-chairs).[9]

Again, there was nothing new in an inner-circle of senior Labour figures meeting to consider aspects of group policy; the system had been in operation throughout the post-war period. However, with Ives's arrival, this body, which had previously met only infrequently to discuss specific issues, now met once a month prior to each full group meeting. Ives, as Secretary, was a permanent member. Of course, as defenders of the system were quick to point out, all recommendations were subject to ratification by the group itself. It was also felt to fulfil a useful function as a court of appeal between warring members and committees, so that publicly at least Labour politicians spoke with one voice.[10] Increasingly, however, the practice of comprehensive reporting on policy decisions fell into disuse, while the Sub-Committee meetings themselves on occasion comprised solely of group officers.

Finally in 1958, led by Coffey, group members 'registered a protest against the practice of [a] certain few members of the Group going into

8 *GJ*, 4 June 1957; *NEP*, 11 May 1960; *The Times*, 2 May 1960; see also Coffey, *NEP*, 3 May 1960.

9 NMLH GS/EMRLP/136, letter from H. B. Bryant to Phillips, 14 Oct. 1958; Block, *Party Politics*, p. 8.

10 *The Times*, 2 May 1960; see also H. V. Wiseman, 'The Party Caucus in Local Government', *New Society*, 31 Oct. 1963, pp. 10–11; H. V. Wiseman, 'The Working of Local Government in Leeds: Part 1, Party Control of Council and Committees', *Public Administration* 41 (1963), pp. 67–70; Jones, *Borough Politics*, pp. 194–99.

private meetings to discuss the policy of the Group and the properties of the city without the approval of the group'.[11] The specifics of the complaint were not solely altruistic, being more immediately anchored in Coffey's personal grievance against the Sub-Committee's refusal to sanction Corporation spending on police housing—an issue which finally led to his expulsion. Nevertheless, the validity of the complaint can be measured by the support it received from other members, and as a result, the base of the Policy Committee was widened, with three 'backbenchers' being elected to attend meetings with the officers. Yet it is indicative of past practice that the group subsequently had to demand 'that in future, decisions taken by the Policy Committee should be circulated to Group members before the Group meeting' and later to insist that the Sub-Committee meet earlier to ensure that such recommendations were indeed received by members prior to group discussions.[12] However, the belated attempts by the group to resecure a greater degree of accountability over its ruling oligarchy were only made after, and because, several controversial and potentially damaging initiatives had already been passed. It was from one of these, an outline proposal for a city planetarium, that the original allegation of corrupt practice arose.

It was later to be argued that the ensuing crises, far from promoting internal accountability, actually increased authoritarian rule within the party. Here, opponents labelled a subsequently elected leadership reactionary: 'a conspiratorial clique of councillors, who made up for what they lacked in talent by considerable expertise in deviousness'.[13] The accusation was made by Ken Coates, a spokesman for the New Left in Nottingham, shortly before his engineered expulsion from the party. Obviously the presence of a peremptory inner caucus was not novel and while, on occasion, the new group leadership exercised a highly developed Machiavellian instinct, primarily internecine disagreement centred on matters of policy. For one major consequence of the 'Popkess Affair' was that afterwards, the Labour group opted to steer a course conducive to normalising relationships within the council chamber, above all avoiding new controversy. This brought it into conflict with a newly strengthened constituency-based radicalism. To them, city councils, both past and present, had been 'notoriously lethargic' in implementing

11 Lab. Group mins, 24 July 1958.
12 *Ibid.*, 30 Oct. 1958, 4 June 1959.
13 K. Coates, *The Crisis of British Socialism* (1971), p. 81.

educational reforms, while their notional 'radicalism' could best be summarised by their past 'appalling housing record'. The resultant internal battle to control council policy, similar in many ways to that seen in the late 1930s, again set right against left and City Party against Labour group.[14]

Gaitskell's own reference to the 'illiberal behaviour' of certain Labour authorities has already been recorded. More precisely, both he and Morgan Phillips were deeply concerned about the adverse publicity this attracted; indeed, this was later to be held by them to have been a significant contributor to Labour's subsequent defeat in the 1959 general election. Nottingham's Labour group was certainly not immune from criticism from this quarter. As Phillips wrote:

> The National Executive Committee have [sic] been especially concerned by the attacks that have been made in different parts of the country upon Labour Groups and their activities. Nottingham has become more than a symbol in recent months because of the national publicity that has been concentrated upon your actions in suspending your Chief Constable. The continuation of this conflict is in our opinion a matter of serious concern at the present time. I have no doubt in my mind that the Conservative Central Office and the Press will give maximum publicity to their interpretation of what has happened at Nottingham.[15]

On balance, Phillips's fears were shared in Nottingham. Ian Winterbottom, the sitting Member for the marginal Nottingham Central constituency, was quick to declare the impact of the controversy to be the most important local factor in his own narrow defeat. At branch level, Popkess and the accompanying 'smear campaign by the Conservatives' against key party members were widely held, correctly or incorrectly, to be largely responsible for Labour's unsatisfactory election results in 1959. Only Ives offered solace, arguing that the 'widespread belief that the results in Nottingham were much worse than elsewhere, because of the local political situation, is a mistaken one. In fact Nottingham did a little

14 *Ibid*, pp. 85–95; see also MRC MSS 9/3/21/295, 5 Nov. 1966; Gosling, *Personal Copy*, pp. 92–111.

15 NMLH GS/EMRLP/136, letter from Phillips to Eric Foster (Lab. group leader), 13 Nov. 1959; report by Phillips on General Election 1959, NEC mins, 28 Oct. 1959, p. 46.

worse than some industrial centres and a little better than others.'[16] If the figures were convincing for the parliamentary elections, where a national swing to the Conservatives of 1.1 per cent could be set against one in Nottingham of 1.8 per cent, they were less so in the municipal elections. Here, national comparisons reveal that in May 1959—immediately after the controversy first burst—the swing against Labour in Nottingham (Table 6.2) was notably four points higher than a weighted average elsewhere in Britain.

Ives and the group were always quick to cast doubt on Popkess's motives for instigating the police enquiries: it was their contention that these were politically based—that his actions amounted to an 'abusive use of police power' directed at publicly besmirching 'the reputations of leading Labour Party members'. It was a charge given greater resonance by the 'malicious' intent governing the release of details of the police enquiries—which had then been under way for some time—to the national and local press on the day prior to the May 1959 municipal elections. The leak was attributed by Ives and the party to Popkess himself, charges that the Chief Constable always denied. An example of the 'crudest kind of politics' perhaps, but as Richard Crossman later pointed out, it was a first-rate piece of 'black-propaganda' for the Conservatives, designed to inflict grave damage on the party at all levels.[17] Ives himself, responding to press and media reports which appeared on polling day, angrily retorted:

> It is a great pity that to the ordinary person it would appear that certain sections of the city police and Scotland Yard should be quite ruthless in an attempt to defeat Labour candidates. The revelation that Scotland Yard have [sic] been investigating certain people's activities on behalf of the city has no doubt had an influence on the result. This is serious, deplorable and contemptible and the Labour Party will not allow the situation to continue.[18]

16 MRC MSS 9/3/3/55, observations of [Labour] Candidates in Marginal Constituencies; NAO LPC 3, Market Ward Lab. Party mins, 8 May 1959, 13 May 1959; NOA LPC Box 10, Ives, report to the F&GP Sub-Comm. Nott'm City Lab. Party, 11 Nov. 1959.

17 Ives, 'Suspension of Chief Constable', 5 Aug. 1959; Mark Arnold-Foster, 'Popkess: An "Observer Enquiry"', *The Observer*, 23 Aug. 1959; *NEP*, 27 Aug. 1959; Richard Crossman, *Daily Mirror*, 29 Aug. 1959.

18 Arnold-Foster, *The Observer*, 23 Aug. 1959.

Shortly after, the city's Labour-controlled Watch Committee suspended Popkess. However, the shock-waves of the disclosure and the ensuing controversy were to reverberate throughout Nottingham for a further two years, by which time many of the key figures involved had either resigned, retired or had been dismissed.

Senior Labour members also maintained that it was 'unfair' press coverage, not their policies and activities, which was largely responsible for the notoriety the city acquired under their control, and which in turn led to the disastrous reversals in the 1960 municipal elections. They cited especially the 'insidious propaganda' disseminated during the media campaign for Popkess's immediate reinstatement (even in the party's own national, *The Daily Herald*), and the persistent 'persecution' of the then Labour leader, George Wigman, who consequently retired from public life. *Tribune* was one of the few national publications to offer an alternative perspective critical of the conduct of the Chief Constable. Perhaps this was to be expected given the paper's left-wing credentials, although its support was by no means guaranteed; by its own admission, the journal was openly hostile to the rigid disciplinary codes and 'powers arrogated to themselves by Labour groups on local councils'.[19] So anxious, however, was the city's Labour party to counter unfavourable media coverage that it took the unusual step of re-publishing this one wholly supportive article in the form of some 70,000 leaflets and via advertising space in the local press.

There were, however, other factors working to compound an intrinsic bias against a balanced local presentation of events in Nottingham. For with the onset of the early debates about the Popkess Affair, the Labour group simultaneously found itself at the centre of a heated argument over press freedom, the result of a national industrial dispute then troubling the newspaper and printing industries. The Trades Council had already 'blacked' attempts by Nottingham's newspaper proprietors to produce a combined 'Emergency Broadsheet' during the trades dispute. The local National Union of Journalists (NUJ) then successfully lobbied support from the Labour group to exclude the said papers' reporters from the council chamber. Nottingham councillors were not alone in adopting this

19 Lab. Group mins, 3 Sept. 1959; Ives, 'Suspension of Chief Constable'; NAO LPC Box 10, Nott'm City Lab. Party Exec. mins, Aug. 1959; *NEN*, 15 March 1960; John Marcullus, 'The Popkess Story', *Tribune*, reprinted and issued by Nott'm City Lab. Party as an advertisement in local newspapers 14 Aug. 1959.

proscriptive strategy; several other large Labour-controlled authorities also barred journalists from council meetings.[20] In Nottingham, however, the embattled local press seized upon the duality of circumstance surrounding the industrial dispute and Popkess's suspension. In addition to publicising extensively the employers' case, they also ran a series of prominent articles pointing to the exclusion of their reporters as yet one further embarrassing example of the Labour group's authoritarian political stamp. Implicit in press coverage at that time were strong hints that the ban was linked to a separate desire to draw a veil of secrecy over the actual circumstances governing Popkess's suspension. Press speculation was only fuelled when it became known that the Watch Committee minutes recording the suspension, contrary to custom, had not been circulated to members. The situation was not helped by resolute procrastination on the part of the Labour group to avoid a debate in council on the Popkess Affair.[21] So strident was the growing tenor of the attacks that the NUJ, which had been instrumental in calling for the boycott, now wrote to the group urging that its members be re-admitted to the chamber to avoid a further deterioration in relations between the city council and the local press. The group, already under severe pressure from central government and fearful that its actions in banning the press were unlawful, readily accepted the opportunity to lift the sanctions.[22]

The next full meeting of the city council on 27 July 1959 was to be a particularly stormy occasion. Conservatives again raised the issue of the missing Watch Committee minutes, but attempts to kindle any debate were quickly and controversially doused by John Kenyon. The main Tory thrust, however, was reserved for an attack on the unlawful 'pretexts' used to exclude the press from the 6 July meeting. Again, once the principal Conservative speakers had moved that the previous meeting be declared illegal, and Wigman had replied through a prepared statement, further discussion was guillotined immediately by Labour. Dyer, the Conservative leader, at least had the opportunity to accuse publicly his

20 For political partisanship, see I. Jackson, *The Provincial Press and the Community* (1971), ch. 12; NUMD TrM Box 2, Trades Council mins, June–Aug. 1959, *passim*; NCC, Council mins, 6 July 1959.

21 *GJ Emerg.*, 11 July 1959, 17 July 1959, 22 July 1959; NAO LPC Box 7, letter from Ives to Kenyon, 28 Aug. 1959; Lab. Group mins, 3 Sept. 1959.

22 Lab. Group mins, 23 July 1959; letter from Dame Evelyn Sharp (Ministry of Local Government and Housing) to Owen, 16 July, full text reprinted in *H.C. Debates*, 609, cols 164–66, 23 July 1959.

opponents of being the 'Wardens of Tammany'. His predecessor, Joseph Littlefair, was no more complimentary:

> Only once before in my fairly long association with the City Council have [sic] either side of the house felt prompted to walk out in protest. It was no easy thing for my colleagues to take that stern step at our last meeting: it is a measure of the seriousness with which we view the Socialists' decision to exclude the Press ... Three years ago, in May 1956, I warned the city in these words 'Democracy as we have known it, and practised it, will become a mockery. The wild men of the Socialist Party are in control and they intend extending that control to the whole of the city's affairs'. The Socialists have since then taken all the committee chairmanships even though they have not got sufficient men capable of doing the job ... I appeal to the city. Do not forget what is now taking place.[23]

Rhetoric aside, these sentiments hardly suggest a past political consensus. There is, of course, a need to impose perspective. Littlefair's comments were made at a time of heightened inter-party tension, while his retrospective analysis is also heavily suspect, being truncated chronologically in terms of the overt disagreement that existed between the competing party groups. Nevertheless, even if partly under Conservative rule, the past decade had seen increasingly bitter local divisions in the council chamber. Indeed, to adopt temporarily Ben Pimlott's controversial template of past national political trends, the atmosphere in 1950s Nottingham would, in many respects, have been irreconcilable to contemporaries as a period of allegedly maturing consensus.[24] More particularly, however, it must be remembered that Nottingham's past co-operative political system had been judged not solely by the lack of overt disagreement but also by the inter-party adherence to earlier power-sharing conventions. It followed, therefore, that the curtailment of power sharing could be, and indeed clearly was, presented as a proposition for comparative local dictatorship—although Nottingham was only, and belatedly, following a post-war trend when adopting single party rule. It was then a short step to the view, as

23 *GJ Emerg.*, 28 July 1959.
24 Pimlott, 'Post-War Consensus', pp. 12–14.

espoused by Littlefair, that the sub-structure for contemporary Labour intemperance was past institutional change.

In what they claimed to be the partisan chairing of full council meetings by Kenyon, Conservatives saw an even more fundamental denial of the basic freedoms of critical opposition, held hostage to the fortunes of single party dictates. Kenyon's decision to vote with his Labour colleagues after the vociferous debate on press freedom only cast a further shadow over his impartiality in opposition eyes. In fact, such conduct was merely a precursor to the Labour group's future conduct, as it sought to manipulate, and indeed exclude, formal discussion of the Popkess Affair. It was only during the last weeks of November that Labour finally sanctioned a council debate on the Chief Constable's suspension.

Six months later, the editor of the local *Guardian Journal* unreservedly dismissed claims that unfair press coverage bore any responsibility for Labour's heavy defeats in the May 1960 municipal elections:

> The chickens have come home to roost with a vengeance in Nottingham. They were sorry birds of ill-omen hatched out during the troubled days of last summer when the city was held up to ridicule and contempt throughout the country by the ill-advised actions of the power-obsessed Socialists who held complete domination over the City Council and all its committees ... They behaved like men possessed; nothing could stop them piling folly on to folly. It is no use the president [sic] of the Nottingham City Labour Party trying to put the blame for their defeat on unfair criticism in the press ... the Socialists can reflect that they have reaped the bitter fruits of the seeds of abuse which they sowed.[25]

If anything, the ebullience of the denial, coupled with the wording of the Editorial, only served to add weight to the original complaint. And indeed, it would be unwise to underestimate the importance of the press, which in this particular case also included the nationals, in determining local opinion; before the introduction of local radio and with only a limited regional television news service, newspapers provided the only primary channel of communication linking the electorate with Corporation affairs. While academic research generally suggests that the ability of the provincial press to sway political opinion was limited, nevertheless it is

25 *GJ*, 13 May 1960.

acknowledged that local newspapers retained the power to mobilise popular protest under special circumstances.[26] Anecdotal evidence collected by *The Times* immediately prior to the May 1960 elections tends to support this conclusion:

> For most people only a hazy impression of what happened remains ... It appears from scores of conversations that the depth of concern, whether on Labour or the opposition [sic] behalf, depends on how closely people have read their newspaper.[27]

Yet the 1960 municipal election results themselves offer a more objective method of determining the impact of anti-Labour sentiment. It is now generally accepted that local election results are determined predominantly, not by local issues, but by the national standing of parties at the time of polling.[28] Even dissenters from this orthodoxy acknowledge the pre-eminence of the national component in determining local results; their disagreement rests on the propensity of specific local factors to influence markedly voter preference.[29] Figures from Nottingham tend to support the view that, in exceptional circumstances, local events could and did exercise considerable sway in determining outcome. As Table 6.2 shows, Nottingham's local municipal election results broadly reflect national voting intentions (cols a and b).[30] A similarly strong correlation

26 Jackson, *Provincial Press*, p. 269; J. A. Brand, M. Margolis and A. L. M. Smith, *Political Stratification and Democracy* (1972), p. 142; Maud Committee, *Management of Local Government, Volume 3—The Local Government Elector* (1967), Tables 32, 36, 38, 40.

27 *The Times*, 3 May 1960.

28 D. Butler and D. Stokes, *Political Change in Britain* (1975), pp. 40–44; P. E. Peterson and P. Kantor, 'Political Parties and Citizen Participation in English City Politics', *Comparative Politics* 9 (1977), pp. 209–13; R. Gregory, 'Local Elections', pp. 31–47; Newton, *Second City Politics* pp. 14–18.

29 Green, for example, attributes some 75 per cent of the swing between parties to national factors; G. Green, 'National, City and Ward Components of Local Voting', *Policy and Politics* 1 (1972), p. 54; see also A. Bruce and G. Lee, 'Local Election Campaigns', *Political Studies* 30 (1982), pp. 247–61.

30 The correlation co-efficient (r) between the two interval sets (col. a and col. b) years 1947–66 is such that r = +0.59 which is significantly greater than zero (no correlation) at the 0.5% confidence level. If, for example, the years 1960, 1965 and 1966 are omitted, then the value of r rises to +0.88 (+1.0 being a perfect positive correlation). Note that in 1960, 1965 and 1966 particularly, the actual municipal results in Britain were considerably closer to Nottingham's results than the opinion poll ratings suggest, indicating

can be noted when comparing the swings to and from Labour in local city elections with those elsewhere in Britain (cols c and d), but it would be noticeably more emphatic were the years 1959-61 surrounding the Popkess Affair excluded.

In fact, 1960 proved to be the only year in which both the percentage vote and swing in Nottingham were at marked variance with national indicators. It had been a bad year for Labour across Britain: 'disastrous' was how the party assessed its national performance in the May local county borough elections, when it recorded a nett loss of some 500 seats over comparable 1957 totals, secured 224 fewer seats than in 1959, and in fact returned only 1,132 councillors, the lowest total since 1951. Greater London, the Midlands and the West Riding of Yorkshire were heavily hit, particularly as the Conservatives, building on their successes of the previous year, made 'unprecedented' post-war gains in the larger city boroughs.[31] 1959 had also been bad for Labour in Nottingham, despite local protestations to the contrary, but 1960 proved to be far worse. Not only did the party lose nine council seats, but it also recorded its then lowest overall percentage post-war vote. Yet the true depth of electoral hostility facing the city Labour camp in 1960 is best measured in the light of comparable national swings against the party. And here there was precious little comfort for city councillors, for the swing across Nottingham against Labour averaged some 13 per cent, approaching three times the national mean in May 1960. Quite clearly there were local factors at work.

The following year, however, the swing to Labour in Nottingham (measured against the national average) was of an equal compensatory order of magnitude (Table 6.3), setting to one side the electoral protests of 1960. The media's message, it would seem, had only a transitory, albeit powerful, influence in determining local voter preference. In 1963, a new 'moderate' Labour party regained control of the city council. The caucus system, however, remained intact, as did single party rule (which was readily adopted by the Conservatives when they took office). For the new leadership, the majority of whom had already held key positions in the later 1950s, presentation and outward conciliation were of primary importance; image and reality merged into an acceptable political

the latter's limitations as an accurate guide for local elections, particularly in predicting large swings.

31 NMLH GS/LE 134, Morgan Phillips, Memo to NEC Meeting, 26 May 1960, Sec. No. 99; Michael Steed, *The Economist*, 21 May 1960.

Table 6.2 *Comparative percentage Labour vote: Nottingham and Britain*

Year	% Labour vote in Nott'm (col. a)	National Gallup % rating (col. b)	Corrected swing in Nott'm (col. c)	National municipal swing (col. d)
1950	47.5	50.5	-	-
1951	48.2	44.4	-	-
1952	56.8	52.6	-	-
1953	49.5	48.9	-	-
1954	51.4	50.5	-	-
1955	46.3	47.9	-	-
1956	56.6	52.7	-	-
1957	57.6	55.4	3.5	0.5
1958	56.4	56.6	0.3	0.5
1959	49.1	49.4	-9.9	-6.0
1960	37.0	48.8	-13.0	-5.0
1961	48.8	48.2	10.9	3.0
1962	52.3	54.0	3.7	4.5
1963	57.9	57.8	5.0	2.5
1964	55.7	56.6	-0.4	-1.5
1965	41.8	51.1	-13.4	-10.0
1966	50.2	60.0	7.9	4.5

Notes

Col. (a) Percentage calculated using the formula:

$$\frac{L_v/n}{(C_v/n + L_v/n)]} \times 100$$

where L_v and C_v represent the sum total of votes cast for the leading Labour and Conservative candidates in each ward contested in Nottingham's municipal elections and n is the respective number of wards fought by each party.

Col. (b) source: R. Gregory, 'Local Elections and the "Rule of Anticipated Reactions"', *Political Studies* 17 (1969), p. 43.

Col. (c) $Sw_c = Sw^1 + Sw^2 + Sw^3 + ...$ where Sw_c, the annual corrected swing, is the sum of individual swings in each city ward, Sw^1, Sw^2, Sw^3 etc., where both Conservative and Labour candidates stood in consecutive years (see P. Fletcher, 'The Results Analysed', in L. J. Sharpe (ed.), *Voting in Cities* (1967), pp. 290–95). Swing calculations are based exclusively on votes cast for Conservative and Labour candidates (see D. E. Butler and A. King, *The British General Election of 1964* [1965], pp. 337–39). 1957 was the first year of new ward boundaries.

Col. (d) source: K. Newton, *Second City Politics* (1976), Fig. 2.2. Figures are approximations only, based on 'two party' swing statistics previously supplied by Michael Steed but unfortunately no longer available in their primary form. They are founded on the results in between 290 and 700 wards across urban Britain, exc. London, and weighted towards county boroughs.

Table 6.3 *Swings to/from Labour in the May 1960 and 1961 municipal elections*

	Nottingham	Nationally
1960	- 13.0	- 5.0
1961	+ 10.9	+ 3.0
Aggregated nett trend	- 2.1	- 2.0

triumvirate of renewed consensual two-party politics of which the third arm, the press, approved.

Transport House viewed the poor overall showing in the 1960 British municipal results as a reflection of the party's unfavourable national image, blame for which 'in honesty' could not 'be laid at the door of local councillors'. Heavy losses, it was pointed out, had been registered in cities where no apparent disunity or public quarrel existed to prejudice Labour's cause.[32] Nevertheless, Morgan Phillips also noted the special circumstances operating in Nottingham and certain other cities which accounted for heavy local defeats. It was an analysis with which city Conservatives and the press concurred. If the local Labour leadership, not unsurprisingly, sought initially to place responsibility for the heavy defeats elsewhere, it too acknowledged the primary cause to be the turbulent events of the summer of 1959. Yet while Nottingham's parties agreed on the illness, they remained sharply divided over the causes. Conservatives, with the support of the press, presented the past era of Labour control as one dominated by an imposed autarchical rule which had attempted to stifle all criticism. Labour, with equal justification, accused the press of bias and its political opponents of distortion. As ever, the Liberals attacked both major parties for their political opportunism and high-handedness. The crisis, for such it was, even spurred the formation of a 'new' fringe party to protest against the mode of city government. The 'Nottingham Vigilantes' was supposedly a coalition of businessmen and ex-councillors. In practice, it centred again on that disparate alliance of former Labour rebels and those prominent in the formation of the Independent party in 1945—notably Jeremiah Lynch and George Twells. What was unique about the Popkess Affair was that, via its attendant coverage, it undoubtedly enabled opponents to focus attention

32 NMLH GS/LE 134, Phillips, memo to NEC, 26 May 1960.

on several of Labour's perceived weaknesses under the cover of one single, and high profile, emotive issue. Here, an existing rigidity and self-imposed disciplinary code, mustered under the pretext of solidarity, ultimately promoted an ethos of self-withdrawal and secrecy which increased exponentially to the hostility generated as the crisis deepened. In this setting, it was the press itself that subsequently called the tune in Nottingham in the summer and autumn of 1959. Yet, as we shall see, the civic ethic of insular detachment was not uniquely attributable to Labour's internal mentality, nor were the circumstances leading to Popkess's suspension as clear-cut as the press suggested. Indeed, Labour's initial impulse was to resist strongly the full range of governmental, political and media hostility ranged against it. It was to be the supreme irony for Labour that accountability was widely viewed publicly to be a wholly one- sided equation, limited to elected but not appointed officials, and that the party's newly found self-assertiveness was, through its portrayal, a key to its misfortunes.

CHAPTER 7
Political Corruption or Police Partisanship?: The Popkess Affair

When, in July 1959, Labour members on Nottingham's Watch Committee voted to suspend the city's Chief Constable, Athelstan Popkess, they gave impetus to a train of events of singular local significance. Yet the decision also had national ramifications. It stimulated academic and political debate on the lawful relationship between the police and local authorities, and provided a key impetus for the establishment of a Royal Commission later that year whose report formed the foundation for the 1964 Police Act. The ambiguity surrounding police accountability was already evident prior to Popkess's suspension; ministers insisted before parliament that jurisdiction was not theirs but was instead vested in local authorities, yet at the same time the Home Office maintained that chief constables particularly remain free from local democratic controls.[1] A series of unconnected incidents in the late 1950s involving senior police officers—notably in Cardigan (poor administration), Brighton (corruption), Worcester (fraud), Thurso (inadequate enquiries into alleged brutality) and, most prominent of all, Nottingham's dispute over political jurisdiction—only highlighted concerns over this very lack of accountability and of an effective complaints procedure. Moreover, doubts over the police's ill-defined constitutional position ran parallel to a broader perception that community police relations were deteriorating. In

---

1 B. Keith-Lucas, 'The Independence of Chief Constables', *Public Administration* 38 (1960), pp. 1–11; D. N. Chester, 'Some Questions', *Public Administration* 38 (1960), pp. 11–15 (interestingly, Keith-Lucas had previously worked for Tom Owen, and Chester's comments are based on Owen's review of his former employee's article; see PRO HO 272/77, letter from Critchley to Willink, 23 Feb. 1961); G. Marshall, 'Police Responsibility', *Public Administration* 38 (1960), pp. 213–26; J. A. G. Griffiths, 'The Changing Shape of Local Government', *Adult Education* 31 (1958–59), pp. 174–75; *H.C. Debates*, 25 April 1958, Vol. 586, col. 1295, 20 Feb. 1959, Vol. 600, cols 767–771; *H.L. Debates*, 8 Dec. 1958, Vol. 213, cols 4–54.

practice, however, the Royal Commission chose to side-step the fundamental questions raised and, in particular, although having taken the evidence, steadfastly refused to comment on the cases themselves.[2]

In consequence, the 1964 Act, and accompanying ministerial explanations, did little to clarify the existing dichotomy between a local authority's statutory duty to maintain an adequate and efficient police force and its lack of formal redress over police conduct. Although the Commission drew attention to the omnipotent powers possessed by chief constables, its recommendation that the legal responsibility for policing be transferred to the Home Secretary was also rejected. Instead, the government chose to reduce further direct political influence so that in future one-third of the membership of watch committees, previously composed wholly of elected local politicians, would be drawn from the magisterial bench. Both the local watch committee and the Secretary of State were empowered to request specific reports from chief constables (one point at issue in Nottingham), although a request from the former could be discarded and the matter instead referred to the Home Secretary. As Marshall concludes:

> nothing was enacted directly about the *exclusive* control of the chief constable or the nature of his powers *vis-à-vis* the police authority. What really happened was that the Government avoided this direct issue, in view of the inherent difficulty of framing any precise prescription, and relied instead upon the Home Secretary's powers to act as a potential buffer between police authorities and chief constables.[3]

Those disciplinary powers traditionally held by watch committees, which the Association of Municipal Corporations wished not only to retain but expand, were abolished. Thus the historic, if seldom used, sanction to appoint, discipline or promote subordinate officers was transferred to chief constables, who in turn could be 'retired' only if they could be proven inefficient, and then only with the active consent of the Home Secretary.

---

2 T. A. Critchley, *A History of the Police in England and Wales 1900–1966* (1967), pp. 270–71; *Final Report of the Royal Commission on the Police* (Cmnd 1728), PP (1961–62), pp. 4–5; G. Marshall, *Police and Government* (1967), pp. 74–75.

3 G. Marshall, 'Police Accountability Revisited', in D. Butler and H. A. Halsey (eds.), *Policy and Politics: Essays in Honour of Norman Chester* (1979), p. 58; see also J. L. Lambert, *Police Powers and Accountability* (1986), p. 36.

In short, further authority was reinvested in chief constables and the centre, at the expense of the political periphery.

When Nottingham's Watch Committee took the unusual step of suspending Popkess, it did so under the powers conferred under the Municipal Corporations Act, 1882, claiming he was 'unfit for the discharge of his duty'.[4] The Committee, Labour maintained, was entitled to demand reports from its Chief Constable—here concerning his recent enquiries into alleged corrupt practices involving city politicians. Popkess refused, arguing that he alone, and not the Committee, was responsible for enforcing the criminal law—an opinion later backed by the Home Secretary. There were two central issues. The most basic was whether the Watch Committee still retained the statutory authority to enforce its wishes. It was an area surrounded by ambiguity. The most commonly cited precedent, Fisher v. Oldham Corporation (1930), held that all police officers derived their powers from common law or statute, not via and from their immediate employers, the local authority. Thus the Watch Committee held no authority to intervene in the execution of a constable's duty, for no master/servant relationship existed. Butler, as Home Secretary, accepted this interpretation. Nevertheless, the parallels drawn between a case where the issue was one of civic liability and subsequent events in Nottingham were thought tenuous by certain authoritative commentators, and indeed contradicted past ministerial pronouncements over police accountability to local authorities.[5] Moreover, Nottingham's Watch Committee claimed that they had prima facie evidence to suggest that Popkess's motives for instigating the investigations into local corruption were suspect, spawned out of past and unrelated disagreements with the Labour group. Such bias, it was argued, made Popkess potentially unfit to hold office. As the Watch Committee was legally responsible for efficiently policing the city, its members not only had the authority to demand reports from their Chief Constable, but also to instigate their own investigation into his conduct, suspending him in the interim.

*

4 NMLH GS/EMRLP/133, letter from Charles Cunningham to Owen, 15 July 1959.
5 Marshall, 'Police Responsibility'; Chester, 'Some Questions'; Cmnd 1728, Mins of Evidence, E. C. S. Wade, pp. 33–35 and AMC pp. 628–32.

Popkess's appointment as Chief Constable in 1929 was in itself controversial, not only because of his past ties with the 'Black and Tans' but also because of his lack of civil police experience (it being unusual for county boroughs to appoint ex-military officers). In fact, Popkess proved an able and innovative chief officer, especially in areas like forensic science and radio communications. It was the authority's refusal to fund a similar pioneering initiative—to establish a traffic warden corps—which saw a rift open between Popkess and the ruling Labour group in early 1959; particularly as this also coincided with the rejection of his repeated demands for greater spending on police housing. These rebuffs, according to Tom Owen (Nottingham's Town Clerk), prompted Popkess to retaliate by instigating three separate and very public enquiries into the affairs of prominent local Labour members.[6]

Whether in exercising a financial veto the Labour hierarchy had deliberately sought to curb the Chief Constable's authority is open to question. Certainly the main objection to the traffic warden proposal was that of cost. Popkess, backed initially by the Labour-controlled Watch Committee, requested thirty wardens for a trial period to tackle the city's burgeoning traffic problems, arguing that scarce police resources were better utilised combating the escalating crime rate. It became clear, however, that the corps was never intended as a substitute for, but a supposed cheaper supplement to, an existing, if temporarily under-staffed, police establishment. As such, it would always be an extra charge to the rates. Moreover, the Home Office refused to confirm that the corps would attract the fifty per cent Exchequer subsidy attributable to local police costs.[7]

Chris Coffey, the Labour chair of the Watch Committee, was the fiercest political proponent of Popkess's various initiatives. He was also a vociferous critic of Labour's inner circle of policy makers, and particularly of the role played by George Wigman, the group leader and chair of the Finance Committee which had repeatedly blocked Popkess's initiatives. Personal and political animosities aside, Coffey quite naturally viewed police expenditure as a priority. Wigman, however, had more ambitious and prestigious projects in mind: notably the construction of a new civic theatre (£200,000) and a city planetarium (£150,000). Coffey

6 Ives, citing Owen's report to Watch Committee, 8 July 1959, in 'Suspension of Chief Constable', 5 Aug. 1959.

7 NCC, Watch Comm. mins, Dec. 1958–Feb. 1959; letter from Owen to Dutton, 9 March 1959, IAP; NCC, Finance Comm. mins, 3 Feb. 1959, 3 March 1959.

entertained serious reservations here, particularly as his own Committee's recommendations on traffic wardens (£10,000 assuming an Exchequer grant) and additional police housing (£21,000 nett) were passed over. It was the rejection of this latter proposal which finally set Coffey apart from the Labour group and ultimately led to his expulsion.

Popkess had originally requested an additional 120 houses, although this was whittled down to 40 by the Watch Committee. However, the Finance Committee consistently deferred this and several other projects submitted by other committees. Here, it claimed, it was only responding to the government's own current policy to curtail capital expenditure. This only prompted Coffey to insist that Owen contact the Home Secretary to point out that the council was ignoring earlier directives to rectify accommodation shortages. Owen—ever anxious to preserve Corporation autonomy—refused, retorting that the government's design here was ambiguous, and that anyway the provision of police housing was a wholly local concern. In late 1957 the Secretary of State, prompted by the Watch Committee, wrote to Owen expressing his serious concern at the lack of progress made over police housing provision. He also rebuked the Finance Committee for its interference and promised that any application for loans sanction would be viewed favourably.[8] Yet while Popkess claimed that the city force was one of the worst housed in the country, Owen told Labour members that Nottingham bore favourable comparison with most other authorities. The Finance Committee and a majority of the group agreed with Owen. Having twice deferred the project, they again passed over the now further emasculated Watch Committee recommendations for only twenty houses in 1958. In fact, the group's inner caucus determined to reject any future application, ruling that an earlier council motion against the provision of tied accommodation also covered police housing.[9]

Neither Popkess nor Coffey accepted this decision. Both continued to argue publicly, and erroneously, that the corporation was obliged to comply with Home Office requests for extra housing. In January 1959, the Watch Committee again decided to press for financial approval for twenty police houses, at the same time forwarding the proposal for traffic

8 Letter from Coffey to Owen and Owen to Coffey, 17 and 23 July 1957, IAP; NCC, Watch Comm. mins, 11 Dec. 1957.

9 *Aide Memoire*, Meeting of Labour Group Officers, 30 June 1958, IAP. Given the significance of this decision on later events, note that the reference in the Group minute accepting this recommendation was typed in at a later date. It was here also that Coffey's motion condemning caucus practice was passed; Lab. Group mins, 24 July 1958.

wardens. Both reports were rejected by the Finance Committee the following month. It was then that Coffey, in an attempt to by-pass Wigman's veto, sought to submit the housing proposal directly to full council. In the process, he rejected an offer to place his case before the group and a call from Labour's policy committee to withdraw the report. Other Labour members of the Watch Committee, however, faced with a stark hierarchical directive, now withdrew their support, and with Owen's help, blocked Coffey's initiative. The group then unanimously endorsed a recommendation that Coffey resign as Watch Committee chair. Coffey refused. Instead, through March, he launched a public tirade against Labour's inner-caucus, assailing them for blocking additional housing but now also demanding that leading members be called to account for alleged financial improprieties in connection with the proposed city planetarium.[10] Not surprisingly, he was expelled immediately from the group.

*

Coffey was to be the most vocal of all Labour's critics in the coming months. Initially, however, it was Stanley Thomas, a prospective Liberal councillor with a penchant for controversy and publicity, who on 6 January 1959 first demanded that Popkess act over allegations of financial impropriety, after himself receiving numerous anonymous telephone calls and letters on the subject. A month later Popkess was again approached by Thomas, and this time the Chief Constable requested substantive details of the allegations. Thomas was again to contact Popkess in April, requesting confirmation of action on his complaints. Popkess was later to claim that investigations began immediately after first being contacted by Thomas. Metropolitan police officers had interviewed the English agents of the 'planetarium' optical equipment company by early February. However, no investigations appear to have been launched locally for almost three months. Nottingham officers inquiring into an alleged improper drawing of loss of earnings allowances by council members made no request to the City Treasurer for the papers 'to begin investigations' into members' expenses until mid-March. Thomas later claimed that the substance of his correspondence with Popkess centred on

10 Eric Foster Diary, Feb.–March, 1959, IAP; Lab. Group mins, Jan.–June 1959, *passim*; *NEP*, 3 March 1959.

the Planetarium visit. Here the Chief Constable only contacted the Director of Public Prosecutions in early April (that is after Coffey's public statements in March) requesting an opinion as to 'whether further enquiry is justified, as much disquiet has been expressed in many quarters, including the local press and a question in the City Council.'[11] The dates were of considerable significance, given Labour's later assertion that Popkess only began the series of investigations after his own proposals on traffic wardens and police houses had been rejected in February.

From the outset, Owen entertained serious reservations about the 'catch-all' method adopted by Popkess in addressing a vague complaint 'that some member of the council is drawing loss of earnings allowance improperly'. Writing to the Chief Constable in March, he commented:

> I think we ought to talk this matter over as I still feel unable to lend myself to a general enquiry by the Police at the place of work of so many [some twenty] members of the Council merely on the vague allegation of an anonymous letter which does not mention names or dates. I am sure that you must agree with me on reflection that it is wrong to make enquiries about members of the Council at their place of business which must embarrass and annoy them.[12]

Popkess denied immediately that this had been his intention and agreed, when confronted with Owen's objections, 'to leave the matter where it is for the present'.[13] It was shortly after this that police attention focused on the specific complaints now being aired publicly against Ives, Wigman and Butler.

The three Labour officials had, in late 1958, visited the Zeiss optical factory in East Germany in connection with a proposed city planetarium. The company paid the fares to and from Berlin, where the local Buergermeister had presented the delegation with two cameras, each worth about ten pounds. In all other respects, the three had met their own expenses, although this was not clear at the time. On Wigman's

11 Thomas, *News Chronicle*, 13 July 1959; Popkess, *NEP*, 27 Aug. 1959; letters from Owen to Popkess and Popkess to Owen, 13 and 17 March 1959, IAP; PRO HO 272/83, letter from Popkess to DPP, 3 April 1959.

12 Letter from Owen to Popkess, 16 March 1959, IAP.

13 Letter from Popkess to Owen, 17 March 1959, IAP.

recommendation, the planetarium proposal was later rejected because of its cost. Labour members themselves were somewhat perturbed at the secrecy surrounding the trip, of which they had no prior knowledge. It was, it was argued, symptomatic of the almost incestuous hierarchical control over policy making at that time.[14] In January, Conservatives had also questioned the cost of the trip in the council chamber. Ironically, however, it was the delay exhibited by Popkess when reacting to the complaints raised first by Thomas, aided by local Conservatives, and finally Coffey, which formed the nexus of Labour's grievance, suggesting that in reversing his earlier cautionary tenor, the Chief Constable had later acted 'without impartiality and perhaps with malice'. The DPP, however, on the basis of the 'facts' as outlined in a less than dispassionate manner by Popkess, concluded that 'the subsequent conduct of these council members and their lack of frankness with the City Council inevitably raises a doubt as to their bona fides and, in my opinion justifies police enquiries'.[15]

Two officers from Scotland Yard, called in by Popkess, subsequently arrived in Nottingham and spent some three weeks conducting wide-ranging inquiries within and outside the council. It would perhaps have been overly optimistic to expect their presence would not be noted and commented upon; indeed, Labour suspected that their arrival had been purposefully timed to coincide with the municipal election campaign. However, the most damning indictment to Labour eyes was that specific details of the investigations were leaked to the press the day before the election itself. As Wigman recalled:

> The reports could only have come from inside local police circles. They even quoted the exact number of people interviewed ... Scotland Yard has denied having anything to do with the release of this information. One is left with the assumption that it must have come only from local police sources. As only a limited number of people in the City Police had this information, one doesn't have to look far to know where it came from.[16]

14 Arnold-Foster, *The Observer*, 23 Aug. 1959; Foster Diary, 25 Nov. 1958, IAP; Lab. Group mins, 30 Dec. 1958, 1 Jan. 1959.

15 Ives, 'Suspension of Chief Constable', 5 Aug. 1959; PRO HO 272/83, letter from Popkess to DPP, 3 April 1959; letter from Popkess to Owen and Owen to Popkess, 4 June 1959, 17 June 1959, IAP.

16 *NEP*, 19 Aug. 1959.

It was this disclosure which, according to the Labour leadership, 'sparked off a situation which did much to create the view of partiality by the Chief Constable in the minds of the Watch Committee'.[17] Shortly after, the Labour officials were informed by the DPP that there were no criminal charges to answer.

Before this verdict had been rendered, however, Popkess instigated yet another round of enquiries: this time into claims that three years earlier Wigman had not fully reimbursed the corporation for materials and labour (later valued at approximately £25) supplied to his house. An anonymous tip to the local press had subsequently been passed to a city councillor who lodged an official complaint. The workman concerned then made a statement to the police alleging that goods had been deliberately cross-invoiced from Wigman's account to a public contract. Wigman, when questioned, produced receipts which failed to marry wholly with the costing later attributed to the construction of his domestic concrete driveway.[18]

Again, it was the lack of discretion exercised during subsequent police investigations to which Owen took strong exception. The Town Clerk, therefore, resolved to take charge himself, forwarding the results of his internal inquiry to Popkess only if he thought further investigations were warranted. Meanwhile, he refused access to confidential corporation files. From this point relations between Popkess and Owen, which so far had been courteous but not warm, deteriorated rapidly. Popkess totally rejected Owen's intervention, for 'enquiries into such alleged offences are a Police responsibility, and the question of prosecution is entirely a matter for the Attorney General'. Owen, citing his own credentials as the city's legal officer and a past police prosecuting solicitor, in turn was now less circumspect in his open presumption that the Chief Constable was strongly biased in his dealings:

> I have already told you that I will consult you if I decide that it is necessary to employ the Police for a prosecution. Your way of dealing with this investigation, with the investigation about the

17 Speech by Foster (Lab. leader), 30 Nov. 1959, from verbatim notes taken by the Town Clerk's staff, IAP; PRO HO 272/77, letter from G. Dutton to Critchley, 11 Feb. 1960.

18 Letter from Popkess to Owen, 15 June 1959, IAP; statement by J. Smith, 18 May 1959, IAP; City Treasurer, investigation into 23 Hilcott Drive (Wigman's home address), 16 Dec. 1959, IAP.

Planetarium and with the investigation about claims by members of the Council for loss of earnings has made it impossible for me to do anything with you about matters of this kind. I take a very serious view of what you have done in these matters to the denigration of the City Council and its members but I have decided that as you have only a few months to serve before retirement I will do nothing about your methods.[19]

Popkess considered the Town Clerk's observations not only 'unwarranted but an impertinence'.[20] Owen, for his part, made it perfectly clear that he intended to relay his appreciation of the Chief Constable's past and current motivations to the Watch Committee.

In fact, the Watch Committee had already instructed both officers to prepare reports on the circumstances leading to the earlier investigations by Scotland Yard. Although at first willing to comply 'as a matter of courtesy', as his conflict with Owen grew so did the Chief Constable's reservations about co-operating with the Committee itself. By now, Popkess and Owen were communicating solely through written retort, with any pretext of co-operation having broken down. When the Watch Committee met, Popkess stated simply that he was within his rights to refuse to comment on any criminal investigation. Owen, in turn, informed the Committee that it was legally entitled to receive a report from its Chief Constable. He then outlined his appreciation of the linkage between the Finance Committee's refusal—notably under Wigman's chairmanship—to fund extra police housing and a corps of traffic wardens, and Popkess's current behaviour. He also commented disparagingly on Popkess's conduct during the three subsequent investigations. The correct action, he insisted, would have been to conduct an internal enquiry so as not to 'denigrate the Council as a whole, both in Nottingham and outside'. Popkess was again asked if he wished to submit a report. Again he refused, adding that after 'so much vilification he intended asking for a public enquiry'.[21] Owen's criticisms found a captive audience amongst Labour councillors, whose hackles being raised

19 Letter from Popkess to Owen, 2 June 1959 and Owen to Popkess, 9 June 1959, IAP.

20 Letter from Popkess to Owen, 2 July 1959, IAP.

21 Letter from Popkess to Owen, 13 June and 25 June 1959, Owen to Popkess, 26 June 1959, IAP; NCC, Watch Comm. mins, 8 July 1959; NCC, Watch Comm. Report, 16 Nov. 1959; *GJ Emerg.*, 9 July 1959.

already by recent events, voted immediately to suspend the Chief Constable pending an investigation into his conduct. Conservatives at the meeting opposed this sanction.

The next day, the Home Office wrote to Owen demanding an explanation of the Committee's actions, and directing that 'the enforcement of the criminal law is a matter for the chief officer of police and that it is a well established principle that he should not be subject to any interference or control by the police authority in carrying out his duties in that regard'.[22] From the outset, therefore, the Home Office explicitly asserted that Chief Constables, like all police officers, held autonomous status by virtue of their standing as officers of the Crown. Nevertheless, as the Royal Commission highlighted by recommending that the legal responsibility for 'efficient' policing be transferred from police authorities to the Secretary of State (confirming past ministerial pronouncements), at that time watch committees also had obligations and duties. Indeed, the related questions of responsibility and accountability, coupled to a definitional ambiguity over what constituted efficiency—the very points of principle raised during the Nottingham dispute—were again ones which the Commission chose not to resolve.[23] Here, the parameters of a local authority's responsibility in guarding efficiency proved central as events unfolded. The Labour group and Owen argued from a broader perspective: as *prima facie* evidence existed that Popkess had, in their view, failed to operate with the impartiality demanded of his office, he was incapable of exercising proper command over the local force, for which the Watch Committee retained overall responsibility. As such, the Committee had a duty to remove a chief officer who no longer retained its confidence. Opponents took a narrow view, regarding responsibilities for efficiency as limited essentially to ensuring adequate financial provision.[24] The Home Secretary, as we shall see, took both lines one critical step further.

From the beginning, local Conservatives opposed the suspension, and immediately set about orchestrating a campaign both in parliament and Nottingham for Popkess's reinstatement. Others also busied themselves on

22 Letter from Cunningham to Owen, 9 July 1959, also reprinted in *GJ Emerg.*, 10 July 1959; see also D. Regan, *Are the Police under Control?* (1983), p. 4.

23 Cmnd 1728, Recommendation 12, see also p. 50; Marshall, *Police and Government*, p. 79.

24 NMLH GS/EMRLP/133, letter from Cunningham to Owen, 15 July 1959; Ives, 'Suspension of Chief Constable', 5 Aug. 1959.

the Chief Constable's behalf. Stanley Thomas, the Liberal instrumental in pressing Popkess to instigate investigations, leafleted the business community to canvass support—from which came a 6,000 signatory petition. Capitalising on this success, Conservatives organised a public meeting to endorse this petition. Originally to be held in a local school hall, so great was the interest that the venue was transferred outdoors to the city's Market Square. Here, the press recorded, a full 7,000 'roared demands for "justice for a great man"', heard tell of the 'gloating faces of the Socialists' immediately after Popkess's suspension, of the illegal exclusion of the press from council meetings and of Owen's formative role in the affair.[25] The public tone was now set.

A week after Popkess's suspension, Owen, hotly pursued by television crews and the press, travelled to London to consult with Home Office officials. Shortly after, the Home Secretary publicised his view that 'the Chief Constable would have been in breach of his duty' had he complied with any instructions to submit reports on criminal investigations, and urged Popkess's immediate re-instatement. However, at a special meeting of the Watch Committee on 23 July, Labour members refused to lift the suspension. Here, Owen rejected both the Home Secretary's interpretation and his jurisdiction: 'Politics come into it and Butler [Home Secretary] is a politician. I say that you [the Committee] and you alone can take a decision on this matter. The Home Office can only come in when the police force is inefficient.' So strong was Owen's conviction on the rights of his case that at one point he flatly refused to discuss the matter further with Conservative members, arguing that he had 'offered advice previously and it had not been well received'.[26] Faced with strongly conflicting legal interpretations, Labour now resolved that the Watch Committee, city parliamentarians and the Town Clerk meet with Butler to resolve their differences. In fact, although Conservatives suspected Labour of filibustering because of Popkess's pending retirement, it was Owen who had suggested the conference which was then arranged by Tom O'Brien, MP (Labour Nottingham West). In adopting a mediatory role, O'Brien reflected the growing concern within Transport House that the adverse publicity being generated might jeopardise the party's prospects at the forthcoming general election.[27] The Home Secretary had

25 News Chronicle, 21 July 1959; GJ Emerg., 21 July 1959.

26 H.C. Debates, 16 July 1959, Vol. 609, cols 52–53; News Chronicle, 23 July 1959; NCC, Council mins, 27 July 1959.

27 Letter from Phillips to Ives, 23 July 1959, IAP.

already once refused to see Owen. Now he agreed, with the proviso that Popkess was reinstated immediately; then removed even that precondition.

On 28 July Nottingham went to London. The meeting, which the local press predicted would be brief—with Butler simply restating his position—lasted for a little under two hours. Owen spoke ably and at length. There was, however, little room for manoeuvre. The Home Secretary, in reiterating his support for Popkess's stance, strategically focused on his central responsibility for ensuring that all local police forces were 'efficiently and properly maintained, equipped and administered'. While not disputing their legal authority to suspend their Chief Constable, he warned that unless Popkess was re-instated immediately, he would deem the force to be inefficiently managed and withhold the city's police grant—an amount equivalent to approximately a three shilling rate. This was an assertion wholly without justification; both parties expressed unreserved confidence in the city's Deputy Chief Constable, to whom command had devolved—indeed, both later sought to confirm his promotion until again blocked by the Home Secretary.[28] Nevertheless, financial imperatives won through and the Watch Committee returned to Nottingham after agreeing reluctantly to lift the suspension.

*

On 30 July, at a hastily convened meeting, the Watch Committee re-instated Popkess, but in a manner unlikely to assuage Conservative antagonism. Labour was particularly critical of Butler's imposed intervention. This, it argued fallaciously, had prevented the Watch Committee itself from quickly resolving the impasse: either by re-instating Popkess, an unlikely scenario given they were firmly convinced of his guilt, or by confirming his dismissal—which anyway attracted an automatic appeal to the Home Secretary. In any case, the dispute now centred as much on political and personal kudos as on any higher democratic principle of police control. The Committee, therefore, formally recorded

---

28 Joint statement by Butler and Nott'm Watch Comm., *GJ Emerg.*, 29 July 1959; Keith-Lucas, *History of Local Government*, p. 6; NCC, Watch Comm. mins, Aug.–Nov. 1959, *passim*.

its lack of confidence in the impartiality of the Chief Constable and having regard to the circumstances set out in this Resolution [restating its past position] and to the fact that the Chief Constable is due to retire the Committee reluctantly reinstates him in office with effect from 9th August, 1959, midnight.[29]

The 'settlement', with its noted lack of an apology (indeed the inference was that Popkess was guilty), criticism of Home Office intervention and its post-dated implementation only added grist to a Conservative opposition which, sensing public support, had every incentive to capitalise on Labour's tenacious refusal to withdraw judiciously.

Yet inter-party tensions were already stretched to breaking point, consequent partially on Labour's insular endeavours to constrict public debate. At a full council meeting on the eve of the delegation's departure to see Butler, Coffey and senior Conservatives set to exploit this further. Why, the ex-Labour alderman demanded, had the minutes relating to Popkess's suspension not been presented to the council as regulation dictated? His attempts to press this point were immediately ruled out of order by John Kenyon, Labour's Lord Mayor, as were subsequent Conservative objections and motions to speak. Questions critical of Owen's conduct elicited little more by way of response. The debate terminated, a martyred Coffey briefed waiting reporters:

I think it is a disgrace that elected representatives of the people should be treated this way ... Lord Mayors have a duty, and as far as I know in the past have exercised it, to extend to members the freedom to express what they feel in the public interest, but this Lord Mayor has not done this.[30]

It was opportune for Conservative propagandists that members then moved immediately to debate Labour's earlier dictum to exclude the press from the previous council meeting.

With local newspapers solidly voicing the opinion that a spectre of Socialist intolerance hung over Nottingham, critical commentary was not dissipated by the lifting of the Chief Constable's suspension:

29 NCC, Watch Comm. mins, 27 June 1959.

30 *GJ Emerg.*, 28 July 1959; NCC, Council mins, 27 July 1959. Note that a transcript of the disputed minutes had appeared already in the press five days before.

> Like the Bourbons, the Socialist members of the Nottingham Watch Committee have learnt nothing and forgotten nothing. The terms of their Popkess reinstatement resolution express the inflated egotism of people of totalitarian temperament who are incapable of gracious admission of the error of their ways. On every count upon which they have been shown to be at fault they proclaim a brazen defiance, and they reduce themselves to complete absurdity by recording their lack of confidence in the Chief Constable and in the same breath reinstating him.[31]

Similar hostility set the underlying tenor of past and future press coverage, consistently asserting that Popkess's suspension was unjustifiable, if not malicious. There was, for example, a noticeable local absence of questioning the Home Secretary's right to impose his will on the city council. Here, exemplar texts state clearly that 'Mr. Butler [was] to define [the] position'. '[H]is patience strained by reproofs issued in Nottingham', he was 'insistent ... that any [joint] meeting must clear the way for prompt reinstatement of the Chief Constable.' Here he 'confine[d] himself to explaining the law', councillors being 'plainly told ... that the suspension should not be allowed to continue'.[32] Butler's pronouncements, axiomatically, were authoritative and beyond dispute. The strains imposed by adverse national and local coverage began to tell. Shortly after Popkess's re-instatement, Wigman abruptly announced his intention of resigning his leadership of the Labour group.

Belatedly Labour, or more precisely Tommy Ives, took to the offensive in placing its grievances before a wider constituent audience. Having first received assurances from corporation officers of Wigman's innocence, the party set about compiling a detailed report on the suspension, citing amongst other things Owen's allegations to the Watch Committee and notably stipulating—for the first time—the party's charges against the Chief Constable. That it had taken one full month for this to occur, and three since the damaging report of police investigations first surfaced, was indeed significant. As Dick Crossman later commented, the very secrecy surrounding the suspension gave the 'false impression that they [the Labour group] had something to hide', bolstering Tory charges

---

31 *GJ Emerg.*, 31 July 1959.
32 *GJ Emerg.*, 16 July 1959, 24 July 1959, 29 July 1959.

of conspiratorial governance. To counter this, Ives said, Labour now had a 'responsibility to publish the facts'.[33]

The facts, as Ives saw them, were these: that Popkess was responsible for leaking details of the investigations to the press; that chief constables should not instigate public investigations, thus jeopardising civic reputations, on the basis of unsubstantiated, anonymous information; and that the correct course, advocated by Owen but rejected by Popkess, was first to conduct an internal inquiry. Instead, three consecutive investigations were initiated and conducted in a manner designed specifically to attract public attention. Why?—because 'it was known from the statements he [Popkess] has made to people that he regarded Alderman Wigman and some of his colleagues as being against him'—as Ives recalled the disputes over police housing and traffic wardens. The report, in identifying locally 'an abusive use of police power', concluded:

> It is deplorable that there should be such a lack of public concern about the present situation. A Chief Constable can institute investigations into any individual, on the slightest pretext, and yet be responsible to no-one for his actions ... There is a vital principle at stake here which strongly affects the liberty of the individual—If what has happened in Nottingham causes people to think more deeply about the powers of Chief Constables and results in a renewed vigilance over Police powers generally then at least some good will have come out of it ... In exercising this vigilance, the Watch Committee has only been doing its duty in the interests of the citizens of Nottingham.[34]

Ives's call for a national, autonomous body—free from political control—to circumvent any abusive exercise of authority by either Chief Constables or Watch Committees was later rejected by the Royal Commission, although a minority did favour the establishment of 'police ombudsmen'.[35] Instead, this meditative function was vested solely in the Home Secretary. To Labour eyes in 1959, this would not have constituted

33 Crossman, *Daily Mirror*, 29 August, 1959; *NEP*, 19 Aug. 1959.
34 Ives, 'Suspension of Chief Constable', 5 Aug. 1959.
35 For a favourable response, see 'Nottingham: Some Constitutional Reflections', *Justice of the Peace and Local Government Review* (7 Nov. 1959), pp. 620–21; Marshall, *Police and Government*, p. 81.

an independent review, for it correctly perceived Butler's actions to be those more of a political enforcer than arbitrator.

Ives's report was carried overwhelmingly by both Labour and Trades Council delegates. It was also widely covered in the local and national press. Popkess's immediate response, relayed through a local Conservative, proclaimed that Labour's charges were so grossly inaccurate as to be 'beneath contempt'. The disclosures, however, demanded a more comprehensive response, and he straightway refuted any suggestion of a linkage between the onset of investigations and the veto of his proposals by the Finance Committee. In this he was aided by Coffey and local Tories, all claiming quickly a prior knowledge (in apparent contradiction of Popkess's already noted private correspondence) of the onset of police investigations well before March.[36]

Yet if Labour was now prepared to levy its charges publicly, it still strove resolutely to avoid debating the 'Affair' in the council chamber on any other than its own dictated terms. Paradoxically, the impulse to maximise political embarrassment only buttressed non-disclosure as Conservatives, contrary to custom, refused to treat in advance as confidential a Watch Committee report on the suspension. Meanwhile, Ives wrote to Kenyon, the Lord Mayor, outlining the various tactics available to curb debate in full council. Kenyon proved an able executor of group instruction, ruling out of order, for example, a motion by Coffey at the September meeting calling for the resignation of all Labour Watch Committee members.[37] Privately, however, attitudes favouring insularity and procrastination were beginning to fracture. Eric Foster, the acting Labour leader, led this call for a policy reversal, arguing

> that a properly constituted enquiry be held and that the findings be made public as in this way, and in this way only, can the confidence of the public at large be restored in a manner in which not only will justice be done, but will clearly be seen to be done ... protect[ing] the Labour Party in general and this Group in particular from further insidious propaganda increasingly built up to the detriment of all we stand for.[38]

36 *GJ*, 18 Aug. 1959; *NEP*, 21 Aug. 1959, 27 Aug. 1959.

37 Arnold-Foster, *The Observer*, 23 Aug. 1959; NAO LPC Box 10, letter from Ives to E. Smyth, 14 Aug. 1959; NAO LPC Box 7, letter from Ives to Kenyon, 28 Aug. 1959.

38 Nott'm Lab. Group mins, 3 Sept. 1959.

Foster's proposal split the group, but by the narrowest of margins it rejected his initiative. He continued to press, however, for a public resolution to the Popkess dispute, spurred on by Transport House and the inter-party rancour that grew by the month as the Watch Committee delayed submission of its report.

Popkess had already moved to re-open investigations into the allegedly improper claims submitted by councillors and the work carried out at Wigman's house. Likewise, the Corporation continued with its own enquiries, instigated by Owen in June, into the workings of the City Engineer's Department: for a broader suspicion existed that expenditures under control of Robert Finch, the City Engineer, had been 'deliberately charged to the wrong account with the object of obscuring the true cost of a particular job'—in short, that Finch ignored Committee directives and mis-coded material when contracts ran over-budget.[39] Confidential material alleging impropriety here was leaked to local newspapers in September.

The public, through the press, had also been aware for some time of Owen's central role in the Chief Constable's suspension, but less so of the antagonisms which divided and grew between the two senior city officials. Now Popkess used the occasion of his last report to the Watch Committee to publicise this rupture. Stressing the criminal sphere of the allegations, he charged, pertinently:

> that the Town Clerk ... instructed both the City Treasurer and the City Engineer not to give information to my officers on these matters. The fact that the complaints have, therefore, never been fully investigated by the Police Department, has quite naturally caused considerable public concern.[40]

Copies of Popkess's controversial speech were promptly distributed to the press, appearing the following day. According to Conservatives, 'when the Town Clerk left [the meeting] he was highly indignant and the atmosphere was very hostile'. Within the week Owen retaliated, releasing to the local papers copies of his private correspondence with Popkess listing his strong objections to any blanket enquiry and the overtly public

39 Memo by the City Treasurer on the Subject of the City Engineer's Cost Accounts, 12 Dec. 1959, IAP.
40 Transcript of Popkess's speech to Watch Comm. of 11 Nov. 1959, IAP.

manner in which the investigations had been conducted by the police. Not
to be overshadowed, Popkess then accused the Town Clerk of deception
and of investigative sloth, as he again reiterated the need for 'the fullest
impartial enquiry' under police auspices.[41]

In early November, Foster sought to pre-empt group objections by
announcing to the press his intention of entering into bilateral talks—if
Conservatives agreed—to instigate a joint investigation into past events.
The Labour group still demurred. Foster, however, was not to be
deflected from his goal of inter-party talks. Straightway he and Jim
Cattermole decided that in light of the pending Watch Committee
report—itself highly critical of Popkess's behaviour—both should meet
with Morgan Phillips to devise a counter-strategy to curtail group
objections to a formal inquiry.[42] Phillips lent a sympathetic ear, for the
national hierarchy remained deeply concerned lest the party's overall
image be tarnished by the activities of local councils. He agreed,
therefore, to write directly to the group, relaying these concerns in terms
which Foster could then use to manipulate internal opinion, concluding:

> I would, therefore, appeal to you [Foster] and your colleagues to
> try and find some satisfactory means of ending this conflict as soon
> as possible. I do not feel it is enough to end merely by a vote in
> the Council chamber, unless that vote gives the impression of
> generosity, constitutional propriety, and is sufficiently convincing
> that your main consideration has been the interests of Nottingham
> rather than the continuation of any kind of feud ... this is no longer
> a local matter. It is one of vital concern ...[43]

The ploy was successfully played, members finally agreeing to 'seek the
co-operation of the Conservative group' in concluding the investigations
into malpractice within the Corporation. In fact, so confident had Foster
been, that the machinery to instigate a joint-party enquiry had already
been set in motion. Yet Foster was not the only player seeking to
manipulate group opinion. That morning, the national press revealed that
the group would shortly place investigations into the hands of the police,
an anonymous Labour source adding that Owen's earlier refusal here

41 *GJ*, 12 Nov. 1959, 17 Nov. 1959.
42 *GJ*, 3–5 Nov. 1959; Nott'm Lab. Group mins, 3 Sept. 1959, 5 Nov. 1959; NMLH,
GS/EMRLP/135, Memo from ILM (Transport House), 6 Nov. 1959.
43 NMLH GS/EMRLP/136, letter from Phillips to Foster, 18 Nov. 1959.

'may not have been fully justified'. This was only the most recent of several occasions where confidential information had been leaked to the newspapers. Only the day before, a verbatim account of the final Watch Committee report had appeared in *The Daily Telegraph*.[44] Clearly the interest generated in, and the antagonisms provoked by, the Chief Constable's suspension remained unsated. Quite simply, Labour's past attempts to stifle debate had failed, for the issue pointedly refused to lie down and die of its own accord.

Nowhere was this more evident than in the council chamber itself. When members met on 2 November, Coffey again attempted to debate the 'Affair'. And as before, Kenyon had already agreed with his Labour colleagues to rule such a motion 'out of order'. Instead he called on Foster—barely audible at times because of the heated protests flying across the chamber—to move that the whole matter be debated the following month. As Kenyon ordered an irate Coffey to be evicted from the chamber, Conservatives sought a motion of no confidence in the Lord Mayor's chairmanship, but before that could be heard, Labour members quickly voted to suspend the sitting. It was partly to prevent a repeat of such unseemly behaviour that representatives of both parties met and agreed an agenda for an extraordinary meeting of the council called for the end of November.[45]

In the interim, the Watch Committee finally met to consider its report on the suspension. Drafted by Owen, yet with a singularly strong political content, the report essentially regurgitated those accusations already cast against Popkess and sought to vindicate the Watch Committee's and Owen's stance—although it stopped short of repeating those charges of malice levied by Ives. Conciliatory, therefore, it was not. Indeed, its nature was such that Owen, prior to its submission to the Committee, cautioned group leaders:

> I have conferred with Counsel on this Report and have to advise
> you that the Report is defamatory and that you are only privileged
> so far as members of the Council are concerned. This means that

44 *Daily Express*, 26 Nov. 1959; *The Daily Telegraph*, 25 Nov. 1959. Both stories were subsequently reprinted in the local press.

45 Nott'm Lab. Group mins, 29 Oct. 1959, 5 Nov. 1959; *GJ*, 3 Nov. 1959; *NEP*, 11 Nov. 1959.

the Report or any part of it must not be shown to or discussed by you with any person who is not a member of the Council.[46]

Such warnings, even though only the two party leaders retained copies of the draft, were of no avail. So strong was the desire to elicit political advantage and so intense the media interest that shortly after, as already noted, its content was leaked in full. Passed by Labour members of the Watch Committee without alteration, the report, together with Coffey's postponed motion of censure, went forward to be debated in special session. It was now some five months since Popkess's suspension, and considerably longer since the original allegations first surfaced. At last, it appeared, all parties had finally acceded to the demands for public debate, explanation and investigation as, behind the scenes, the machinery turned to draw opposition politicians into the political process of reconciliation. The exceptions here, perhaps, were Owen, who consistently re-stated his jurisdiction in all city matters, and certain senior Labour politicians on the Watch Committee—those at the heart of the dispute, and subject to the greatest criticism, who resisted the control of events passing from their hands.[47] On balance, however, Labour's redefined imperative to place the Popkess Affair behind them speedily but with propriety neatly dovetailed with the opposition's repeated clamour for debate and explanation. When this finally occurred, it acted as a release for the tensions and bitterness of the preceding months.

The six-hour debate itself was an occasion of long speeches. Coffey, in leading the attack, was bitterly critical of past delays where, 'throughout this time much has been said in many quarters but least of all by the Watch Committee', adding that 'if it is conceivable for the Labour Party to extract and compile [a report] I should think the time would be ripe for this Council to have the same sort of information'.[48] Popkess, he said, had refused to answer Watch Committee questions, not out of contempt or guilt, but because he had an obligation of confidentiality. Owen's verbal evidence given before the Committee that day (unrecorded because a request for a stenographer had been refused) had mistakenly been taken as definitive fact, whereas in reality it was merely an opinion.

46 Letter from Owen to Foster, 16 Nov. 1959, IAP.

47 Letter from Owen to Foster, 18 Nov. 1959, IAP; Eric Foster, Notes on the Popkess Affair, 1989, IAP.

48 Council Debate, 30 Nov. 1959, verbatim notes taken by the Town Clerk's staff, IAP.

In equal measure he attacked Labour for its autocratic structure and a compliant Town Clerk for suppressing information on the suspension and earlier Watch Committee affairs. Foster, in replying, quickly endorsed the need for past and future police investigation—even at a member's place of work—once complaints had been levied. Nor was he supportive of the private and unauthorised trip to East Germany: an 'unfortunate' decision, he thought, for 'such conduct was open to criticism and therefore [necessarily] investigated at source'. It was on the lack of co-operative spirit exhibited by Popkess in his dealings with Owen that Foster focused:

> It is the Town Clerk's duty to advise on legal matters concerning police activities, for he is not only the legal officer of the Corporation in Nottingham, but he is also the police legal advisor. It has, so I understand, been the customary practice in Nottingham for the Chief Constable of the City and the Town Clerk to work together, to consult, to examine and to decide the proper course of action, legal or otherwise, on any matter of this kind which may happen in this City. But for some reason, these matters were not conducted in this manner, and this has given rise to much doubt, and much conjecture was created in the minds of the Watch committee'.[49]

Why, Foster asked, had such co-operative spirit been lacking, when before and since, the Chief Constable had co-operated with Owen? Popkess, he insisted, had failed to interpret the 'spirit of the law' protecting members from 'prolonged bias, suspicion and hurt'. In short, albeit in measured tones, the failure to investigate the criminal charges, and the reason for the Watch Committee's subsequent actions, rested squarely on disagreements between Owen and Popkess, as he skated lightly over Labour's own contributions. Finally, in espousing a spirit of reconciliation, Foster requested that Coffey withdraw his motion of censure and 'accept the assurances that both Parties will jointly ensure a full enquiry into the allegations'. Coffey, in turn, accepted this olive branch; but before it could be formally agreed, Kenyon intervened and Labour members, as instructed, defeated the original motion.

The later debate on the Watch Committee report proved a considerably more rumbustious affair, with Labour speakers vigorously defending the

49 *Ibid.*

past actions of both the Committee and Owen. Here, it was maintained, 'ample' evidence existed of Popkess's bias to warrant his dismissal. Even Ernest Purser, Labour's mild-mannered former leader, demanded that it was 'the Chief Constable who ought to apologise to ... those people he has vilified by his actions', and not as Conservatives craved—in between their eulogistic tributes to Popkess's character and past service—vice versa. In fact the latter, set as a precondition by Tories for normalising inter-party relations, was instantly rejected by Labour. Continuing and vehement disagreement, however, did not prevent the establishment of an inter-party committee of investigation; like much else during recent months, hyperbole, albeit successfully employed, was window dressing for a wider audience in a situation where 'political emotion had run riot'.[50]

Representatives of both political parties met subsequently, and established a sub-committee of enquiry consisting of Foster, Roland Green (Labour's deputy leader) and their Conservative counterparts. Owen, the City Treasurer, and later Porter (as acting Chief Constable), attended with the results of their own investigations. In late 1959, the Finance Committee invited the police to instigate criminal enquiries into the work done at Wigman's house. Concluding, the DPP reasoned that, although evidence existed that work had indeed been improperly debited, it was 'wholly insufficient to support a criminal charge against the Alderman or Finch', adding that in any event the incident had occurred three years previously and totalled only some £25. Nevertheless:

> The plain fact is that once these rumours circulate and suspicions are engendered in matters affecting public administration, the cloud, no bigger than a man's hand at the start, can soon cover the whole sky and darken many lives. When this happens it becomes urgently necessary, both in the interests of the community and for the sake of the persons more directly affected, that there should be a proper and thorough scrutiny. Perhaps a good deal of concern and uneasiness would have been avoided if the City Council had arrived at this conclusion earlier.[51]

City politicians were less inclined to adopt a benign attitude. The confirmation that Finch, for twenty-five years the City Engineer, had been

---

50 *Ibid.*; *GJ*, 1 Dec. 1959.
51 Statement issued by Porter, citing DPP, 15 March 1960, IAP; *GJ*, 16 March 1960.

party to falsifying expenditure led both political leaders to press for his dismissal—no doubt partly because of the furore precipitated by his actions. It was a fate he avoided only because of his pending and accelerated retirement.[52] The city's own enquiry report was later approved unanimously by both political parties.

The suspicions of criminality aroused by Popkess's investigations proved to be substantially unfounded. Popkess had by this time left the city to live in Torquay, and whilst both he and Wigman promised repeatedly to publish their memoirs on the 'Affair', neither did. Wigman, meanwhile, rarely attended either party or council meeting. Attempts were made by the group to rehabilitate its former leader's reputation, most notably by proposing him for an Honorary Freemanship of Nottingham. Perhaps the most highly prized of civic honours, in practice its award was invariably tainted by much internal intriguing, inter-party negotiation and bartering. Wigman was to have been nominated immediately prior to Popkess's suspension, but consultations were placed in abeyance with the outbreak of party hostilities. After Wigman's resignation, negotiations resumed, although it was agreed to defer his candidacy (with those of the Conservative nominees, Littlefair and Mitchell) until 1962, by which time it was expected that the machinations of previous years would have subsided. Unfortunately, Wigman died in December 1961.

Within the Labour group and party itself, those closely associated with the pre-Popkess regime suffered markedly from a fall in support. Charlie Butler, widely tipped as Wigman's preferred replacement and his past confidant, lost heavily when standing against Foster for the vacant leadership (having been only narrowly defeated by him in the deputy elections the previous year). Tommy Ives, also reputedly working hard behind the scenes to secure Butler's succession, was the next to fall from grace. With Butler and Wigman, Ives had been party to the ill-fated deputation to East Germany in late 1958 to which certain group members objected vigorously. Ives's role in particular attracted internal criticism: that as a 'mere' official he had had prior knowledge of, and a policy input on, a major initiative ahead of his elected peers, irritated many within the Labour group. As the crisis developed, so Ives's public profile grew. In itself, this further engendered petty jealousies amongst his colleagues, as it only reinforced the already evident bitter and

---

52 Letter from Owen to Foster, 22 March 1960, IAP; interview with Foster, 12 Jan. 1989.

personalised hostility of Conservative members.[53] Ives himself was well aware from an early stage that his high profile was having a detrimental effect on his career within the party. Nevertheless, he continued in the vanguard of moves to promote the anti-Popkess cause, on occasion without first consulting the Labour group, and so fuelling the resentment against himself.[54]

Consequent upon his enhanced notoriety, rumours spread that Ives was considering abandoning city politics for a career in the media. However, it was not until the following May that he announced his pending resignation (post-dated until later that year), ostensibly because national restructuring devolved authority from the City Party to individual constituencies. In fact, Ives's influence had diminished considerably with Foster's succession to the leadership and Morgan Phillips's intervention in Nottingham's affairs. Shortly after the disastrous 1960 May elections, the group met to consider Ives's position. He himself wished to remain as Secretary until he found a new post. Instead, ungraciously, the group immediately terminated Ives's employment, replacing him not with a full-time official but with an elected member from within its own ranks. Ives, it was said, accepted the decision 'reluctantly'. Noel Heward, an early critic of Ives's conduct—and of the planetarium trip—replaced Ernest Smith as Chief Whip, and was charged with enforcing the group's now enhanced disciplinary policy. The next day, the City Party also confirmed that Ives's employment as its Secretary would cease in August.[55]

Foster's new broom, seemingly, had swept the decks clean of those from the previous regime closely associated with the Popkess debacle, and, with it, residual internal opposition to his programme of moderation and a rapprochement in inter-party relations. Yet the tensions following Popkess's suspension were not easily dissipated. Certainly, despite Labour's consensual overtures, the electorate was not in a forgiving mood in May 1960. Nor, judging by the polemics employed, were local Conservatives or the press inclined towards political

---

53 NAO LPC Box 10, letter from Heward to Ives, 27 Dec. 1958; Nott'm Lab. Group mins, 30 Dec. 1958; Foster Diary, 25 Aug. 1959, IAP; *GJ*, 18 Aug. 1959.

54 NAO LPC Box 10, letter from Ives to E. Smyth, 14 Aug. 1959; interview with Foster, Nov. 1989.

55 *GJ*, 16 May 1960; Nott'm Lab. Group mins, 15 May 1960, 9 June 1960.

clemency—continuing to describe Labour as that 'Socialist Dictatorship'.[56] And, indeed, under the party system as it then stood, there was no ready reason why Conservatives should not play to the natural political advantages accrued over the previous twelve months. Moreover, although the events of 1959 predicated a nadir in inter-group post-war relations, quite clearly the roots of overtly conflictory practice were tied contextually to the earlier 1950s. A movement with this heritage, having reached a crescendo, was not likely to abate overnight. If the warp of such disagreement centred on the changing structures within party and city governance, inter-woven throughout we find the weft of confrontational populist appeal being exercised by both parties—of which Popkess provides only the bitterest example. No sooner had this particular crisis passed than each group embarked on yet another bitter crusade, this time over the proposed cancellation of the new civic theatre. The construction of the Playhouse was an issue on which city politicians had been deeply and publicly divided for the previous five years. Here, however, Conservatives were unable once again to mobilise public antipathy, despite running a high-profile and pointedly concentrated campaign promoting civic economy in this sphere; a campaign which dominated disproportionately the electoral and broader political agenda of the late 1950s and early 1960s. It is to the reasons behind this Conservative failure and Labour success, each contrasting markedly with their Popkess experience, that we now turn.

---

56 Letter from Dyer to all Conservative candidates, 1960 municipal election, cited *GJ*, 11 May 1960; Editorial, *GJ*, 13 May 1960.

CHAPTER 8
Controversy and the Arts: Building the Nottingham Playhouse

Despite the considerable controversy surrounding the existence or otherwise of a newly found political consensus during and after the Second World War, islands of academic agreement can be found. One such centres on the war and post-war national enthusiasm for promoting the arts generally, and arts subsidy in particular. If commentators disagree over its function, they nevertheless accept that state-subsidised cultural provision received war and post-war bi-partisan parliamentary support, and attained an important, integral place within Britain's new welfare state. Future joint party agreement was to be expressed centrally through a continuously rising government grant-in-aid to the arts—a consensus which lasted until the arrival and triumph of Thatcherism.[1] That this new emphasis took form was the more extraordinary given the country's perilous economic position in 1945: as John Pick records, it was 'an astonishing time for Britain to begin wholesale financial support of the arts'. Nevertheless, nationally, cultural developments during the war, and under the Labour government after it, did strongly favour public arts subsidy. Underpinning what was perceived by many to be a 'cultural renaissance', Marwick notes, lay the experience of the war itself: 'the sense that Britain was fighting for what was best in civilisation, the sense of pride in British culture, the sense that the best in that culture should be more widely shared out'.[2]

---

1 J. Minihan, *The Nationalization of Culture: The Development of State Subsidies to the Arts in Great Britain* (1977), pp. 215–49; R. Shaw, *The Arts and the People* (1987), pp. 20, 41; A. Sinfield, *Literature, Politics and Culture in Postwar Britain* (1989), pp. 47–58; A. Beck, 'The Impact of Thatcherism on the Arts Council', *Parliamentary Affairs* 42 (1989), p. 362.

2 J. Pick, 'The Best for the Most', in J. Pick (ed.), *The State and The Arts* (1980), p. 9; A. Marwick, 'The Arts, Books, Media and Entertainments in Britain since 1945', in J. Obelkevich and P. Catterall (eds), *Understanding Post-War British Society* (1994), p. 180; A. Marwick, *Culture in Britain since 1945* (1991), pp. 14–24.

The success of the Council for the Encouragement of Music and the Arts (CEMA) in attracting a new, vibrant and previously largely untapped mass audience to its wartime productions was much commented on by contemporary enthusiasts for the arts. Of course, CEMA was a wartime expedient, its 'new' audience in many ways one held captive geographically and emotionally to the wartime experience and the lack of alternative entertainments. However, as Minihan unequivocally concludes, it was and is widely held that 'the war [undoubtedly] stimulated the growth of large and lasting audiences for the arts'. The unsated demand from local amateur societies for assistance and the better known enthusiasm that greeted professional performances and tours provided contemporaries with the evidence needed to support calls for a permanent post-war organisation 'devoted to fostering art throughout the country'.[3] Thus the Arts Council, which replicated CEMA's central remit to aid professional productions, was founded in 1945 and enchartered a year later. Arts audiences, however, were to remain predominantly middle-class, and not drawn from those culturally 'deprived' workers so enthusiastically identified by CEMA staff.[4]

The wartime experience also promoted local initiatives. Nowhere was this more evident than in repertory theatre, where the war and post-war years saw the rapid multiplication of non-profit-sharing companies.[5] Politically, too, developments during and immediately after the war suggested the emergence of a more positive policy towards municipal arts support. It was, for example, local authorities themselves who spearheaded collectively the successful campaign to end the legislative prohibition of the municipal sponsorship of theatre and increase their local

3 A. Calder, *The People's War* (1969), pp. 372–3; B. I. Evans and M. Glasgow, *The Arts in England* (1949), pp. 16–20; J. S. Harris, *Government Patronage and the Arts in Great Britain* (1970), pp. 33–36; F. M. Levenstal, '"The Best for the Most": CEMA and State Sponsorship of the Arts in Wartime', *Twentieth Century British History* 1/3 (1990), pp. 289–317; E. White, *The Arts Council of Great Britain* (1975), pp. 34–37; Minihan, *Nationalization of Culture,* pp. 225–28.

4 Pick, 'Best for the Most', p. 17; Evans and Glasgow, *Arts in England*, pp. 44, 94–95, estimated that only two per cent of hostel workers had experienced live theatre prior to the wartime tours.

5 Arts Council of Great Britain (hereafter ACGB), *Housing the Arts: Tenth Annual Report 1954–55* (1955), pp. 5–7; Evans and Glasgow, *Arts in England*, pp. 94–95.

revenue raising capacity to fund arts and entertainments activities.[6] The subsequent 1948 Local Government Act, in enabling local authorities to spend the product of a 6d rate on entertainment services, undoubtedly furnished 'the means to enrich the cultural life of the country as no previous measure had ever done'. Yet, infamously, the tangible benefits accruing proved perpetually disappointing. From 1951, the Arts Council initially regretted and then annually lamented the disparity between its expectations and the realities of local authority sponsorship.[7] As the Association of Metropolitan Councils' journal recorded in 1964, when commenting on the latest Arts Council Annual Report:

> One turns with foreboding to the introductory paragraphs to seek out the customary castigation of local authorities for their failure to exercise with sufficient generosity their powers under Section 132 [of the 1948 Act]. Thus the ball is placed again firmly at the feet of local authorities, who have to decide how far they are justified in spending on the ratepayers' behalf, in such a way as to help create as well as follow public taste.[8]

Such was to be the general ambience between local authorities and the Arts Council. 'One of the uglier faces of the post-war arts establishment' is how one critic depicts a patronising metropolitan-based Arts Council, which in defining cultural values in its own elitist setting, devalued traditional local authority contributions in the fields of library, museum, gallery and amateur provision as not being part of the 'real' arts.[9] Yet, although later set to rise dramatically, by 1961/2 local authorities were spending only around £2.5 million nett annually on all forms of 'popular' and 'high' entertainments (approximately the product of 1d rate). Of all

---

6 *Municipal Review* (July 1945), p. 158, (May 1946), p. 115, (April 1948), p. 59; see also S. K. Ruck, *Municipal Entertainment and the Arts in Greater London* (1965), p. 24; Harris, *Government Patronage*, pp. 116–17.

7 Minihan, *Nationalization of Culture*, p. 241. For a contemporary reaction, see Evans and Glasgow, *Arts in England*, p. 66; and for the Arts Council's comments see, for example, ACGB, *Partners in Patronage: Sixteenth Annual Report 1960–61* (1961), p. 6.

8 *Municipal Review* (Jan. 1964), p. 6.

9 J. Pick, *Managing the Arts in Great Britain? The British Experience* (1986), pp. 75–77; see also R. Hutchison, *The Politics of the Arts Council* (1982), p. 122.

gross expenditure (£7.5 million) under Section 132, only some 12–13 per cent went directly to the sponsorship of high culture.[10]

Marshall has subsequently stressed that municipal attitudes to the arts can only be understood within the limiting context of a broader traditional operating rationale, bureaucratically bound to areas of major statutory service provision. Here, little incentive existed to cater for 'locally discovered needs and optional and novel tasks'. Indeed, across Britain, councillors questioned the need to offer rates support in the presence of a competing and historically viable commercial theatre sector (in much the same way as city politicians had rejected Corporation intervention in housing earlier in this century). As Hutchison indicates, it took 'enthusiastic individuals' of 'strong personality' to counter this inner conservatism.[11] Others, in seeking to explain the lack of municipal arts sponsorship, have stressed the importance of 'ratepayer' or 'independent' groupings standing on a rates reduction programme.[12] While such associations generally had a limited presence in major cities after 1945, their influence and heritage in Nottingham immediately prior to the war has already been noted; nor should there be dispute over the centrality of 'the rates' as a central preoccupation in post-war local government politics.

*

Nottingham's Reconstruction Committee, in degrees, reflected the wartime enthusiasm for arts promotion. The all-party Committee received reports from a number of extraneous bodies, amongst them the Nottingham Playgoers' Club which requested Corporation support for the establishment of a civic theatre. The reconstructors were not unsympathetic to the objectives of cultural regeneration, their final report noting with 'satisfaction [and profit] the evidence in our midst of much constructive thinking'. Nevertheless, it was upon the more utilitarian aspects of renewal that the committee focused, provision for arts activities being limited to a proposed 'Public Hall or Halls for exhibitions, concerts

10 Institute of Municipal Entertainment, *A Survey of Municipal Entertainment in England and Wales for the two years 1947/8 and 1961/2* (1964).

11 A. H. Marshall, *Local Government and the Arts* (1974), pp. 17–18; White, *ACGB*, p. 85; Hutchison, *Politics of Arts*, p. 122.

12 N. J. Abercrombie, 'The Approach to English Local Authorities 1963-1978', in Pick (ed.), *State and Arts*, pp. 65–66; Harris, *Government Patronage*, p. 119.

and other activities' to be located within a newly envisaged civic centre campus.[13] The question of municipal subsidy, however, was not forgotten. Simultaneous with the publication of the reconstruction report, a local solicitor, Hugh Willatt, chaired a committee to press further the claims for a civic theatre. Willatt had close ties with the local co-operative arts movement (becoming its Drama Director) and later the Arts Council itself, rising through its drama panel to become Secretary General in 1968. The committee's detailed proposals were submitted to the Corporation in 1946, but were immediately rejected by city councillors. The absence of civic backing and suitable premises forestalled further developments until in 1948 the reconstituted Nottingham Theatre Trust, as it was to be known, was offered the tenancy of an Edwardian converted cinema. The Lord Mayor, Conservative John Mitchell, subsequently launched an appeal which quickly raised some £4,000 to finance the venture. Significantly, a year later Mitchell resigned in protest as a near bankrupt Trust again pressed the Labour-controlled Corporation to grant it civic theatre status and/or a regular subsidy. Thus, while the experiences of war stimulated local Tory civic interest in voluntary arts provision, as Mitchell pointed out, a subsidised municipal theatre 'was against his whole ideology'.[14] Equally, the ruling Labour group's initial response was less than generous–a £500 grant for two years. In 1951, however, the now Conservative-controlled Corporation did agree to provide a £5,000 loan to enable the Trust to purchase the theatre's lease. As the Arts Council and Trust now noted optimistically, Nottingham's senior city officers were sympathetic to aiding the Playhouse and the 'City Fathers' were 'also coming into line nicely.'[15]

The other principal patron was the city's Co-operative Society (NCS). Aside from financing its own theatre and arts centre, the NCS continued to act as loans guarantor and financial benefactor to the Trust. Such philanthropy contrasted sharply with the past lack of private arts patronage in Nottingham and with the post-war decline generally in commercial and private arts sponsorship. The managing secretary of the NCS was Cyril Forsyth, a charismatic figure passionately committed to the arts, and whose voice held considerable sway within the city's Labour party. Indeed, the educational ethos promoted by the co-operative

13 NCC, Reconstruction Comm. mins, 11 March 1943, 15 July 1943; NCC, Report of the Reconstruction Committee on Post-War Development, 9 Sept. 1943, pp. 5–6, 30.
14 NJ, 19 April 1949; NCC, F&GP Comm. mins, 13 Sept. 1949, 8 Nov. 1949.
15 PRO EL 3/35, minute to Williams, 15 Oct. 1951.

movement in many ways encapsulated Labour's own post-war ambitions for the increased recreational provision for working people.[16]

The 'Little Theatre', however, was far from ideal: indeed, it was 'desperately inadequate' according to the *New Statesman*, for

> its stage (12' x 20') is believed to be the smallest in any professional theatre. It has practically no wings and five tiny subterranean dressing rooms. Noise from a busy road junction, and occasionally from the fire station across the street, interrupts the plays; regular patrons buy their seats as far as possible from the traffic lights.[17]

In a similar vein the Arts Council's Drama Director, Joe Hodgkinson, described the artistic standard achieved as 'nothing short of a miracle', given the surroundings.[18] Nevertheless, its high artistic standards explain why the Playhouse was one of the few provincial theatres in regular receipt of an Arts Council grant by the early 1950s.

Within Labour circles, enthusiasm for the establishment of a new municipal theatre continued to surface. Any immediate uptake of Section 132 was always unlikely; local authorities simply had more pressing priorities. Even in more prosperous times local councillors, with puritan piety or a weather eye to elections, retained a common, lingering suspicion that expenditure on cultural provision was 'frivolous' or made them unnecessarily vulnerable to hostile criticism.[19] In Nottingham, the explosive opposition so successfully orchestrated during the earlier 'Houses First Campaigns' against inter-group plans to complete the city's inner-ring road stood as a vivid reminder of popular priorities in the immediate post-war period. Indeed, those Labour councillors who

16 T. Driberg, 'This Proud City', *Reynolds News*, 5 July 1959; *The Times*, 3 May 1960; J. Bailey, *A Theatre for all Seasons. Nottingham Playhouse: The First Thirty Years 1948–1978*, (1994), p. 49; for similar attitudes in Coventry, see Tiratsoo, *Reconstruction: Coventry 1945–60*, p. 50.

17 *New Statesman*, 20 Jan. 1960; see also Bailey, *Theatre for all Seasons*, pp. 60–61.

18 ACGB Arch, letter from J. L. Hodgkinson to Sir William Emrys Williams (Sec. Gen. ACGB), 21 Feb. 1958.

19 M. Foot, *Aneurin Bevan—Vol. 2, 1945–60* (1973), p. 100; Harris, *Government Patronage*, pp. 91, 119; P. Crane, *Enterprise in Local Government—A Study of the Way in which Local Authorities exercise their Permissive Powers* (1953), p. 16; Evans and Glasgow, *Arts in England*, p. 64; Marshall, *Local Government* pp. 17–18.

remained unenthusiastic about the new theatre project continued to employ the same housing priorities theme in pressing a dissenting case. It was an argument to which the Labour group and leadership continued to feel vulnerable. Nevertheless, with the passing of the worst deprivations associated with post-war austerity and shortages, in 1954 an internal enquiry committed the party to the imminent provision of suitable theatre premises. Local Conservatives were already campaigning against this proposal, objecting principally to a rates subsidy of 'other people's enjoyment'. Nottingham's Labour politicians, on the other hand, increasingly saw 'municipal enterprise'—that is intervention—as the key to widening social access to the arts. 'Providing for [the] people's leisure', it was argued, was 'almost as important as jobs, housing and education.' 'Let them [the people] have gardens, books, music, singing, entertainment, plays, parks, sports fields, festivals and everything else possible and practical for making life brighter and happier.'[20] Such sentiments were to find a place in Labour's national innovative programme in the increasingly affluent late 1950s, where homage was paid to Nottingham's pioneering role (with that of Coventry) in promoting municipal provision.[21] But amidst broader ambitions for an arts festival, the ill-fated planetarium and improved sports facilities, the political showpiece locally was always the new civic theatre.

Electoral defeat in 1955, however, temporarily halted Labour's plans. The Conservative group leader, Joseph Littlefair, in any case also had strong and fixed ideas about how best to rehouse the theatre company. Littlefair, a combative free-marketeering traditionalist, was less inclined than his predecessor to take a conciliatory or consensual line generally. Yet he was also an early subscriber to the Theatre Trust appeal and his later caricature as an 'anti-Playhouse' die-hard needs qualification. What he continued to favour was economy, notably through a joint development with Nottingham's Mechanics Institute on the site of the proposed civic centre. Here provision would be made by the Institute to lease premises to the Theatre Trust. Municipal Conservatism in this sphere for Littlefair and other senior Tories meant an ideological rejection of direct

20 NAO LPC Box 10, Nott'm City Lab. Party, Notes to Prospective Candidates for the 1954 Municipal Elections; LPC Box 10, letter from Ives to A. Greenwood, MP, 25 April 1959; Nott'm City Lab. Party, Municipal Manifesto 1954 and 1957, IAP.

21 Labour Party, *Leisure for Living* (1959), pp. 9, 23, 25; NAO LPC Box 10, letter from Greenwood to Ives, 30 April 1959.

Corporation provision—that is, a civic theatre—and an emphasis on voluntarism with its associated curtailment of rates expenditure.

Thus, both parties agreed that the Trust was badly housed and that the existing premises needed replacing or refurbishing; what was lacking was the qualified unanimity that existed between political leaders at Westminster on arts sponsorship. Initially, however, inter-party agreement through compromise, the traditional approach adopted within Nottingham's ruling political circles to civic projects, seemed possible. If tensions were mounting between the groups, a consensus had been reached eventually over transport and spending on education while, despite differing emphases over housing, the major programmes at Clifton and Bestwood continued unabated. Moreover, the sums involved in connection with the theatre were limited, relative to other areas of responsibility. If Hallward, the Trust's chair, favoured a 'bold' expansive policy, the promise of adjacent land from the NCS initially limited thinking to a £40,000 appeal to be raised jointly from industry, the Arts Council and the Corporation. Inevitably, however, lobbying centred on local politicians; Arts Council support already underwrote the proposal while industry proved generally unresponsive. To oil civic wheels, Willatt and Labour politicians pressed for the establishment of an independent advisory Civic Trust (50 per cent of whom would be local councillors) to guide the local authority on the provision of arts-related buildings and support in Nottingham. It, the argument ran, could then 'provide that mandate which a City Council can at present naturally claim is lacking in expenditure on these matters'. Indeed, both Willatt and Labour agreed that 'it would be quite wrong if this [the Playhouse] were to become a party matter'.[22] The rationale behind establishing a Civic Trust was obvious. Extra community-based funding and advice aside, the central objective was to gain consensual inter-party backing for direct Corporation intervention on the Playhouse's behalf, for past practice suggested that civic improvement schemes required a broadly based political support.

Meanwhile, Willatt invited the redoubtable W. E. Williams, the Secretary General of the Arts Council, to Nottingham to speak at a business luncheon in the presence of prominent local politicians. The Arts Council, and Williams in particular, was already campaigning vigorously to promote local authority participation in rehousing the arts in key

---

22 ACGB Arch, Willatt, undated paper, Nott'm Theatre Trust Exec. Comm. meeting, 26 Oct. 1955.

regional centres. The Council, of course, had twin, and arguably conflicting, obligations towards both regional diffusion and raising artistic standards—epitomised in the so-called 'Raise and/or Spread' debate initiated in the 1950s.[23] Launching its arts rehousing campaign in 1955, Williams had argued:

> To deplore without discrimination the closing of theatres in so many towns is to beg the whole question of theatre provision. The fewer theatres, for the time being the better ... For, in a select number of well-based, well-mannered and well-equipped [regional] playhouses, the living art of drama is more likely to be sustained than ... in precarious establishments committed to a suicidal policy of weekly 'reps', or ... mobile missions to play Shakespeare on improvised stages in village halls.[24]

Critics have since suggested that this focus on promoting 'metropolitan' standards in a limited number of regional centres further alienated many town hall politicians and staff; that because it had only a restricted regional organisation, the Arts Council failed to provide the broader leadership required to stimulate municipal interest in developing their new powers and responsibilities.[25] Nottingham's experience was atypical of this genre or response. Williams began by hinting that Nottingham Playhouse—because of its past artistic achievements—was high on the list of provincial theatres to be submitted to the Chancellor both for permanent subsidy and help with capital expenditure. But the final selection depended on 'how much local support could be expected'. 'If the local authority', he said, 'would, for example, provide the land, the Government would provide the money for the building. From then on the project would rely on income taken from the box office, helped by Arts Council grants and assistance from the rates.' The local press responded

---

23 See Hutchison, *Politics of Arts*, pp. 60 ff; N. M. Pearson, *The State and the Visual Arts* (1982), pp. 52 ff; K. King and M. Blaug, 'Does the Arts Council Know What It Is Doing? An Inquiry into Public Patronage of the Arts', *Encounter* 41 (1973), pp. 6–16.

24 ACGB, *Housing the Arts: Tenth Annual Report 1954–55* (1955), p. 10; see also Hutchison, *Politics of Arts*, pp. 96–99.

25 Hutchison, *Politics of Arts*, ch. 8; King and Blaug, 'Does the Arts Council?', pp. 11–14; Pearson, *State and Visual Arts*, pp. 56–61. For a rebuttal, see White, *ACGB*, p. 85. Hutchison, *Politics of Arts*, pp. 101–02, acknowledges the ACGB's key role in promoting local authority involvement in theatre reconstruction.

enthusiastically. Sir William, proclaimed Arts Council sources, had clearly 'laid the foundation stone for a new Playhouse "well and truly".' Labour, in launching its 1956 municipal manifesto, declared its willingness to take to up Williams's challenge and provide civic finance.[26] In fact, the Secretary General had jumped the gun. The Treasury had as yet made no specific financial commitment, where anyway the needs of London had taken, and were to continue to take, priority. Yet it was only some twenty months later, when local opponents reiterated Williams's as yet unfulfilled promises in an attempt to delay the project, that it was finally acknowledged that government support for provincial capital arts expenditure was highly unlikely—a fact which Willatt, for example, had suspected for some time.[27]

Labour's own proposals at this stage remained somewhat embryonic. Tommy Ives, then newly appointed and wholly committed to the cause of expanding municipal cultural provision, favoured a new building. Willatt, however, thought it most unlikely that the Corporation could be persuaded to build afresh. After considerable discussion, the Theatre Trust rejected the establishment of a broadly based advisory Civic Trust—that is, the most likely vehicle for political compromise—because of the delays this would cause, and with it the idea of a new building. Instead, it opted for the more limited objective of renovating the existing premises. Yet the Trust also had little clear idea of the costs involved. Thus, even the scale of fees to be charged by architect Peter Moro, appointed on the Arts Council's recommendation, reportedly 'left the Board a bit breathless' and wanting to think again.[28]

Ives's championing of the Playhouse cause further infuriated local Conservative opinion; their 'amateur' ethos saw no role for professional organisers in municipal policy making. Indeed, his key involvement was unjustifiably to be cited as the principal reason why the Playhouse proposals so divided the parties. According to Conservative accounts, Ives simply foisted unwanted ideas upon an unwilling Labour leadership; Conservative views, on the other hand, were either not sought or just

26 GJ, 21 Jan. 1956, 20 March 1956; ACGB Arch, letter from Hodgkinson (Drama Dir. ACGB) to Willatt, 26 Jan 1956.

27 Written answer by Brooke to Linstead, HC Debates, 21 Dec. 1955, Vol. 547, col. 335; ACGB Arch, letters from Hodgkinson to Willatt, 12 Oct. 1956 and Willatt to Williams, 23 Aug. 1957.

28 ACGB Arch, memo from MacGregor to Hodgkinson on Directors' Meeting Nott'm Theatre Trust of 10 Jan. 1956.

ignored.[29] In essence, these allegations were simply untrue. For example, the decision finally to opt for a new theatre was taken by George Wigman, during an extensive private interview with Willatt shortly after Labour's 1956 election victory. Then, one of the first actions of the new administration was to establish a committee of enquiry upon which Conservatives had equal representation.[30]

Without doubt, disagreement over the Playhouse did reflect broader and widening divisions in the council chamber which was further spurred by Labour's imposition of majority rule. It was the project's misfortune that it came to fruition during a period of escalating inter-group tension; a tension which, as already noted, pre-dated both Ives's arrival in Nottingham and the immediate pedigree of the theatre proposals itself. Yet in other ways, party reactions to the theatre proposals were symptomatic and expressive of the disparities which then increasingly separated city politicians: notably an unwillingness to compromise (here particularly on the part of Conservatives) tied to a key disagreement on the function of local government once beyond the widely endorsed agenda and impetus provided by reconstruction. For Conservatives this meant adherence to what might be labelled civic minimalism, measured here in their rejection of the permissive powers granted to expand cultural provision, and allied to a reassertion of more fundamental tenets (regarding the sanctity of the rates, for example, and an emphasis on voluntarism) which rejected adding further to the functions and remit of city responsibilities.

This is not to deny Ives's dynamic back-room endeavours on behalf of the Trust, nor the mythically piratical influence with which Conservative opponents endowed him. Indeed another key to understanding why the Playhouse project acquired overtly political overtones rests on the incessant championing, by influential local leaders, of conflicting proposals that made compromise impossible. As the Trust's board later noted, it fully believed that ordinary Conservative councillors were perpetually kept in a state of ignorance, being fed only the standard derogatory—and minimalist—party line.[31] In Nottingham, the presence of

29 Ald. Dyer, *GJ*, 26 Jan. 1961; Ald. Coffey, *Daily Telegraph*, 7 April 1959; Ald. Littlefair, *NEP*, 7 May 1958; *The Times*, 2 May 1960.

30 ACGB Arch, letter from Willatt to Hodgkinson, 3 July 1956; Nott'm Lab. Group mins, 5 July 1956, 25 July 1956, IAP.

31 ACGB Arch, Memo from Linklater to Hodgkinson, 7 Nov. 1960; memo from Linklater to Hodgkinson, 13 Sept. 1961; *Manchester Guardian*, 21 May 1960.

'enthusiastic' 'strong personalities' of the sort identified by Hutchison was certainly not wholly beneficial to promoting the arts. Indeed, their actions increasingly led to the intransigent polarisation of local political opinion generally, in a reaction seemingly out of all proportion to the relative cost of the project, and noticeably at odds with the pragmatic co-operative tradition operating during the inter-war and immediate post-war periods.

Nor should we accept, unreservedly, Marshall's concept of an inner conservatism within local government circles tied to the provision of existing services against set standards. To cite Tom Driberg again, in his aptly titled article 'This Proud City', civic self-esteem was an important local component:

> One tradition lacking here is a tradition of patronage of the arts. Yet so far as I know, no comparable city in Britain has a programme of cultural development anything like so bold and comprehensive as Nottingham's ... In the great advance—'the break-through' some of those concerned call it—the Corporation, now Labour controlled, provide the main leadership; but the University works closely with the Corporation, and the Co-operative movement makes a noticeable contribution ... What is most important in all this cultural ferment is that there is a good chance that Nottingham will succeed better than any other place in bridging the gap between 'highbrow' and 'lowbrow', between the arts—especially the living theatre—and ordinary working people ... Nottingham, as I found it, [was] ... lively, tolerant, rich in history, yet alertly progressive and, above all, proud.[32]

Undoubtedly, the proposed civic theatre was, as Driberg labelled it, Labour's 'revolutionary' idea of the period. Yet, as we have noted elsewhere, civic pride was not wholly the preserve of politicians. Moro's estimates for refurbishment had greatly exceeded the original budget. This prompted the Trust to consider building afresh, a decision almost immediately sanctioned informally by Wigman. Moro estimated this cost to be in excess of £150,000. Meanwhile, Willatt enlisted the support of Tom Owen. Although initially perturbed by the cost, he agreed that the new Playhouse was 'important, that it was fairly urgent and that it must involve substantial expenditure'. Owen now collaborated closely in the

32 *Reynolds News*, 5 July 1959.

preparation of a detailed memorandum from the Trust to the city's General Purposes Committee (GPC); for as Willatt remarked, Owen 'knows his people pretty well and felt that it gave him the necessary ammunition to deal with all the anticipated points that might be raised'.[33] Indeed, the Town Clerk proved a valuable ally, both to the Trust and Labour proponents of a new theatre.

*

On receipt of the Trust's application, the GPC immediately set up a four-man bi-partite sub-committee of inquiry, chaired by Labour's Charlie Butler—another Playhouse enthusiast—and also including Littlefair. Three options were put before them: to renovate the existing theatre, to build on land owned by the Mechanics Institute, or alternatively on a near vacant site at East Circus Street. It was this last scheme which was favoured by the Trust, the Arts Council and Owen, who clearly intended that the Corporation retain overall control of the project and completed theatre. Majority opinion by now favoured not only a new building, but providing additional facilities including a restaurant, bars, broadcasting studio and ancillary accommodation. This, combined with the necessity of closing down the existing theatre for an extended period during renovation, effectively ruled out the first option. Of the remaining two, the East Circus Street proposals were certainly less complicated and more economical. Not only was the land already owned by the Corporation, but development was not tied, as was the case with the Mechanics site, to an extensive joint retail and property venture. East Circus Street was therefore commended to, and accepted by, the GPC. The proposed theatre would, they thought, cost some £150,000 plus £25,000 for the site. Approval of the overall project containing an additional £175,000 studio/office development was deferred, pending negotiations with the BBC.[34]

Even over this more limited scheme, however, the political parties remained deeply divided. Butler, in a later television interview, recalled that 'the sub-committee ... had run into trouble from the start', as he went on to accuse Littlefair of political 'bigotness [sic]' in viewing modern

33 ACGB Arch, letters from Willatt to Hodgkinson, 13 July 1956 and 4 Oct. 1956.
34 For a full breakdown, see NCC, Draft Report to the General Purposes Committee of the Sub-Committee Appointed to Examine and Report on Proposals Relating to the Nott'm Playhouse, 1957, copy IAP.

drama as mere 'Socialist propaganda'. Indeed, on the same programme, the editor of the local *Guardian Journal* ruefully reflected that historically any scheme put forward by one party was 'almost automatically opposed by the opposite side.'[35] While this misrepresented the policy agreement of earlier years, his comments carry a greater resonance the farther one strays into the 1950s, where individual expression and committee esprit de corps were increasingly subsumed by the party machines. With Conservatives actively campaigning against the civic theatre proposals, once in office Labour undoubtedly saw the Playhouse as a manifesto commitment to be enforced. Nevertheless, in instigating an inter-party inquiry, it honoured the tradition of bi-partisanship by providing a forum for consensus. But then it was in its interest so to do. Annual municipal elections dictated that no party was guaranteed the extended period of office necessary to carry through major projects. Since 1950, when Labour's post-war domination ended temporarily, local party majorities had fluctuated first one way, then the other (Table 3.1) —which in itself promoted political discord as each group sought temporary advantage.

Why, then, did Labour fail to reach a compromise? Quite simply, both parties approached the project from diametrically opposed positions. One wanted to spend very little, and certainly opposed municipal participation in commercial ventures. The other favoured an expansive remit. With Conservatives repeatedly citing their basic tenet that all the schemes being considered, including renovation, were either wasteful or extravagant—indeed, of benefit to only a minority interest—a political deadlock was assured. Labour members, with the tacit support of the Corporation's officers, then pressed ahead unilaterally.

It was planned to finance the Playhouse using £200,000 from the city's Gas Fund Trust, those capital receipts realised from the nationalisation of Nottingham's municipal gas industry and set aside to be 'utilized for any amenity likely to be for the general benefit of the community'.[36] The financing of the theatre was debated by the full council in February 1958.

35 *GJ*, 29 Sept. 1961. See also *GJ*, 4 Feb. 1958 and *NEP*, 14 June 1960, *Manchester Guardian*, 21 May 1960, for Littlefair's comments on contemporary Playhouse productions damaging the cultural climate in Nottingham. For Burnett's views, see his editorial, *GJ*, 8 May 1958. Marshall, *Local Authorities*, p. 19 argues that local politicians were particularly sensitive to charges that moral standards were being endangered by rates sponsored arts.

36 NCC, Draft Report of the Sub-Comm. appointed by Finance Comm. re Financial Implications of Re-Housing the Playhouse, 10 Aug. 1960, IAP.

Here Littlefair rightly cast doubt on the validity of the capital cost estimates, over which Willatt also had reservations. He also questioned the Trust's cash flow projections which, on the basis of a peppercorn rent, predicted that the new theatre would be self-supporting. In a pithy statement of minimalist thought, he labelled the project a 'reckless and feckless proposal' which ought not to be loaded on to already overburdened ratepayers. A redundant cinema, he claimed, could be utilised at 'infinitely less cost'—an option already rejected as uneconomic by the Trust, the Arts Council and the sub-committee upon which he sat.[37] Other Conservatives were less scathing but adhered to Littlefair's general lead. Nevertheless, a division along party lines saw the report carried. Paradoxically, while at a national level both major parties were to praise Nottingham's ambition, the time for local consensus seeking had passed.[38]

Moro was soon to be confirmed as project architect. Indeed, so impressed with his past work for the Royal Festival Hall were Owen and Butler that, after a promotional visit there arranged by Williams, both left not only convinced that Moro was the right man, but (civic pride to the fore again) that 'they must try to arrange for more money to be available if it were needed!'[39] The Arts Council also underwrote the cause by guaranteeing a minimum annual subsidy of £5,000 to the Playhouse in its opening years. In the event, it was to be considerably larger. Yet the final adoption of the East Circus Street proposals depended entirely on Labour's fortunes in the forthcoming municipal elections.

Labour's position in May 1958, although not secure, was less precarious than during the years immediately before; the party entered the elections with an eight seat advantage (Table 6.1) and the Macmillan government also was nationally unpopular. The party previously had campaigned vociferously on its Playhouse proposals. On this occasion, however, in seeking to avoid local controversy, Labour's utterances were limited to the odd defensive denial on costs and subsidies. The Conservatives, by contrast, sought to focus attention squarely on the new theatre. Claims to have unearthed considerable opposition to Labour's

37 *GJ*, 4 Feb. 1958.

38 See, for example, the comments of future Conservative Party Chairman, Peter Thomas, *HC Debates*, 23 Jan. 1959, Vol. 598, col. 561; R. Careless and P. Brewster, *Patronage and the Arts*, Conservative Political Centre (1959), pp. 41, 44; Labour Party, *Leisure for Living*, p. 25.

39 ACGB Arch, Letter from Willatt to Williams, 2 May 1958.

plans (although a later opinion poll indicated the reverse to be true)[40] preceded full-page advertisements on the eve of poll in all local newspapers lambasting the cost of the project. The same papers' correspondence columns also saw Littlefair claiming to have found his alternative—the ideally situated cost-cutting redundant cinema site. The Arts Council was intrigued, and wrote to Willatt asking for details. His reply provides an apt commentary on contemporary civic affairs:

> Yes indeed I saw Littlefair's letter and a great deal else, including the whole back page of our evening newspapers the day before the election, featuring as the main reason for getting the Socialists out 'the mad Playhouse scheme'. I suppose it is something that an artistic matter was treated as so important. Anyway, the Conservatives lost even more seats than they expected and there was no doubt that the matter was raised at this stage in a desperate attempt to whip up extra votes. No-one knows what Littlefair's suitable premises were. I don't think anyone dare ask him! I don't think it matters very much because it was mainly an election stunt anyway.[41]

Both the Arts Council and Willatt were dismissive of the Conservatives' unsuccessful attempts to exploit the theatre project for political gain, which indeed contradicted the broad national political consensus that arts policy remain above party politics. This, of course, did not deter the Trust and its supporters from themselves repeatedly attempting to manipulate the local political decision-making process. Yet the greatest inconsistency rested with city Conservatives. Throughout the 1950s, they continually accused Labour of politicising the local civic agenda. Yet measured by their own future conduct over the Playhouse, it soon became clear that here Conservative opposition set no limits, for civic principle came a poor second to party dogma or expediency.

In April 1959, Moro presented his detailed proposals to the Corporation's Theatre Sub-Committee. His most difficult task, he reported, had been to marry his £200,000 budget allocation to the Trust's rising expectations and the practical knowledge gained from Coventry's new Belgrade civic theatre. Including an additional wing (containing,

40 *NEN*, 18 May 1960.
41 ACGB Arch, letter from Willatt to Linklater, 14 May 1958.

amongst other attributes, a restaurant and art gallery), Moro now estimated the theatre's cost at some £295,000. Nevertheless, the GPC, impressed by his proposals and the critical acclaim afforded them, authorised the preparation of tender documents. Further support for the now financially ailing Playhouse (for attendances, having peaked in 1957, were falling), came from the Arts Council in the shape of a 75 per cent addition in grant aid to £10,000 annually by 1961. The Council insisted that much of this increase should go to raising further artistic standards. Nevertheless, increased Arts Council support was seen as particularly important in allaying Labour fears that the theatre, when open, would be a 'continual drain on the rates'. With this in mind Butler and Willatt invited Williams to Nottingham in March 1960, primarily 'to keep up the morale of the Labour people' but also, if possible, to 'smooth out' the divisions between the two political parties in the run up to the municipal elections.[42]

Williams thought the visit a great success. Owen, too, thought real progress had been made in bringing the opposing factions together. Congratulating Williams, he wrote:

> It was obvious to me that what you said did have some very real effect on one or two of our leading members who are inclined to carry their opposition to the civic theatre to the ultimate length. I think there were signs that their feelings against the project will be toned down in future discussions.[43]

But whatever leading members were saying in private, the approach of the annual elections stifled any public reconciliation. With demolition work due to start shortly after polling day, Bill Dyer (the newly appointed Conservative leader) announced that, if returned to power, he would immediately suspend all work on the new theatre. This, as later became clear, meant its cancellation. As we know, the 1960 elections proved disappointing for Labour nationally, and disastrously so in Nottingham in the aftermath of the 'Popkess Affair'. Having lost nine seats, the party was forced to rely on the casting vote of the new Lord Mayor, Roland

---

42 ACGB Arch, letter from Willatt to Williams, 5 March 1960; Letter from Linklater to Hodgkinson, 26 Feb. 1960.

43 ACGB Arch, letter from Owen to Williams, 11 March 1960.

Green, to retain control of the council. The new theatre's future, once again, appeared to be hanging by a political thread.

Yet the Conservative threat to postpone construction galvanised support from the arts fraternity and Nottingham's theatre-going public, where over 3,300 signed a local petition. Given the middle-class composition of theatre audiences, Conservative supporters were unsurprisingly well represented. More unexpected, perhaps, some signatories were prominent party members—those whom Dyer later claimed on radio to have signed 'under the misapprehension' that the Conservatives were against the Playhouse, as he once again floated the idea of a converted cinema.[44] Leading Young Conservatives were also calling for an end to delays, while individual Tory party activists criticised the lack of leadership consultation over Playhouse policy.[45] Uncertainty was certainly aided by a paucity of reliable information over costs. The press was still speaking of a project valued at £200,000 (some £95,000 below Moro's 1959 estimate), while critics were glibly talking of £500,000. Finally Butler, in a belated attempt to stem the wilder rumours, publicly committed Labour to a figure of around £300,000, drawn solely from the Gas Trust Fund. Tenders above that would lead to design cuts.

Further disagreement arose over future rental arrangements. Owen, Ives and the Trust favoured charging only a nominal sum—in effect, a hidden subsidy. But Labour's new leader, Eric Foster, insisted on the need for a full economic rent, which included the cost of servicing and repaying the loan in order to finance future projects. This was to be partially offset by an annual subsidy, thereby limiting the Corporation's liability. The Trust was then predicting an annual trading surplus (excluding rent) of between £11,000 and £20,000, depending on audience attendance. However, a bi-party Corporation Finance Committee report took a considerably less favourable view of these projections, which in any case ignored the economic return on the loan now demanded by the city. On this basis, it concluded:

---

44 *NEN*, 1 June 1960. The cinema Littlefair and Dyer had in mind was the Gaumont, seating some 2,500 and rejected in 1956 as being too large.

45 *NEN*, 26 and 27 May 1960; ACGB Arch, memo from Hodgkinson to Linklater, 13 Sept. 1961.

The suggestion is well founded that the net loss to the City would be at least £20,000 per annum, assuming a continuation of the £10,000 grant from the Arts Council.[46]

However, an inventive and politically inspired redrafting of the final sub-committee report relayed a totally different account, predicting instead an annual Corporation subsidy of only some £7-12,000 per annum. Any subsidy, of course, effectively reduced the rate of return to the fund and the time taken to replenish it. But as Labour and Owen were quick to point out, an economic rate of return was not a covenantal requirement; nor was it the fund's *raison d'être* to provide a cheap pool of internal funding for miscellaneous items of Corporation expenditure—purpose for which it was currently employed. Thus Labour was able to reaffirm that both capital cost and annual subsidy 'could be met from the Trust fund without recourse to the rates'.[47] As this was now seemingly the central political issue at stake, Dyer and Littlefair, not surprisingly, dissented from such an interpretation. Conservatives, anyway, had long publicised the somewhat pedantic view that any loss of profit currently accruing to the Gas Fund would necessarily lead to an additional charge to the rates.

Labour, however, was soon facing larger and more immediate problems; namely, a lowest tender bid of £358,000 which, with professional fees, brought the total figure to some £400,000. As senior Labour figures were pledged to guillotine any scheme over £300,000, Moro set to pruning the specification. Meanwhile, Hallward, in a desperate attempt to save the project, proposed the Trust realise its own assets. With Moro promising a saving of £30,000, the Trust wrote to the Corporation guaranteeing to contribute £60,000 itself.[48] Green was then instructed to use his casting vote in the council chamber for the Moro proposal. This further inflamed Conservative opinion for it again compromised the traditional impartiality of the Lord Mayor's office. Indeed, two weeks later Green abruptly refused to sign the building contract on the city's behalf because of this enforced intervention.[49] The

46 NCC, Draft Report of the Sub-Comm. appointed by Finance Comm. re Financial Implications of Re-Housing the Playhouse, 10 Aug. 1960, IAP.

47 NCC, Report of the Special Finance Sub-Committee Appointed to Report on the Financial Implications of the Civic Theatre Proposal, 21 Dec. 1960, IAP.

48 ACGB Arch, letter from Hallward to Owen, 23 Jan. 1961.

49 *Birmingham Post*, 4 July 1969; Nott'm Lab Group mins, 2 March 1961; Foster Diary, 21 Feb. 1961, IAP.

matter was quickly and quietly suppressed (necessarily as it jeopardised Labour's mandate to govern), and Green was again instructed to comply with group policy, on pain of expulsion.

Local Conservatives, unaware of Labour's internal problems, but realising that in effect they had little chance of stopping the project before May, only now offered to resurrect inter-party talks. Here Dyer proposed that the city provide the Trust with an interest-free loan of £100,000, pay all professional fees and offer the site at a peppercorn rent. The Trust was then to raise the balance through a debenture issue offered to the market. It was a wholly impractical scheme commercially. As the city treasurer's internal assessment indicated:

> Far better investments are available in first class industrial companies where there is much greater security of capital and where debenture interest is covered several times over by the earnings of the company. The interest on the Theatre debenture would not be covered by earnings at all but only by the Arts Council subsidy. Such a debenture would only be likely to be taken up by a benefactor.[50]

The Trust's reaction was unequivocally negative. As one director remarked, the Conservatives were 'trying to deal themselves a winning hand with marked cards'.[51] Yet, hopeful of obtaining alternative sources of finance, the Trust opted to delay any formal response until after the elections.

Predictably, May 1961 saw the return of a Conservative administration fully committed to killing the Moro project. Implementing this policy, however, presented difficulties. A complete cancellation was thought contractually to be too expensive, while using the site for a suggested car park was presumed to contravene the terms of the Gas Trust. Dyer, therefore, pursued his 'debenture' discussions with the Trust, which it in turn now formally rejected. The Trust, however, remained optimistic of securing a compromise. Indeed, Hallward confidently predicted 'the whole thing would simmer down in time but that clearly the Conservatives had

50 City Treasurer's Office, comments requested by Ald. Foster for the Corporation to Assist in the Financing of the Building of a New Playhouse, 1 March 1961, IAP.
51 ACGB Arch, memo from Linklater to Hodgkinson, 3 May 1961.

to find some way of saving face and it might be wise for the Trust to help them to do it'.[52]

The Trust, however, was operating under a misapprehension. Littlefair, granted carte blanche by the Conservative group, had already secretly contacted the entertainments chain Moss Empires, then seeking a new site for the city's Theatre Royal. He now proposed that in exchange for accepting the Corporation's existing liabilities, Moss Empires take over the Circus Street site. Moss Empires agreed to enter negotiations. To do this, Littlefair required the permission of the GPC. It was left to Owen to extract from a reluctant Littlefair that the theatre chain was in fact to be given the £75,000 site free of charge. Not only did this make commercial sense, Littlefair argued, leaving the Gas Fund largely intact, but Nottingham would also acquire the most up-to-date theatre in Britain at no future charge to the rates.[53] It was, he said, the Trust's own fault that it was to be left unprovided:

> They have, throughout, acted on what can only be considered as unsound advice, and the opportunity of securing substantial assistance from the Corporation has been jeopardized ... The next move must rest with the Trustees of the Playhouse to put forward some valid scheme which is not subject to the same valid criticism as the project now foiled.[54]

Littlefair's measure of what constituted 'substantial assistance' remained, as it had always, central to the divide between the parties. If Labour, aside from any ideological commitment, saw major municipal intervention as a prerequisite to broadening access to the arts, Conservatives viewed the Playhouse in voluntaryist, static terms: a 'useful amenity' of minority interest to be funded sparingly. With Littlefair predicting, incorrectly, that popularist commercial theatre in Nottingham 'would not survive a heavily subsidized municipal competitor', he went on to speculate that 'so extravagant a project' as the Moro design would, in any case, be patronised by 'less than 5 per cent of [city] ratepayers': 'the burden on

52 ACGB Arch, memo from Andrews to Hodgkinson, 20 June 1961.
53 NCC, GPC mins, 7 Sept. 1961; *GJ*, 18 Nov. 1961.
54 *GJ*, 8 Sept. 1961.

the rates would be ... out of all proportion and I repeat that it is on financial grounds that we have been justified'.[55]

The Trust, with Owen's tacit approval, now reluctantly sought advice on the legality of the proposed transfer. It also agreed, with the assistance of the Arts Council and Equity, to lobby Moss Empires. Owen himself wrote to the Arts Council requesting the chairman to visit Nottingham to discuss the future financing of the Playhouse with local Conservatives—a meeting subsequently vetoed by the Tory group hierarchy. Finally, the Trust, still desperately seeking a compromise, examined the possibility of itself raising further finance, although as Willatt admitted privately, he thought they would 'find it difficult to raise [the] £60,000' already promised—a prediction which proved all too correct.[56] Work on site, however, was still proceeding apace, adding daily to the cancellation costs. Indeed, Moro remained wholly optimistic. In his view the site, and particularly the foundations work, was totally unsuitable for the 1,500 seater which Moss Empires proposed. Meanwhile, Willatt and the Labour group had both been advised that there were several favourable grounds on which to seek a legal injunction against the proposed transfer by the Corporation. Moss Empires' interest, however, was already subsiding. In November, they approached the Corporation for permission to include a new theatre in a planned redevelopment complex on their existing site. In fact the straight choice, as presented by the Conservatives, of either a new playhouse or a self-financing commercial theatre had always been illusory; the Corporation had a long-standing agreement with Moss Empires to make an alternative but compatible site available on favourable terms when and if required.

To date, all discussions between the city and Moss Empires had been handled exclusively by Littlefair. Owen's services, however, were required to conclude any transaction. He arranged to meet Moss Empires on 15 November. Yet before he could lay his detailed instructions before them, the company terminated the negotiations. According to Conservative accounts, Owen happily accepted this rebuff—his only reaction being quickly to pass the news to the press.[57] An annoyed Littlefair and Dyer, therefore, only learnt of the abortive negotiations the following day when reading their morning newspapers. Littlefair's

55 *GJ*, 4 Feb. 1958, 8 Sept. 1961, 18 Nov. 1961.

56 ACGB Arch, memo from Linklater to Hodgkinson, 13 Sept. 1961; letter from Willatt to Hodgkinson, 16 Oct. 1961.

57 *GJ*, 16 Nov. 1961, 18 Nov. 1961.

subsequent claims, however, that the talks had been abandoned because of minor financial disagreements were promptly denied by Moss Empires. Instead, they cited their 'wish not to become involved in local politics', nor to be portrayed as 'the people who wished to prevent the building of a civic theatre in Nottingham'.[58] Ironically, it appeared, local Conservatives had fallen partial victim to their own propaganda in presenting the choice as one between a subsidised or commercial theatre. Instead, Littlefair chose to blame the scurrilously inaccurate campaign conducted against his proposals and, more justifiably, the weight of the arts lobby.

The new 760-seat theatre was officially opened in December 1963. In the interim, the Civic Theatre Sub-Committee and Trust agreed the terms of a 21-year lease: an annual rent of £26,000 to be offset by a £13,000 per annum subsidy from the Corporation, fixed for seven years. The Trust's contribution to the capital cost, as Willatt had predicted, fell markedly short of the £60,000 promised. The Trust, however, neither offered payment of the £25,000 collected nor showed any readiness to meet with city councillors and officials to discuss the debt. After confirming that Hallward's promise to raise the capital was legally binding, Owen was instructed to write to the Trust requesting an explanation. Meanwhile Foster, under pressure from 'Playhouse enthusiasts' within his party to settle on generous terms, but faced equally with Conservative protests over the lack of repayment, forestalled any final agreement until after the municipal elections.[59] Once re-installed in office, the Labour leadership was faced with two options: either to renege on its own commitment to the electorate and party by accepting that capital expenditure on the Playhouse would rise above the set cost limits—risking a political storm; or alternatively, to abandon the moral high ground of cultural provider and insist that a financially stretched Trust fulfil its legal obligations. Foster chose the latter course. Characteristically of the post-Popkess era, however, he sought to defuse inter-party conflict—and thereby limit potential damage to his own party—by involving his political opponents in the decision-making process. With Hallward already demanding further subsidies before the debt was honoured, and complaining bitterly in the interim that it was like

58 *NEP*, 16 Nov. 1961.

59 Letter from Foster to Owen, 5 May 1964, IAP; NCC, Gen. Purposes (Civic Theatre) Sub-Comm. mins, 4 May 1964; NCC, Gen. Purposes Comm. mins, 13 July 1964.

'negotiating with the USSR', dubbing the Corporation a 'recalcitary authority', a united front-bench finally extracted some £42,000 from the Trust. The financial balance was added to the rent.[60] Hallward, politically isolated, resigned in protest.

The Playhouse's financial legacy having being finally resolved, the Corporation, Trust and Arts Council met in November to outline future policy. Given the predicted poor state of Playhouse finances, both city party leaders were now faced with the more difficult task politically of approving increases to Corporation subsidies. Pre-warned, however, that the other agencies favoured an expansionary policy and budget, Foster and Bill Derbyshire (the new Tory group leader) arrived fully briefed and determined to keep future increases in expenditure and subsidy to a minimum. Costs, they were told, were escalating primarily because of the Trust's decision to adopt a policy of 'true repertoire', which although increasing audience potential also added significantly to production and labour costs. Foster neatly summated Labour concerns:

> We were all aware of the increase in costs, but the possibility of the Theatre becoming a rate borne project was more serious, for the Press and the Tories had predicted this in Council and would most certainly attack ... What we are being asked to do, is to write off the [Gas] Trust Fund, for there will be no money to put back and also to give the Theatre £3,000 [per annum] as well.[61]

Nevertheless, estimates were predicting an overall annual deficit of some £14,000. It was on this basis that senior members from both parties bilaterally agreed to raise the city council annual grant by a further £9,000, a decision later endorsed by both groups at full council. Drawn into the political process, Conservatives had little option but to participate positively and actively. This was made all the easier because of Labour's 'new realism'—that largely negative, if understandable, response to the political uncertainties spawned by the debacles of the late 1950s—so that shared civic objectives once again placed limits on past disagreement. With the new theatre constructed and operating as a civic and artistic beacon, it was simply in nobody's interests for the venture to founder.

60 ACGB Arch, letter from Hallward to Hodgkinson, 27 June 1964.
61 Nott'm Lab Group mins, 24 Nov. 1964; see also letter from Owen to Foster, 18 Aug. 1964, IAP.

Indeed, measured in artistic terms, the Playhouse was a singular success, critically acclaimed as one of the best examples of the 'utopian' type of facility for which Jennie Lee had been calling.[62]

*

Undoubtedly, the public acrimony over the new Playhouse centred principally on the 'rates factor'. Nevertheless, Conservatives consistently objected, both financially and philosophically, to any permanent annual subsidy of 'other people's entertainment', and centrally to the concept of a civic theatre itself. Indeed, Conservative agitation against Labour's 'revolutionary' initiative intensified with time: witness the extreme lengths to which they were eventually prepared to go to foil the Moro project. Yet paradoxically, leading Conservatives had been among the earliest supporters of the post-war initiative for a voluntary aided city repertory theatre. This support had been extended to the granting of limited municipal funding when required by an ailing Theatre Trust and by plans to re-house the company elsewhere. Indeed the scale of Conservative generosity also increased as the political crisis escalated. It simply became politically inexpedient to be caricatured as wholly 'anti-playhouse', the more so given the class basis of Tory support. Aid, however, was always to be limited to a single payment, whether by way of a grant to the Mechanics Institute or later an interest-free loan to the Trust to finance partially the new theatre. It remained Littlefair's oft repeated central preoccupation to resist what he considered 'reckless and feckless' spending on a major civic arts initiative in order to protect already overburdened ratepayers.[63] Minimalist instincts guided local Conservative thought, here rejecting the permissive new responsibilities for the arts instigated in 1948 as part of the national post-war welfare settlement. That Conservative objections and resistance pre-dated the later, broader divides so evident in Nottingham in the second half of the 1950s is also significant. There was simply no solid foundation for consensus between one party wedded to private or voluntary provision and another to expansive civic arts intervention. Thus, while the war, and the impetus for reconstruction which it engendered, undoubtedly promoted local

62 *A Policy for the Arts: The First Step* (Cmnd 2601), PP (1964–65), pp. 5–6, 12–14; Dept. of Education and Science, *Circular 8/65* (June 1965).
    63 See, for example, *GJ*, 4 Feb. 1958, 18 Nov. 1961.

enthusiasm for the arts amongst practitioners and politicians alike, it failed to breach traditional core Tory political values at a local level. The parameters of agreement, over both reconstruction and the extension of civic responsibility, had clearly defined limits.

There is, however, a danger in oversimplifying the later political division. Majority Labour opinion fully intended that Trust repayments refurbish the Gas Fund. Theatre finance, in terms of capital cost, was viewed as a loan, albeit one made on increasingly favourable terms, not the gift which by circumstance it finally became. Noticeably, the party became increasingly sensitive to Conservative charges of local financial frivolity, as Hallward later found to his cost. Indeed, had Labour initially known the true capital and revenue cost involved, it seems probable that the project would initially have been deferred. This is not to doubt its commitment to the Trust. The party, and particularly many of its leading lights, were enthusiastic interventionists on behalf of the arts. But municipalisation here, as in other areas like direct works, while remaining an important historical tenet of local party philosophy, increasingly acquired a pragmatic and financial character. In local politics during the 1940s, the 1950s, or 1960s, only the confident or the foolish set to one side, albeit temporarily, the political centrality of the rates.

What, then, of civic and political pride? Certainly, the nearer the planned theatre came to fruition, for proponents and opponents alike, the greater the influence of party and individual vanity. In large measure this reflected, and indeed extended, the party political division of the time. Initially, however, the two constituents were more closely bound, linked in supporting a key theatrical company held in high critical esteem by providing a civic amenity of equally high architectural stature. In this objective, Labour was able to draw on a wider support and consensus outside and within the town hall—where ultimately the final decision rested. Local Conservative minimalism, isolated from this consensus, misjudged contemporary opinion, which in itself was partly formed by a self-assertive Labour group and leadership. Only in this way was the subsidised municipalisation of local culture, keenly advocated by the Arts Council and Westminster, able to defeat the utilitarian financial imperative.

CHAPTER 9
Discord and Harmony: City Politics in the 1960s

The 1960s are usually portrayed, pejoratively or not, as an era of reform and change—even of revolutionary change. In Nottingham, however, the legacy of the previous decade cast a counter-acting but strong, immobilising shadow on city politics as the Popkess fiasco—a memory etched distinctly into the Labour group's collective psyche—dissolved progressive confidence. To combat this traumatic past, the new leadership determined on a more consensual brand of city politics. While *rapprochement* was not always possible (notably over the construction of the Playhouse), the general tenet of future Labour policy was to be less visionary, and indeed frequently hesitant. In achieving its objectives, through a blend of co-operation and caution, the group was to be remarkably successful. But there was a price to pay. Commenting on city politics in 1964, Antony Howard cynically noted:

> The weakness of the present Labour Party in Nottingham ... is not administrative incapacity: it is a failure of imagination. Perhaps Aneurin Bevan put it best when he announced at one Labour Party conference: 'You know, I sometimes think that some of our comrades are alderman first and socialists second.' In Nottingham his words attain a vivid meaning. So close is the liaison between the top municipal brass on both sides that the Conservative leader on the council is in all but name deputy leader of the Labour Group; there is the usual ex-Lord Mayors' 'club'; and a time-honoured tradition still lays down that whereas committee chairmanships should go to the majority party, deputy chairmanships should, where possible, be given to the other side. All this naturally makes for a comfortable atmosphere in the Council House—but it has led to political atrophy in the rest of the city.[1]

1 Howard, *New Statesman*, 21 Aug. 1964.

Howard was concurrently expressing a sympathy for a local New Left which, through its control of the City Party policy-making apparatus, sought to curtail traditional councillor autonomy. In demanding fundamental change on a broad ambit of policy issues, friction with an inwardly conservative Labour group was inevitable. In fact, the scale of the acrimony unleashed surpassed even the party's earlier post-war factionalism.

The task of rebuilding shattered group confidence had fallen largely to its new leader, Eric Foster. After first cajoling support for a bi-partisan enquiry into council corruption and Popkess's dismissal, he then set further to restoring the party's tarnished image. Foster preached moderation in both policy and action. As Bert Kirk (Group Secretary, 1965) later recounted:

> Ald. Foster ... since being 'pitchforked' into Leadership at a critical time for the Labour Party, ... [when] addressing the much depleted Council Group in 1960, [had] said it was the duty of all the Councillors present to adhere to a strict rule to regain the lost confidence of the citizens[.] He did not mince his words, stating any foolish action by a Councillor could place us in the wilderness for x number of years. But if we presented the right policy both in and out of the Council we could be in control again in 3 years. That policy followed faithfully during the '60, '61, '62 Councils is now shown in the successful majority of today.[2]

Controversy was to be avoided. Electoral success, in Foster's eyes, depended above all on the pragmatic adoption of a restricted, politically safe agenda: one geared primarily to the economically competent management of council services largely unfettered by ideological considerations. Thus, the first product of the group's 1963 overall policy review on its return to office was, at Foster's suggestion, the appointment of outside consultants to investigate the efficiency of the Corporation's housing and estates departments.[3]

A cautionary approach in itself, however, provoked internal controversy and external ambiguity. To take but one example, in 1960 the group had been reluctantly persuaded that cuts in central subsidies and

2 Letter from Kirk to Cattermole, 15 Feb. 1965, IAP.
3 Nott'm Lab. Group mins, May–July 1963, *passim*.

greater repair bills made housing rent rises inevitable. Three years later, the outgoing Conservative administration controversially removed Exchequer and rate fund subsidies completely from those tenants considered able to pay a full economic rent—increasing average rents by 6/11d per week. The Labour group (although not the constituency parties and trades unions) was not wholly opposed to means testing per se. It was, however, anxious not to offend its bedrock working-class constituent. Nor did it want to alienate those who had subsidised council rents through rates contributions. Lacking a principled criterion, uncertainty prevailed. Labour members remained wholly divided in their response: whether to be 'courageous enough to say that we shall scrap' the Tory arrangements or merely to 'introduce a more equitable scheme'.[4] Indeed, ultimately it was decided not to issue an election manifesto, while public comment on that most politically sensitive of issues—housing rents—was simply side-stepped.

In fact, it had already been decided to abolish the Tory scheme. However, as local ward supporters feared, the rates component subsidy—the ending of which had been at the core of past Labour objections—was not re-introduced. With Foster repeatedly warning that a failure to modernise properties or operate a policy of financial prudence in respect of housing reserves would 'adversely affect our [broader] public image', it was thought more expedient to offer small, though not compensatory, across-the-board rent reductions rather than revive local cross-subsidies.[5]

The group felt particularly vulnerable to charges that it would, as a matter of course, increase city expenditure. Aside, therefore, from an early concentration on tackling departmental inefficiency, conspicuous attempts were also made to limit expenditure. Thus, in finalising details of their first budget the following March, Labour members were in a congratulatory mood on learning that thus far, they had set the third lowest rate of any comparably sized city, after cutting committee spending by some £420,000. As Table 9.1 indicates, local taxation under Labour in the three years following continued to run counter to perennial

4 *Ibid.*, 29 Jan. 1963, 28 March 1963; Nott'm Lab Group, Notes on Election Policy Discussion, March 1963, IAP; NCC, Housing Comm. Report, 18 Nov. 1963; Nott'm City Lab. Party (hereafter NCLP), Annual Report 1962–63, IAP.

5 Nott'm Lab. Group mins, 25 July 1963, 7 Nov. 1963. For a brief outline of Conservative attempts to encourage councils to operate differential rents schemes, see Merrett, *State Housing*, pp. 177–84.

Conservative charges of extravagance, with rate levels set considerably below those of most other county boroughs in England and Wales. This contrasted sharply with their earlier record. Indeed, a preoccupation with efficiency and the rates, a return to the classical nexus of value for money in local government, became the hallmark of post-Popkess Labour administrations, drawing praise from even the local Chamber of Commerce for doing 'a very good job in curbing expenditure'.[6]

Good housekeeping apart, the other notable Popkess legacy centred on a collective fear of initiating fresh controversy. The task of 'presenting the right picture both in and out of the Council Chamber' was, as already noted, one on which the post-Wigman leadership set great store. This policy found its clearest form in a renewed insistence that the group speak with one voice—through its leadership and committee hierarchy structure—on all matters of policy. Foster, particularly, was always quick to draw attention to occasions when this procedure was not scrupulously observed, curbing debate and dissent from his own moderating line by frequent reference to previously agreed policy decisions pushed through by the hierarchy.[7] For the most part, the group acquiesced to centralised regimentation—even on matters deemed apolitical. There were, however, practical reasons for the introduction of a re-invigorated whipping system. Popkess left group morale at a low ebb, evidenced by the lax attendance of Labour members at committee, group and council meetings. In itself, this warranted the introduction of counter-disciplinary measures. It was against this largely homogeneous body, bonded as much by past shared insecurities as by a commonality of moderate belief, that the left, having secured a foothold in the constituency and city parties, set their cap.

*

For those who held views on the leftward margins of Labour orthodoxy, entry into the party in Nottingham at the turn of the decade remained a hit and miss affair. Certainly, those governing the local parties were more tolerant of leftist dissension than a decade before; but then enforcing local congruity was difficult when, nationally, the party was so openly split.

6 *GJ*, 14 Feb. 1967.
7 Nott'm Lab. Group mins, 28 Jan. 1960, 22 March 1960, 29 Sept. 1960, 7 Nov. 1963, 28 Nov. 1963.

Table 9.1 *Rates poundage set in Nottingham compared with other county boroughs in England and Wales*

Year rate set	Party in control[a]	City rate poundage	Av. county borough poundage	City Ranking (lowest)[b]
1958	Lab.	19s8d	19s4d	41st
1959	Lab.	20s8d	19s11d	49th
1960	Lab.	23s0d	20s11d	59th
1961	Lab.	23s0d	21s9d	50th
1962	Con.	23s0d	23s5d	31st
1963[c]	Con.	7s11d	9s11d	3rd
1964	Lab.	8s4d	10s4d	6th
1965	Lab.	10s4d	11s2d	21st
1966	Lab.	11s0d	12s3d	14th
1967	Lab.	11s0d	12s9d	8th

Source: Institute of Municipal Treasurers and Accountants, *Return of Rates and Rates Levied per Head of Population (England and Wales)*, 1959–67

Notes: [a] Poundage levels were set annually in March/April, prior to the municipal elections. The political classification refers to the party in charge when that figure was set.

[b] Ranking refers to the level of city rates set compared with that of other county boroughs. Thus in 1958, Nottingham's rate was the 41st lowest in England and Wales. Between 1958-68, there were on average 83 county boroughs.

[c] The 1963 poundage reduction followed a national revaluation.

This gave a certain immunity from the abuses practised earlier. It was only when those on the left achieved notoriety or undue influence that party officials, or local right-wingers, considered acting; the rationale in Nottingham, as elsewhere, was that until this stage was reached, it required a disproportionate effort to expel them. That said, national intelligence was made available to local officials on those thought to be engaged in clandestine political activity in order that surveillance could be maintained.[8]

8 Intelligence was passed from, amongst other sources, Transport House and the security services; NAO LPC Box 10, letter from Cattermole to Nellie Bailey (Sec. NCLP), 10 March 1960; interview with Foster, 3 March 1989.

The City Party Executive itself remained firmly under the control of those from Labour's right and centre until 1963, after which the left gained a foothold. Here it continued to vet municipal candidacies, acting as a constitutional filter to block the nomination to winnable seats of those of radical persuasion. It remained equally determined to obstruct entry into its own ranks to those of doubtful allegiance.[9] The most contentious of these cases initially involved delegates from affiliated unions, who were under no obligation to be Labour party members if they paid the political levy and did not belong to any proscribed body. The Executive, however, interpreted its own rules illiberally, and withheld City Party credentials from several union-nominated delegates because of their former Communist membership—a delaying ploy generally, and incorrectly, justified on the grounds that eligibility here was a matter on which individual constituencies had to rule.

In turn, constituency parties themselves could be equally unsympathetic to the enrolment of former Communists. The best documented case involved Arthur West, a one-time Communist prospective parliamentary candidate who left the party in 1956. First nominated as an Amalgamated Engineering Union delegate in 1959, the City Party Executive rejected West's application despite his willingness to sign a declaration of loyalty. The matter was then duly parcelled out to Nottingham West constituency, where it rested uncomfortably for several years. In 1963, constituency officers were still privately assuring Jim Cattermole that under no circumstances would West's repeated application be accepted. Rather, they placed him on twelve months' probation, a deferment which again brought forward a furore of protests. Indeed, it was indicative of the changing tide that, to the surprise of local officers and Cattermole alike, West's local Labour branch then narrowly voted to accept his application. Two years later, the City Party Executive itself endorsed his candidacy for the 1966 municipal election—although he was allocated an unwinnable seat. It was not without a degree of self-satisfaction, therefore, that Cattermole was immediately able to report that before the election, West had signed the nomination forms of a Communist candidate standing against Labour in Broxtowe ward.[10]

9 Gosling, *Personal Copy*, pp. 98, 102. For membership rejections, see NAO LPC Box 10, City Party Exec. mins and correspondence 1960–63, *passim.*
10 MRC MSS 9/3/19/111, 3 April 1964, 9/3/21/162, 10 May 1966.

It was later to be alleged by group officials that it was the active recruitment particularly of trade unionists with Communist sympathies to the City Party which allowed the New Left to expand and consolidate its position in Nottingham Labour politics. Attendances at City Party meetings certainly blossomed around 1964, the year in which Ken Coates—a prominent New Left publicist and the central figure in the ensuing controversy—was narrowly elected its chair. This contrasted markedly with previous years when attendances had been 'extremely poor'.[11] In part, however, past indifference was a direct product of earlier nationally-imposed structural reform, where the centralised political functions of conglomerate city parties were transferred to individual constituencies. A transfer resisted locally, the early 1960s saw a slow return to the practice of holding monthly, and not the decreed quarterly meetings, as delegates sought their own forum to debate national policy and later to oppose the activities of the Labour group.[12] The procedural device adopted was the calling of special delegatory meetings. In turn, this led the group to charge that the City Party was now being prostituted for functions outside its legitimate remit (group liaison, candidate selection and manifesto preparation). As Kirk bitterly declared to Transport House officials:

> this group [the New Left] are using our platform to forward their activities in opposition to National and local policy. The pattern follows much of what has happened before, 'suspension of standing orders', 'Special Meetings' timed for Friday, (a bad night for Trade union officials) and similar moves. The Group have [sic] become so arrogant that when genuine members have spoken in opposition or in correction of policy, insults have resulted and these without check or apology from the President Chairing [sic] the meeting. Staunch Labour Members have vowed never again to attend.[13]

Certainly, City Party meetings routinely became of 'inordinate length', more frequent (during 1965 there were 16 executive and 13 general

11 Letter from Kirk to Sara Parker (Lab. Party Nat. Agent), 29 Nov. 1965, IAP; NCLP, Annual Report, 1961–62 and 1962–63, IAP.

12 R. T. McKenzie, 'The Wilson Committee Report and the Future of the Labour Party', *Political Studies* 4/1 (1956), pp. 93–97; NAO LPC Box 14, letter from Ives to Williams (Nat. Agent), 3 June 1957; NCLP, Annual Report 1962–63.

13 Letter from Kirk to Barker, 29 Nov. 1965, IAP.

meetings) and held in a mutually antagonistic atmosphere. For their part, delegates were equally condemnatory of councillors' poor attendance records and verbosity, while even those openly hostile reported that Coates had attempted to 'carry out his duties with impartiality'.[14] Animosity, in short, was only a surface expression of a more serious rift between competing ideologies, clipped to the battle over formulating and implementing municipal policy.

The New Left was born out of a disillusionment with existing forums of radical politics in the aftermath of the 1956 invasions of Hungary and Suez and the apparent escalating nuclear threat. Yet New Left influences, unlike CND, remained predominantly an intellectual preserve.[15] In the local field, Gyford suggests that exponents concentrated initially on 'community based action against local authorities rather than with involvement in the party politics of local government', the latter being very much a product of the 1970s and 1980s.[16] In Nottingham, the New Left sought, through its control of political office, directly to determine Corporation policy well before this date. Foster and the Labour group, however, were unconcerned as to its origins. In evidence later before a National Executive Committee enquiry for which they, and their supporters within the constituencies had called, Foster accused Coates of 'using his office to further the principles of [entryist] Trotskyism': establishing an inner-caucus to disrupt the City Party and vilifying those who stood 'loyally by the leadership of the Party and its policies'. Or as a co-defendant on the City Executive put matters, a separate campaigning caucus existed 'to ginger up the [city Labour] Group's work'.[17]

Such an admission, while hardly revelational, was unlikely to endear them to those seeking reasons for exclusion. And indeed, Coates remained convinced that his subsequent expulsion was engineered because of his vocal and written criticism of the national leadership at the 1965 Party

14 NEC mins, 25 May 1966: Report of an Enquiry into the Affairs of the Nottingham City Labour Party, Conducted by Lord Hilton, Mr. E. S. Taylor and Miss Sara Barker at Nottingham, 12/13 February 1966, pp. 5–6; letter from Coates to Foster, 11 Dec. 1964, IAP.

15 For a philosophical synopsis, see R. Currie, *Industrial Politics* (1979), pp. 196–200. A more eclectic symposium of New Left founding thought can be found in E. P. Thompson (ed.), *Out of Apathy* (1960).

16 Gyford, *Politics of Local Socialism*, pp.1–20, esp 16; see also S. Hall, R. Williams and E. P. Thompson, 'Mayday Manifesto', in C. Olgesby (ed.), *The New Left Reader* (1969), pp. 111–43.

17 Enq. into NCLP, pp. 1, 7.

Conference, particularly over Vietnam and incomes policy.[18] It was also the case that his behaviour caused some little resentment back in Nottingham: 'the last straw which broke the camel's back' according to 'loyalists' within his own constituency party. This only fuelled an existing pique against his co-editorial line in the *Nottingham Voice* news sheet (then sponsored by the City Party) and other publications, and his general campaigning activities and associations with, and on behalf of, the radical left on both national and local issues, which had already set in motion local resolutions within his constituency for his expulsion (later carried by 26 votes to 15).[19]

*

How did this essentially internecine conflict conflate with public and private perceptions of a broader political consensus within configured mainstream political opinion? Nottingham's *Guardian Journal* had, in the preceding months, carried several leading articles commenting on the leftward trend in local Labour politics, arguing that this could

> ultimately lead to a return to fierce political disputation within the City Council itself. Considerable efforts have been made by the leaders of both the local parties in recent months to bring about a more thoughtful and responsible attitude to local affairs ... It would be a disservice to Nottingham and its citizens were this new restraint to be replaced by Left-wing militancy, and it is to be hoped that those serving the interests of moderation will endeavour to reassert their influence.[20]

18 K. Coates, *The Crisis of British Socialism* (1979), p. 95; see also K. Coates, *My Case Against Expulsion* (1966), IAP. For his comments at conference, see The Labour Party, *Report of the Sixty-Fourth Annual Conference of the Labour Party: Blackpool, 1965* (1965), p. 176 and K. Coates, *Briefing*, 30 Sept. 1965, reprinted in *The Week* 4/14, 14 Oct. 1965.

19 NEC mins, 25 May 1966: Report of an Enquiry into the Appeal of Mr Ken Coates against his expulsion by the Nottingham West Constituency Labour Party, Conducted by Lord Hilton, Mr. E. S. Taylor and Miss S. E. Barker at Nottingham, 11 Feb. 1966, p. 2; Nottingham West Constituency Exec. mins, 7 Oct. 1965, IAP; MRC MSS 9/3/20/292, 9 Nov. 1965. Also cited was G. Thayer, *The British Political Fringe: A Profile* (1965), pp. 137–38.

20 *GJ*, 9 March 1965. See also, for example, *GJ*, 7 Oct. 1965.

Of course, the left had little interest in fostering consensual inter-party co-operation, which anyway it largely blamed for the city's ills and past political inertia. The Labour group leadership, however, was of a different mind. With the press paying particular attention to the alleged 'Trotskyite' domination locally, its immediate concern was for such imagery not to be allowed to 'drift' beyond control as it had during the Popkess Affair five years previously.[21]

Stark differences had, in fact, emerged several years earlier between the Labour group and those now controlling the City Party. As Coates commented, 'there was a great deal of civic dead wood in the Nottingham Party' then in need of delicate pruning. The left, however, was not alone in seeking to oust group members. Jack Dunnett, Nottingham Central's Prospective Parliamentary Candidate in 1961, and elected three years later, also favoured moves to de-select several 'less energetic' city councillors. Dunnett's primary concern was housing. Arriving in Nottingham, he recalled, he was 'absolutely appalled by the state of the housing in what I hoped would be my constituency ... very little effort seemed to have been made to re-house their occupants and to clear the slums'. Indeed, in an attempt to force the pace, he later threatened to resign his seat if action on housing was not taken.[22]

Overall, this pessimistic view was fully justified. 'Competition for housing', for example, had been held to be a key element in the racial tensions that erupted in Nottingham in 1958.[23] Between 1955 and 1960, the Corporation completed some 5,500 new dwellings. Completion rates, however, dropped by some 40 per cent by the end of the decade on their 1955 level. In total, shortages had improved significantly by the mid-1960s, 1964 seeing a post-war low of some 4,300 on the waiting lists. But little progress had been made in slum clearance. Of the 3,250 houses represented since 1955 (which by national standards was anyway low), by late 1960 only 1,300 had been cleared and a second programme comprising an additional 4,000 dwellings had to be postponed. Estimates in 1965 suggested that 12,500 unfit houses still remained, which at the then current rate of attrition would take a further 28 years to clear. Finally

21 Enq. into Appeal by K. Coates, p. 4; Coates, *Crisis of Socialism*, pp. 81–82; Coates, *My Case*, p. 16; letter from Coates, *GJ*, 16 Nov. 1965; *GJ*, 7 Oct. 1965; letter from Kirk to Barker, 24 and 29 Nov. 1965, IAP.

22 Coates, *Crisis of Socialism*, pp. 81, 93; letter from Dunnett to author, 27 June 1991; MRC MSS 9/3/20/69, 2 March 1965.

23 PRO CAB 128/32 CC 69 (58), 8 Sept. 1958.

the Corporation, under government pressure, embarked on a greatly enhanced redevelopment programme which in 1970 saw a record 2,036 houses demolished (compared with a yearly average between 1955 and 1968 of only 330).[24]

De-selection was an option open to all wards dissatisfied with a councillor's performance, if not one frequently exercised. Prospective Labour members had also, of course, to have their candidacy ratified by the City Party, although for sitting councillors a tacit understanding existed that this was a mere formality. In 1965, Jack Caughtry, the councillor for Byron Ward, found to his cost that this was no longer the case. It was clear from the start that there were specific and personal circumstances operating here which defied the simplistic, reactive labelling attached by both the press and group. Nevertheless, surfacing as it did at a time of rising internal tension, concurrent with Coates's Blackpool speech, it was treated perfunctorily as an extension and proof of a growing left/right divide within Nottingham's Labour party—not least because de-selection struck at the very heart of the group's power base.

In fact, several months prior, in siege-like terms, the group had relayed to Cattermole rumours of a pending putsch against sitting councillors. If Cattermole offered reassurances of intervention here, he also suggested that little could be done for Caughtry when his own branch unanimously supported the City Party's decision. As Jack Flewitt, a fellow ward councillor opposed to the de-selection, recounted, not only had Caughtry's own nomination three years previously—'against all the odds'—been the product of intrigues against veteran left-winger Councillor George Dutton, but he had since alienated local party workers, being 'repeatedly criticised ... for either not turning up for canvassing or being late, some of his excuses being remarkable'.[25]

The controversy only increased when Byron ward unanimously nominated Peter Price, one of those Executive members subsequently debarred by the NEC, as Caughtry's replacement. Encapsulating the group's view, Foster later responded:

24 NCC, Nottingham Position Statement, May 1974, pp. 3–9; Slum Clearance (Cmnd 9593), PP (1955–56); Central Housing Advisory Committee, Our Older Homes: A Call for Action (1966), Table 1; MRC MSS 9/3/21/23, 26 Jan. 1966.

25 Letter from Kirk to Cattermole, 4 July 1965; letter from Cattermole to Kirk, 8 Oct. 1965; Letter from Flewitt to Kirk, 14 Oct. 1965, IAP.

> Cllr. Caughtrey [sic] has been a good member of the Group and in its view he has been rejected in order to clear the way for the selection of Peter Price. It has been said that Mr. Caughtrey [sic] had been rejected because he did not contribute to the work of the ward and was late for nearly all his appointments. If this criticism was sound then it is difficult to understand why Byron Ward had [initially] nominated Mr Caughtrey [sic] for the 1966 Panel.[26]

Caughtry himself professed to be 'dumbfounded and flabbergasted' at the charges against him; he was, he said, being 'kicked out of his council seat by an extreme element in the party', as he set about exposing, with the help of a compliant press, its activities. Within two days, Caughtry's deselection and Price's nomination—originally viewed by local papers as having 'no political significance'—suddenly became the centre of public controversy. Demands for a full NEC enquiry came from all quarters: as the Editor of the *Guardian Journal* suggested, the real issue was one of

> control over the city's affairs and involves the rights of councillors, party members and the ratepayers themselves. In a nutshell it is a question of whether the present policy of moderation is to continue, or whether there is to be substituted a form of militant Socialism. Were all members of the local Labour Party convinced of the need for militancy, little more could be said. They are not, however, and it is the suspicion that they are being jockeyed into a false position that calls for immediate investigation.[27]

The battle of words in the columns of the press continued unabated; prominent supporters of each side entered the fray, each claiming to speak for the broader party membership.[28] Meantime, attempts to adopt Bob Gregory (also soon to be disbarred from office) in place of 'a loyal retiring member' was only defeated when Cattermole, having been warned in advance, attended the selection to find City Party Executive members present whom the branch erroneously thought were entitled to vote.[29] One month later, an acrimonious meeting of the City Party saw the Labour

26 Enq. into NCLP, pp. 3–4.
27 *GJ*, 7 Oct. 1965, *NEP*, 7 Oct. 1965.
28 *NEP*, 12–19 Nov. 1965.
29 Enq. into NCLP, p. 4; MRC MSS 9/3/20/271, 18 Oct. 1965; letter from Kirk to Cattermole, 23 Sept. 1965, IAP.

group and its supporters stage a mass walk-out when a significant minority of delegates sought to support Coates's re-admittance to the party. It was shortly after this that the NEC was formally requested to intervene.

Predictably, perhaps, Coates's expulsion, and the subsequent exclusion of three City Party Executive members (Price, Gregory and Geoff Coggan) from office for three years, was duly upheld and implemented; 'Mr. Coates', it was concluded, had 'gone beyond fair criticism in both the written and spoken word', while 'no doubt [existed] that the continual disputes ... have been incited by an organised group within the City Party', itself now instructed to end immediately the abusive practice of calling special meetings.[30] In the aftermath, it was hardly surprising that altruistic concerns for the right to express alternative views were firmly ignored. Instead, party officials, with the support of Transport House, sought to press home their advantage by embarking on a further series of investigations and encouraging whenever possible 'loyal' supporters to stand for office. As a result, there were many bitter encounters in local committee rooms. Nevertheless, generally the 'moderates' prevailed, strengthening their grip over constituency affairs in the months following, and persistent attempts to resurrect the cases of those disciplined were comfortably defeated.[31] It was to take three years of persistent lobbying before Coates finally secured his re-admittance. The trio debarred from office at first sought to ignore their exclusion, until steps were taken physically to prevent them from so doing. Finally they sought legal redress. The case never came to court, the restrictions were lifted and the NEC agreed to meet legal costs. Nottingham's New Left was quite simply ahead of its time.

*

If any single issue clearly delineated Labour's internal divisions in the early to mid-1960s, it was the introduction of comprehensive education. It was certainly not a new controversy. Siren voices within the party, notably the National Association of Labour Teachers (the forerunner of the Socialist Education Association), had, from 1944, repeatedly attacked

30 Enq. into Appeal by K. Coates, p. 8; Enq. into NCLP, p. 8.
31 MRC MSS 9/3/20/315, 321, and 9/3/21/18, 19, 46, 120, 175, 178, 221, 274, Dec. 1965–Sept. 1966.

the social inequity promoted by selection at age eleven—more so when the ubiquitous inadequacies of secondary modern provision became readily apparent. In 1951, the adoption of comprehensive schooling became Labour policy. However, many within the party, particularly at a local level, were reluctant converts. Indeed, through the 1950s 'the uneasiness which the utterances of some of the more zealous protagonists of the comprehensive schools had evoked in the minds of many electors' saw leading Labour politicians minimise the party's commitment in this area, especially in abolishing grammar schools.[32] Labour's 1964 victory, on a pledge to abolish selection, ended this reticence. One year later, all education authorities were instructed to submit proposals for the introduction of local comprehensive systems.

Progress towards this goal in Nottingham had been slow and sporadic. In 1954, a group working party surprisingly had recommended the phased introduction of comprehensives. Although adopted, it was not a policy acted upon: a reflection not only of a lack of political will but also of the canons attached, which insisted on the artificial creation of socially balanced intakes within such schools. This meant creating large institutions, or, more precisely, amalgamating existing schools to form one theoretical campus. Such a fundamental restructuring was a recipe for division and inertia; daunting in its scale, it invited objections from the uncommitted or lethargic, while those who rejected the comprehensive system could now also point to the impractical nature of split-site schooling. It also opposed the strongly rooted tradition of community schooling locally, which was organically linked to the city's inter- and post-war spatial housing structure. Thus, by 1964 there was only one city comprehensive—a purpose built 1,500-pupil boys' school at Clifton. Here, Labour had also attempted to amalgamate three existing girls' schools. This, however, became the focus of heated controversy, being presented and represented to council in increasingly bizarre forms and was abandoned immediately on the Conservatives' return to office in 1961.[33]

Yet Nottingham's Labour administration, with Conservative support, was not wholly wedded to Butler's tripartite divisions. True, many city councillors continued to see grammar schools as an avenue of

---

32 D. E. Butler, *The British General Election of 1955* (1955), p. 87; Morgan, *Labour in Power*, pp. 175–77; Pelling, *Labour Governments*, pp. 114–17; for a brief overview of the politics of post-war education, see Lowe, *Welfare State*, ch. 8.

33 *NEP*, 25 Jan. 1961, 28 Sept. 1961; *NEN*, 27 April 1961.

working-class self-improvement.[34] However, in 1957 Labour introduced a bilateral system of education. This did not abolish selection at age eleven. Instead, bilaterals offered grammar streams within locally contained mixed ability schools, although those scoring highly through newly introduced verbal reasoning tests and overall teacher assessment were first offered a traditional grammar school place.[35] Neither were secondary moderns to be abolished straightway, instead being gradually converted into bilaterals. Nevertheless, by 1965, city Labour leaders had already announced the imminent closure of all remaining secondary moderns. Indeed, city proposals now closely mirrored those originally espoused by Crosland, who as Secretary of State for Education was passionately committed to closing grammar schools, but who, a decade earlier, had specifically cautioned against this forthwith; in fact, he still favoured retaining academic streaming within any comprehensive system.[36]

The principal critics of bilateralism within the city's Labour movement remained predominantly outside the group. In 1960, Nottingham's branch of the National Association of Labour Teachers produced its own blueprint for reform: an end to all selective testing, streaming and the grammar system, complete with the amalgamation of all schools into neighbourhood educational units. Such a recipe, of course, ran counter to the group's gradualist approach. But matters only came to a head several years later. Successive Labour manifestos in the early 1960s repeated the Party's intention of moving towards a comprehensive system. However, in 1964 Roland Green, the Chair of Education, reneged on this commitment; announcing instead his Committee's intention not to depart from promoting the bilateral model. Cattermole, trying to placate irate constituency and City Party delegates, suggested joint discussions. Green rejected the idea. In fact, tensions had been rising throughout that year over education policy. Critics held firm to the opinion that Green and the

34 M. Parkinson, *The Labour Party and the Organisation of Secondary Education 1918–65* (1970), p. 85; Newton, *Second City Politics*, pp. 203–05; *GJ*, 2 Feb. 1965.

35 Ironically, the latest research suggested that working-class children were more disadvantaged by verbal than written testing; B. Bernstein, 'Social Class and Linguistic Development' based on 'Some Sociological Determinants of Perception, *British Journal of Sociology* (June 1958), in A. H. Halsey, J. Floud and C. A. Anderson, *Education, Economy and Society* (1963), p. 291.

36 C. A. R. Crosland, *The Future of Socialism* (1956), pp. 268–77; Lowe, *Welfare State*, p. 224; Morgan, *People's Peace*, p. 248.

group were deliberately obscuring the key issue, 'describing patently selective and discriminatory policies as "comprehensive with a small c"'. Green, for his part, spoke of the financial and other obstacles to implementing a fully comprehensive system, while at the same time commending bilateralism and reformed testing methods. It was shortly after that Ken Coates narrowly defeated Ald. Len Mitson, the incumbent President accused by him of deliberately attempting to 'muzzle discussion at the City Party' to protect the group's education policy.[37]

Initially it seemed that Cattermole's mediatory attempts might succeed. Ignoring Green's veto, he contacted Foster and arranged that both group and City Party representatives meet to thrash out their differences. It was by all accounts an amicable affair, given their already publically-aired grievances. Here, the latter enthusiastically outlined the various options currently being implemented elsewhere, with their own strong emphasis on social integration. Apart from a commitment to end testing, which they viewed as a priority, what was required was 'a concrete scheme for the next two to three years'; not to 'wait but press ahead' so that

> when the Secondary Moderns were phased out we should take stock of what other Local Authorities had done and pick out the best parts for ourselves. There was a need for consensus of opinion in favour, and this could be obtained by consultation and wide publicity.[38]

It was, in fact, an invitation to plan rather than immediately revolutionise local educational provision. It soon became clear, however, that the group viewed the comprehensive challenge more as a problem than an opportunity. Lack of finance, union opposition, the physical constraints of existing premises were all cited, not as reasons for caution, but for inactivity. Green, in particular, was singularly opposed to the abolition of testing. He began (echoing Harold Wilson's sentiment) by advocating the right of all children to a grammar school education, then continued:

> I myself was converted to Comprehensive education many years ago and the system of education [bilateral and grammar] now in

37 MRC MSS 9/3/19407, 23 Nov. 1964, 9/3/19/60, 24 Feb. 1964; Lab. Group mins, 2 April 1964; Coates, *Crisis of Socialism*, p. 87.

38 Coates, NCLP, Mins. of a Special Meeting of Lab. Members of Educ. Comm. and Officers of City Party, 17 Dec. 1964, IAP.

existence in Nottingham will lead to the best type of Comprehensive in the country.[39]

Viewed retrospectively, this was more than an exercise in semantics; it was a message structured around a completely different emphasis in which the group clearly signalled its intention of retaining executive control over policy and implementation—Foster, for example, ruling that 'the question of when was [solely] the Group's prerogative'.

The aftermath saw any pretence of harmony rapidly evaporate. Coates immediately declared the minutes of the meeting to be a distortion: particularly the deliberate exclusion of overt reference to the lack of a timetable for reform. Shortly after, Green purposefully discarded a survey indicating 'slightly better' exam results in fully comprehensive vis-à-vis the traditional system, declaring 'the figures provide no support whatsoever for proposals to rush ahead with schemes for making Comprehensive Schools out of old buildings miles apart ... There is not a scrap of evidence to justify a change in the Education Committee's plans for developing the Bilateral Schools alongside the Grammar Schools.'[40] The rejection of the Socialist Education Association's 'campus' proposals, and more universal calls for an end to selection, elicited an immediate response from City Party delegates; they now overwhelmingly endorsed the introduction of 'all through [11–18 years] comprehensive schools as soon as practicable'. It was this latter commitment, delegates maintained, that would form the basis of Labour's May manifesto. Green, at this juncture, appeared to capitulate, publicly affirming that the Education Committee intended to phase out grammar schools (turning them into sixth form colleges), although again he refused to speculate when this would occur.[41]

His actions, however, need to be set in a national context. Labour parliamentarians had two weeks earlier voted to endorse electoral pledges to end selection. Consecutively came Crosland's appointment as Minister for Education, and with it a dictum that local authorities would shortly be

39 Ibid.; B. Pimlott, *Harold Wilson* (1992), p. 512; Lowe, *Welfare State*, pp. 224, 362. For similar attitudes in Coventry, see R. Burgess, 'Aspects of Education in Post-war Britain', in Obelkevich and Catterall (eds), *Understanding Post-War British Society*, pp. 132–33.

40 Coates, statement on mins of joint meeting, (undated), IAP; transcript of Green's Speech to City Council Meeting, 1 Feb. 1965, IAP.

41 *NEP*, 5 and 6 Feb. 1965; *GJ*, 8 Feb. 1965.

required to submit proposals for secondary re-organisation. But government, it was claimed, was only responding to external pressures for reform from local authorities—providing a lead which was 'only a little ahead of the consensus of opinion'. Nottingham's press, however, saw matters differently, quickly insinuating that Green's moderate aspirations were being undermined locally by a 'noisy', 'left-wing' element, which was conducting a 'shrewd tactical campaign' against the city's declared education policy, and in the process, 'splitting the Party from top to bottom'.[42]

In many ways, this was a wholly accurate assessment, albeit one which underplayed governmental intent. Coates's riposte only exacerbated matters:

> No Labour councillor in Nottingham is subject to 'outside pressure' on education policy. The constitution of the Labour party ... lays down that the policy of Labour councillors shall be determined by the City Labour Party ... The Labour Group ... does not, and will not, ignore decisions on policy by the City Labour Party. Indeed, the boot is on the other foot. It is the City Labour Party which decides who shall carry its colours into the Council Chamber.[43]

His comments were ideal meat upon which the press could readily feast. As the Editor of the *Guardian Journal* wryly observed the following day:

> However 'fully representative' it might claim to be, the [City Labour] Party has lost sight of the salient fact that it is not the local Labour Party which places its representatives in the Council Chamber ... The way democracy is understood in this country, only elected representatives have the right to make these [policy] decisions. The way the present system operates, local government apparently is not conducted in the committee rooms of the Corporation but in the offices of the local Labour Party.[44]

42 I. G. K. Fenwick, *The Comprehensive School 1944–70: The Politics of Secondary Reorganisation* (1976), p. 133; D. Rubenstein and R. Simon, *The Evolution of the Comprehensive School 1926–1972* (1972 2nd Edn.), p. 94; *GJ*, 9 Feb. 1965.

43 Letter from Coates, *GJ*, 12 Feb. 1965 (later used in evidence against him at the NEC enquiry).

44 *GJ*, 13 Feb. 1965.

For their part, Labour city councillors viewed Coates's discourse as further evidence that their traditional independence was under attack, a trend they traced back several months as, one by one, prominent members were 'put in the dock' to account for their actions and policy. Green particularly was a marker for group resistance (or petulance), proclaiming that 'he would see the City Party in hell before he would appear before its executive to discuss policy'. Strictly, Green's stance was constitutionally correct; group, as opposed to election, policy formation and its implementation was an internal responsibility.[45] The 'rules of the game', however, were never applied impartially. When the City Party, some six months later, asserted its legitimate authority in seeking to de-select certain councillors, it faced sanction as the internecine dispute entered its most combative phase, culminating in the later expulsions and exclusions.

Cattermole, at this juncture, was still acting as an intermediary. The commitment to abolish pre-16 grammar schools saw both sides agreeing temporarily that bilateralism was an acceptable 'form of comprehensive education'. Again, Cattermole's chief concern was to avoid further 'argument and controversy in the press', exhorting that policy disputes be resolved internally. Indeed, characteristic of his general dealings with and opinions of local politicians, he expressed some little impatience, being at a loss to understand 'why the differences between the Group and the party have arisen', given that the present compromise conformed generally to embryonic national options for educational reform.[46] The armistice proved short-lived. As relations between the group and the left failed to improve, the specific form that re-organisation should take and, more particularly, the date of implementation, again rose to the fore. Crosland, in his July circular, had given local authorities a year to submit their proposals. By September, locally, however, there was already a marked impatience with the deliberations of the Education Committee, group members being harangued for still debating the comprehensive principle, rather than formulating plans for its implementation.

45 Letter from Kirk to Cattermole, 15 Feb. 1965, IAP; Coates, *Crisis of Socialism*, p. 87; Nottingham City Labour Party, *Constitution, Rules and Standing Orders* (1956), p. 22; see also letter from Cattermole, *GJ*, 25 Feb. 1965.

46 Letter from Cattermole to Kirk, 23 Feb. 1965, IAP; MRC MSS 9/3/20/49, 18 Feb. 1965. For the six models advocated re comprehensive education, see C. Benn and B. Simon, *Half Way There: Report on the British Comprehensive School Reform* (1970).

The left also claimed that with the agreement on the 1965 manifesto came an implicit commitment from the group to offer full consultation with the City Party, an undertaking subsequently 'flagrantly violated'. It was certainly true that the group sought to keep Party delegates at arm's length until its proposals had been finalised. In particular, Green refused to talk to the local Socialist Education Association, a decision which infuriated key cross-members of the Executive, particularly as he held discussions with other extraneous bodies. Once a decision had been taken, the group met with the City Executive in April 1966. Here, after prolonged discussion, it was 'generally agreed, without dissent, to accept' Green's preferred option of 11–16 comprehensives and separate sixth form colleges.[47] Peter Price, at equally short notice, then sought an emergency meeting of the Executive to insist that selection be abolished within twelve months. It was symptomatic of the left's waning influence since Coates's expulsion six months earlier that this motion was rejected. Price immediately resigned his Presidency, and proceeded to issue a series of press statements critical of group policy. These appeared in the run-up to the May 1966 elections. Already a city councillor, that July he was brought before the group on unconnected disciplinary charges to affirm his future conduct according to standing orders. Typically, he agreed, with the proviso that Alderman Green, who was chairing the meeting, gave a similar undertaking. A predictable refusal saw Price abruptly leave and shortly after the whip was withdrawn. It was perhaps a fitting commentary on the previous division and reticence that the Department of Education and Science refused to approve the city's two-tier secondary re-organisation plan. It was not until 1973 that Nottingham, as one of the last remaining authorities, finally went comprehensive.

*

The battle over comprehensive education was by no means the only policy issue to divide group and City Party, or indeed to be cited before the subsequent NEC enquiries, where attempts were made to discredit the group hierarchy by charging that it routinely acted in a duplicitous manner, not only in its dealings with the City Party but also with other local bodies. Foster was accused, amongst other things, of having

---

47 Coates, *Crisis of Socialism*, pp. 88–89; Enq. into NCLP, pp. 4, 6; MRC MSS 9/3/21/148, 3 May 1966.

deliberately misled his group, the City Party and Nottingham Anti-Apartheid over a supposed ban on the purchase of South African goods by the Corporation. In fact, a formal ban had never been enforced.

It could be, and indeed was, argued by many at the time (including Foster and certain other senior group members) that boycotts of this nature had no place in local politics per se, and particularly the consensual, utilitarian politics of post-Popkess Nottingham. The same could be said of, but never applied to, proposals dealing with local boundary alterations. Once again, substantial political friction was generated here between adjacent local authorities and between political parties. But the controversy also extended to within Nottingham's Labour party and ultimately saw the Labour and Conservative groups collaborate to protect the city's unitary status—a campaign perceived jointly to be in their mutual and the city's greater interest.

The late 1950s and 1960s saw successive initiatives at local government re-organisation. Initially, in operating to an essentially political rationale, the city Labour group opposed any extension to city boundaries, not least because the Commissioner's initial draft favoured the inclusion of several predominantly Tory areas. Conservatives, not surprisingly, supported the extension. For different reasons, so did Tom Owen. The Town Clerk considered it essential that Nottingham fight to secure the building land needed for future expansion. But he also deemed extension to be a necessary prerequisite to providing the expanded financial revenue base required by the city 'to provide the services both existing and new which the exigencies of modern times called for'.[48] Civic, as opposed to overtly political, interest was henceforth slowly ingested into the city Labour group's position. Appearing before a public enquiry in May 1963, Owen was instructed neither to support nor oppose any extension by the newly elected Labour group: a compromise which Owen thought to be against city interests but which nevertheless represented an uneasy shift in Labour past position from one of opposition to passive acceptance of the Commissioner's past findings. Indeed, as several senior Labour members acknowledged privately, 'the Commission proposals seemed logical and as we could not argue on purely political grounds (i.e. that Labour would lose control of the City)

48 Letter from Owen to members of Gen. Purposes Comm., 23 May 1963, IAP; Nott'm Lab. Group mins, 3 May 1962. For post-war re-organisation, see P. W. Jackson, *Local Government* (1967), pp. 30–49.

objection seemed superfluous'.[49] The Commissioner's report, published a year later, recommended the establishment of a Greater Nottingham authority slightly larger than originally envisaged. This further disadvantaged Labour's future election prospects. It was at this juncture that the idea gelled within city Labour circles that the inclusion of Hucknall Urban District (a safe Labour area) within Nottingham would redress the political balance. Exactly who originally floated the idea became a matter of considerable contention, primarily because nobody thought to consult Hucknall Labour Party prior to its formal discussion or before it was leaked to the press. Both Coates and Foster declared the other to be culpable, which did nothing to improve the then embryonic relationship between the two.[50]

Meantime, the city's Labour-controlled General Purposes Committee met to discuss the Commission's report, and in taking one further step against immediate political party imperatives, declared itself 'content to accept the recommendations of the Local Government Commission'. Owen was then instructed to prepare a memorandum supporting the extension of city boundaries. This was presented to the ruling Labour group in January 1965. Here, Owen presented a mix of logistical fact with a calculated appeal to civic aggrandisement. In this he was helped by the recent declaration that Nottingham was set to become 'the Capital City' of the newly formed East Midlands Region—George Brown's initiative for provincial economic planning and a supposed precursor of a new form of regional government. Foster, with several other senior members, clearly supported Owen. A majority, however, chose to adhere to their previously neutral stance. Nevertheless, one week later, the General Purposes Committee met, and with one final twist, resolved not only to accept the Boundary Commissioner's recommendations but to 'make an order for consideration by Parliament' supportive of its findings.[51]

It was a decision kept confidential until the day of the local ministerial enquiry into the planned extension. As Cattermole, who was aware only that group resolve was weakening and was thus busily co-ordinating a political lobby to resist this, recorded bitterly:

49 Nott'm Lab. Group mins, 4 Dec. 1963; NCC, Gen. Purposes Comm. mins, 27 May 1963.

50 Coates, *Crisis of Socialism*, pp. 83–86; Enq. into NCLP, p. 2; letter from W. Whitlock, MP, to Bailey, 20 July 1964, IAP; *NEP*, 17 July 1964.

51 NCC, Gen. Purposes Comm. mins, 28 July 1964, 8 Feb. 1965; Nott'm Lab. Group mins, 28 Jan. 1965.

After all the careful negotiations that we have had with the City Party and the County Council and the Labour controlled authorities which the Boundary Commission were recommending should be included in the City, the Nottingham City Council kicked the ground from under my feet at the opening. Everybody had been led to believe by the City Council Labour group that they would go to the enquiry saying that they were making no territorial claims ... but at the opening of the enquiry ... the Town Clerk of Nottingham intervened to say that he had been instructed ... to support the Boundary Commissioner's recommendations.[52]

The Labour group was accused by others of 'duplicity', and of engineering a 'volte-face'; indeed, Coates was later to cite this (and the Hucknall fiasco) as conclusive evidence that it was Foster, not he, who should be charged by the NEC with disruptive behaviour. A majority of Labour and Conservative city councillors, however, viewed matters in a different light. A specially convened meeting of the all-party General Purposes Committee rejected any criticism of Owen's presentation, as did the Labour group as a whole: it being commonly understood that the case put by the Town Clerk lay within the remit of protecting the city's greater interest.[53] In the event, it mattered little; the ministerial enquiry rejected the planned extension to the city's boundaries. In February 1966, after seven years' intensive study, the Commission's work was suspended pending a more radical review of English local government. In the interim, local inter-party unity over boundary reform evaporated, as both groups displayed a penchant for political in-fighting over subsequent ward and parliamentary changes on a par with the destructive battles of the mid-1950s.

The major break in the Corporation's post-war, and indeed twentieth-century, history occurred some time later with the abolition of county boroughs under the Local Government Act, 1972. The *Maud Report*, upon which this was based, was published in June 1969. Here, with a touch of sweet revenge for a County authority which had fought successive battles against encroachment by the city, the majority report

52 MRC MSS 9/3/20/87, 16 March 1965.

53 Letter from Whitlock to Foster and Foster to Whitlock, 25 March 1965, 8 April 1965, IAP; *NEP*, 16 March 1965; NCLP Exec. mins, 29 March 1965; Enq. into Appeal by Coates, p. 5; *GJ*, 2 April 1965.

recommended that Nottingham be relegated to the status of a district council within an enhanced county council structure. A few days after its publication, the ruling Conservative leadership called an emergency meeting of the city's Finance and General Purposes Committee. Political enmities discarded, both groups agreed to meet immediately with representatives of surrounding local district, borough and county borough authorities to lobby against the Maud proposals. Within the month, the City Council had produced its own alternative regional restructuring plan advocating the creation of a Greater Nottingham authority, covering some 764,000 people and incorporating much of central and southern Nottinghamshire; at the same time it proposed the amalgamation of the north Nottinghamshire and Derbyshire mining districts under a separate authority, and similarly the creation of a combined administrative area centred on Derby.

Launching the proposals, Bill Derbyshire, the Conservative group leader reasoned that:

> The committee's concept is, in our collective judgement, closer to the economic, social and geographic realities of the situation and would serve the obvious requirements of the electors in the best possible way.

Foster, who shared the platform at the press launch added:

> We feel that we are at the grass roots and know what the local situation is and so we have tried to draw up a scheme which we feel is in the best interests of the people in the area. The people in London, who have drawn up the Royal Commission report, have not got this understanding of the local situation.[54]

Both might have added that, real as their collective sense of civic identity and purpose undoubtedly was—being grounded on a century and a half of municipal traditional and some fifty years of active, joint leadership—the Maud proposals which they so strongly opposed also sought to undermine their own political power and prestige, and that of their respective groups.

54 *NEP*, 16 July 1969; NCC, *Reshaping Local Government—The Nottingham Viewpoint*, 1969.

If the Labour group supported the revised plan for an expanded civic Nottingham, the local party always opposed what it openly dubbed a Tory proposal. Here, in common with Cattermole, members saw their primary objective differently: measured in terms of securing local political control for the party, an interest best served by transferring authority to a county council which had been Labour dominated since 1945. In scenes wholly reminiscent of the Hucknall dispute four years earlier, Cattermole was publicly to accuse the Corporation, and by inference the Labour group, of 'dividing up territory outside the City without consulting the [interested] parties concerned'; at the same time, he actively sought to dissuade outside bodies and representatives from meeting city leaders.[55] In fact, given the limited time at their disposal, city representatives made strenuous and largely successful attempts to meet with all the surrounding local authorities. It was in their interests so to do, if they were to gain support for what remained essentially an extension of those boundary revisions proposed by the earlier Local Government Commission, and already rejected as such by most adjacent authorities. Indeed, critics argued that the city was not so much consulting as simply pressing upon other councils an alternative to Maud to suit its own advantage.

Nationally, the reaction to the *Maud Report* was much as it was locally, the County Councils' Association welcoming the proposals against the opposition of the Association of Municipal Corporations. Ultimately, however, the decision rested not with individual authorities or their associations, but with Westminster and the Cabinet. Here, apparently, debate remained confused and ill-focused, and it was left to the incoming Heath government to enact the reforms. Apart from the specific creation of six metropolitan areas, undoubtedly the greatest change was the loss of unitary status of the former county boroughs. For Nottingham, this truly marked the end of an epoch: the transfer of long held political responsibilities for education, social welfare, highways, fire and ambulance services, sewage disposal and a myriad of lesser tasks to either the county council or other regional authorities. Of their former primary functions, only housing remained as a major item of capital or revenue expenditure. It was to take another two decades before those outside city circles were to question seriously this decision.

55 *GJ*, 17 July 1969; *NEP*, 21–23 July 1969, 12 Aug. 1969; Nott'm Lab. Group mins, 24 July 1969.

CHAPTER 10
Some Conclusions

That Nottingham's political system exhibited symptoms of major change in the twenty years after the war is obvious; that the form these changes took is readily discernible in the terms prescribed by the inter-party agreements which sub-divide the period is also axiomatic. Most noticeable was the newly found emphasis on party, aptly illustrated by the adoption of majority rule and formal negation of the remaining vestiges of individualism in 1957. The end of bi-party responsibility for committee management, and indeed the earlier transitional curtailment of committee independence (both structurally and in terms of enhanced party obedience), marked a noticeable break with a more liberal pre- and post-war practice never wholly repaired. Now a system existed which, far from encouraging joint participation, actively segregated members at all stages of the local political process, placing a psychological, if not a physical barrier, on co-operation and consensus.

It remains tempting to view the late 1950s, with its propensity for overt party conflict, as an extension of this separation. And in many respects, such a perspective is perfectly valid. Majority rule further encouraged a rigidity in city policy-making, linking it exponentially to partisanship to degrees that, in the case of the new Playhouse, attempts were finally made to cancel an already semi-completed project. Yet that a minor item of expenditure so dominated the local political agenda clearly bespoke of more fundamental divides: in this case between an expansionary civic ethos seeking to open new areas of responsibility against a limiting and pervasive minimalist ethic. In origin, both pre-dated 1957, as did the outline of the project itself. Nevertheless, the transfer to majority rule coincided not merely with a moratorium on agreement; it also produced overt and lasting controversy in a number of separate areas. All, according to Conservative accounts, were the product of the same dictatorial mentality, which itself was said to be a response to past structural change.

There are problems with such an analysis. Firstly, Nottingham's previous adherence to a system of shared committee responsibility placed it in a minority amongst industrial cities. Comparatively, therefore, there was nothing exceptional in the city Labour group opting for single party rule; nothing that, when compared with practices elsewhere, accounts for the bitter antagonisms which located the city to the fore of local political intolerance. Nor were the years immediately preceding 1957 politically tranquil; indeed, they were increasingly marked by division as both groups studiously avoided compromise in a number of key areas. By way of contrast, the 1960s were generally thought of as a period of political *rapprochement*; yet it too was governed by the principles of majority rule which by then local Conservatives had also accepted and legitimised. Structural change by itself, therefore, did not automatically decree conflict per se; neither did a stable bi-party framework ensure a local political consensus. Past and future agreement was more firmly embedded in a foundation of shared policy parameters. Nevertheless, alterations to the political framework, which impinged not only on party but also on personal kudos, did rupture the self-contained status quo, providing a local focus for extensive division. The impact, however, is best viewed as transitory. The abolition of power-sharing exacerbated rather than initiated consensual breakdown. It provided a very immediate, and indeed a residually potent, icon which fired indignation and intolerance, just as it reinforced structural division. Yet the effects were to be tempered significantly over time. Long-term, the concordats essentially reflected the temperature of existing inter-party relations; in emphasis, they mirrored rather than transformed predominant attitudes.

There was, of course, another perspective offered predominantly from those on the left—namely that structurally little changed in Nottingham in the two decades after 1945. Here, attention is drawn to the many aspects of joint rule retained: that the minority party continued automatically to nominate committee vice-chairs; that a correspondingly close liaison existed between the two group hierarchies especially; that the closed traditions of shared civic patronage still governed. More particularly, criticism centred on past and present Labour policy (notably over housing and education). Placatory attitudes here, it was said, reflected the congenial atmosphere of city politics generally. It is a rationale with certain attractions, particularly when viewed from the mid-1960s, as both groups made conspicuous efforts to place the rancour of the previous years behind them. But if it exposes a species of consensus reborn, reactively set in its infancy within fixed parameters of civic responsibility and provision, nonetheless in stressing an overall pattern of continuity it also fails to differentiate between the marked variations in inter-party relations of earlier periods.

In contrast to recent interpretations of political life elsewhere, it is to the immediate post-war period that we must turn to see a local and purposeful consensus operating full force. This built in part upon pre-war practice: an early accommodation of Labour's aspirations which promoted co-operation, not lasting antagonisms, and a strong progressive Conservative instinct which valued social provision. Yet the immediate inheritance of the inter-war years should not be overstated. By 1939, progressive imperatives and joint responsibility were both under threat. The city's wartime experiences altered this. Bi-party co-operation re-emerged under the umbrella of shared emergency objectives, while paradoxically the disputes over the status of independent members underwrote the benefits of formal agreements. Above all, however, consensus was rooted in the urgent requirements of post-war reconstruction.

The all-party 1943 reconstruction report provided the physical expression of this inter-party and broader social consensus—a civic blueprint for corporation provision for the next twenty years. Opposition was limited essentially to those Conservatives who thought its encompassing purpose too grandiose or utopian, or those firmly wedded to free market solutions (that rump which most strongly opposed co-operation pre-war). Although the report dealt with a myriad of issues—from nursery provision to technical education, and roads to entertainments—attention remained firmly focused on housing. Here, a clear majority in both party groups, in common with the electorate, thought positive civic intervention to meet wartime deficits essential. The result was a pragmatic mix of local authority primacy, interspersed with secondary speculative provision, to maximise building effort.

The key question, of course, is whether a consensus built predominantly on these terms was predestined to be temporary—dependent on post-war need—or whether past and present shared values bespoke a potential permanency which, for specific reasons, was later to be undermined by local ideological divides and circumstance. In part, the answer lies in the sea change in the political axis in the post-war period. Here Labour, from being the minority party, became electorally predominant. This had two noticeable effects. Initially, the 1945 election results rocked Conservative morale (notable in their early ineffectualness as a party of opposition). More importantly, the scale of early successive victories enhanced Labour confidence. Moreover, victory encouraged the belief that its policies now rightfully formed the foundation of a future consensus; in short, that the political agenda had changed, which indeed, nationally, it had. Any dissipation of this conviction as its local majority slowly fell was fully compensated for by the continuing pressures of post-war social needs. Many local Conservatives were in any case content to work within a system which pragmatically promoted consensual policy within a semi-autonomous and specialist committee structure.

To Labour, however, public housing was always more than simply the practical provision of urgently needed accommodation; it became a universal star to which was hitched both its political fortune and ideological commitment. The first frictions between the Labour group and Conservatives—who also sought to stimulate commercial enterprise—centred on the former's determination to delay even minor projects which might interfere with this overriding housing objective. Initially, this difference in emphasis was relatively unimportant, for government policy remained firmly wedded to a public sector near monopoly in new housing—Labour's local political agenda. A Conservative victory at Westminster altered this balance. Local circumstances, too, changed. Inter-group discipline tightened in the years straddling 1950 as party majorities languished, with committee independence itself an early casualty of increased political competition. Slowly, a more adversarial system re-emerged as the more immediate needs of reconstruction were fulfilled. As councillors turned their attentions (and loyalties) elsewhere, political pragmatism increasingly fell victim to ideological obligation.

Where did responsibility lie for this reversal? Undoubtedly the Labour group provided the greater impetus for structural change—reducing committee independence and formally tightening group discipline. In terms relative to each party's own past practices, however, regimentation increased proportionately to degrees that still further diminished Conservative claims to individualism. However, Tory revisionism after the defeat of 1945 also encapsulated a strong gradualist instinct. Its propagandist image, in promoting idealised notions of independence and non-party, ensured the group was an unlikely vehicle for enforcing abrupt change to the local political system which publicly set aside such scriptures. And if both groups had a tendency towards hierarchical domination, Conservatives still retained the less formal of internal disciplinary codes. A Tory group (although not all elements in the party), in openly espousing civic traditionalism as a core value, remained essentially a public resistor to reform, although it quickly adhered throughout the post-war period to all alterations once enacted.

More particularly, in other ways both groups after 1945 saw themselves as guardians of the status quo: Labour in defending local state-led welfarism and those collective rights deemed central to a new post-war agenda; Conservatives, who saw many of the post-war policies as temporary and quantifiable expedients, consequently placing a greater emphasis on the pre-war values of voluntarism and private provision wrapped around a paternalistic core which fluctuated against cost and need. Again, housing clearly illustrates the division. Here Labour fought determinedly against any transfer of Corporation land to speculative builders. With the relaxation of central regulations, however, Conservatives moved quickly to extend private construction. That they sought this at a time of land shortage and high city waiting lists Labour construed to be a key marker against agreed post-war policy, which in its ideological immediacy overshadowed other continuing mass housing initiatives. But it was not only here that disagreement arose. The early 1950s saw the groups battling laboriously over issues as diverse as a new city car park to trade union rights, slum clearance to school bus fares, ward boundaries to committee allocations. Inter-party antagonism, it seemed, had become a prominent feature of everyday political life.

It was in this atmosphere that Labour finally sought to end joint group rule. It appears a natural progression; the culmination of a move from a pre-war system dominated by one party, but which nevertheless placed great emphasis on committee independence through the controlling activities of individual members, to the more open bi-partite realities of post-war Nottingham, where control passed frequently from one ruling party to the other. Consequently, individuals were more closely tied to group direction. And had the parties retained a unity of purpose and willingness to compromise, then modified agreement would still have been possible. There were, however, fundamental differences over political emphasis and policy separating the groups which now impinged directly into everyday council affairs. The degree of consensus achieved during reconstruction was a predominantly temporary state, possible only because of the economic and social circumstances of the day. It was not the norm, nor was it the logical climax to an earlier golden apolitical era of city government. When agreement subsided, so the party machines took over. And quite clearly, by 1945 Nottingham, in common with other large industrial centres, possessed a well defined and regulated party system. What happened subsequently was that this system simply became more all-embracing.

That this was part of a singularly broader trend in local government is not in dispute. An emphasis on the national, however, fails to explain a distinctly parochial and overlying chronology of continuity and change. It was local views and circumstance which predominantly determined civic perceptions of political consensus: initially setting an overtly co-operative framework which regulated local inter-party relations and individual behaviour, mirroring a broader consensus around reconstruction; determining the subsequent degrees of rancour accompanying the structural dissolution of power-sharing, and the fundamental disagreements over policies, personnel and practice which ran parallel to this; or finally, the neo-consensus of the 1960s which once again promoted images of inter-group harmony amid a basic agreement on the fundamentals of city government, albeit ones tied more to past than future expectations.

Within these chronologies also lay distinctly local interpretations of welfarism. Here, a Conservative resistance to provision as a right, where even key services and expenditures were subject to the rule of continual justification, also found its voice across a gamut of permissive responsibilities. The most notable, particularly in terms of polarised inter-party interpretation, centred on civic cultural subsidy. It could, of course, be argued that such provision was always of marginal importance within the totality of the post-war welfare state. And certainly in resisting an expansive remit, city Conservatives more readily reflected majority opinion in British town halls than did their local opponents, who were seeking to break new ground. Nevertheless, that Labour was exhibiting an innovative approach, questioning the limits of overall civic responsibility, in itself highlights a fundamental disjuncture in the respective party approaches. Stretching the boundaries of civic involvement, or resisting the contraction of existing civic provision, remained essentially a Labour trait. It was they, for example, who sought to retain civic restaurants as an extension of local welfare provision, or who promoted travel concessions for the elderly as a proper area of civic responsibility not to be viewed as a subject of local charity. In more matter-of-fact areas, Labour, with the strong support of the Corporation's principal officers, sought wholesale slum clearance in lieu of patch and mend, or opposed the provision of hostel accommodation of archaic standards. Yet if this suggests a Conservative preoccupation with pre-war values and standards, it also needs to be remembered how progressively oriented inter-war Tory paternalism in Nottingham was deemed to be. Indeed, Conservative opposition post-war to general needs housing provision remained heavily qualified. If Conservative rhetoric professed a strong preference for home ownership and choice, in practice this found its voice only with the limited substitution of private for public provision and, more controversially, in the ending of a rates subsidy of rents.

The promotion by local Conservatives of the private provision of council services in the early 1960s, against the backdrop of recent inter-party rancour, provides a clearer rejection of past agreement over civic working practices. Indeed, in emphasis it was reminiscent of local Conservative policy of the 1920s, when the battles between private and public provision in construction services formed a divide on which 'progressive' and 'minimalist' members polarised. And nowhere was a continuity with pre-war values better illustrated than in the group's conduct during the Fire Brigade dispute. If a *rapprochement* with trades unionism had infused the party nationally, it failed to permeate Nottingham's ranks where local Tories remained resolutely determined to prosecute and discipline those taking industrial action. This thinking placed them noticeably at odds with the more pragmatic (although hardly enthusiastic) responses of the city's Labour group, with their own political peers in other local authorities and with the more flexible approach adopted by the Conservative leadership at Westminster.

Other key areas of provision did receive bi-party support. Despite early Conservative rhetoric against an expansive state educational remit, or a Labour emphasis against technical provision, the application of subsequent policy significantly more united than divided the parties. This common purpose soon extended to local educational reform, a process aided by Labour's resistance to the introduction of socially integrated comprehensive schooling. Nevertheless, across the two decades as a whole, the limits placed on disagreements between the two parties were frequently underpinned by inherited and shared core values which had little to do with the tenets of a post-war social democratic settlement. In chronological order, for example, Bowles's resistance to the nationalisation terms for local authority services, joint agreement that the city transport system should operate without a general rates subsidy or later still the final debates over council house rents. Indeed, of all the shared bonds, financial prudence within set boundaries remained undoubtedly the strongest. When this was even partially severed (as with the Playhouse) it evoked the most robust of reactions. Inherent agreement also partly rested on such nebulous traditional concepts as members' common perceptions of civic pride and duty. For example, in the office of Lord Mayor and Sheriff, which many saw as a fitting pinnacle of a local political career, councillors had before them a traditional model of apolitical behaviour to emulate. Competition for civic office was frequently fierce; indeed, the founding rationale of the concordats in the 1920s was to order and limit such disagreement. And notably, the distribution of patronage remained a common kernel in all subsequent texts. In other ways, too, civic politics provided a traditional fabric for collaboration. Much committee work, even after the structural reforms of the 1950s, remained self-contained and essentially administrative, while even within the potentially explosive atmosphere of the council chamber there remained an essential concentration on what might best be described as municipal nuts and bolts issues.

Yet Nottingham did acquire, with certain other Labour-controlled authorities, a national notoriety for political intolerance in the late 1950s. Locally, this always centred on Popkess's suspension, deemed by political opponents and local newspapers alike to be the unholy incarnation of a caucus dictatorship. Coupled with the exclusion of the press, the prosecution of the new theatre (and the earlier politicisation of non-controversial items), here we reportedly have glaring examples of how expected standards of political behaviour had been breached by the city Labour group. Transport House was sufficiently concerned by such negative images that it effectively directed the group to end its anti-Popkess campaign and reach a political accommodation with local Tories. Yet the Popkess issue was never that clear cut; never simply a case of a Labour leadership, with a newly acquired monopoly of civic power, exercising dictatorial control over an 'independent' police force. Throughout, Labour was primarily on the defensive, not setting the agenda but responding to an immediate chronology largely dictated by others. Nor, necessarily, was it consequential to a post-war tightening of internal group discipline. Under Wigman's and Ives's stewardship, the executive did acquire greater authority, but this rested more on the latter's temperament, organising abilities and drive. Finally, the largely erroneous charges were not connected directly either to the group or its caucus structure, until account is taken of Coffey's strong opposition to Labour's priorities and his close links with Popkess.

Group confidence, however, was high. Labour had commanded the chamber for several years with steadily increasing majorities. To this was added the weight of Owen's support and encouragement. The decision to suspend the Chief Constable, by its very nature, was predestined to be highly controversial—the more so given the existing inter-party tensions. It was not, therefore, a step taken lightly. It was, however, the product of discussions only within a self-reinforcing coterie of opinion which ignored external sentiment; indeed, Popkess's subverting actions only reinforced Labour's sense of inner solidarity and discipline. Two consequences followed: first, in closing ranks the group determined to do battle with Popkess, local Conservatives, the press and even central government. But paradoxically, in facing the external threat, group attentions retreated inwardly, as in a siege-like state they resolutely sought to stymie open debate and discussion. Yet decisions taken in private had to be justified publicly. It was here that the weaknesses of a caucus mentality were most evident.

How, then, do we assess the impact of Labour policy on inter-party consensus, particularly during the 1950s? As the instigators of change to the 'rules of the game', there is merit in the argument that Labour, rather than the Conservative group, determined the disciplinary and inter-group tone. Public alteration to the formal and informal structure was always strenuously opposed by city Tories post-war. Yet the militancy so readily identified in their political opponents by Conservative rhetoric itself defies a ready definition outside this very specific context of inter-group relations in Nottingham. Nor is this made easier because Conservatives, in tending towards a more minimalist and abrasive code as the reconstruction phase of city politics passed, themselves 'debased' the contemporary currency of consensus politics upon which assessments must largely rest. Nevertheless, the rationalist core of Conservative protest focused on Labour's apparent enthusiasm for reforming, or as they saw it revolutionising, the local political structure and in setting aside past practice. Again clearly events in Nottingham reflected change elsewhere, albeit in a dilatory fashion. However, while alterations in Nottingham can, and should, be viewed as essentially evolutionary (springing from existing and growing inter-party antagonisms), at the time both groups saw the transfer to single party government as a major step. For Labour it became a key campaigning issue; for the Conservative group its forced adoption underpinned later allegations of autocratic rule. Condemnation was not limited to antagonisms over committee patronage. Equally bitter recrimination followed the decision by Labour ward activists to oppose Bill Cox after his ceremonial year because it breached custom, although not the letter of the inter-party agreement. Thus, a high public profile was assured any breaking of past practice by Labour; Conservative indiscretions, by contrast, received considerably less publicity. Similarly, the appointment of Tommy Ives broke an unwritten Conservative taboo, placing civic political activity in and outside the council chamber on a professional footing. Notably, Ives's standing placed him and, by extension, the Labour executive at a natural advantage when dealing with part-time councillors. Indeed, it was not only Tory members who objected to his status and influence and Ives was eventually replaced, the cult of amateurism restored.

Yet measured in Labour party terms, the city group was certainly not militant; indeed, it was only during the relatively brief period of Ives/Wigman hegemony that the group was anything less than openly hostile to the left. Yet there is evidence to suggest a measured radicalisation during the late 1950s in broadening the civic agenda. Here the group tentatively supported a limited (if quickly abandoned) programme of direct works, forging civic links with the eastern bloc, nuclear disarmament and breaking a past moratorium on civic arts and entertainments provision—all policies keenly opposed by city Conservatives. It was, however, only a partial transition. In more utilitarian areas Labour quickly abandoned an early flirtation with comprehensive education, preferring instead the politically safer path of bilateralism which built on local past practice. Moreover, the other major sector of local provision, housing, saw only limited progress in slum clearance; it was not until the 1960s, after some judicious prodding from central government, that some of the worst concentrations of bad housing in Britain were finally demolished.

That the Labour group attempted to moderate both image and action after 1959 supports interpretations which not only paint earlier Labour group rule as authoritarian, but also which see the period as one where the pulse of reform quickened and the breadth of civic activity spread. The concrete application of either reform or an expansionary remit notably depreciated local inter-group consensus. Equally, the subsequent rejection of both by Labour secured a new basis for agreement. Indeed, *rapprochement* in the early 1960s was aided significantly by the projection of a temperate group persona (which in part explains the later ferocity levelled at unsympathetic elements within the party). Of the Popkess incident itself, public image through the local press was the key determinant of city opinion. It, in turn, therefore moulded future policy in both the short and medium term. Nevertheless, ignoring central government directives (which conflicted with Owen's legal advice), or responding angrily to attempts to undermine its position by the Chief Constable, do not in themselves substantiate those charges of extremism or dictatorialness which were instantly and successfully applied to Labour at the time of the suspension. Perhaps, the most apposite assessment of

Labour's actions from 1956–1960 was that, apart from the Playhouse, in terms of policy it implemented little that was new or radically different; in terms of ideology it became more tolerant of its own left; and in terms of strategy on occasion it badly miscalculated its own strengths and weaknesses under the new system of single party rule.

Nottingham's problems were not unique in post-war Britain; housing shortages, slums and inner city poverty were common elsewhere. Local experiences, therefore, provide some insight into many aspects of contemporary British life. Primarily, however, a local study addresses local questions set in a local context. Reconstruction, built around post-war political and social expectation, dominated Nottingham's political agenda until the early 1950s. Upon this was built a political consensus which only fell with the completion of these more immediate aims. Indeed, local consensus in 1945 always contained more than a singular party political component; the broader social focus on housing as a priority signalled its presence in local surveys and polls, notably in the battle over the inner ring road. But party political consensus on Nottingham's city council itself remained an intrinsically different animal to its Westminster counterpart: inter-group co-operation ran deeper, disagreement was less frequent, civic unity was more all-embracing. It is against such an outline that subsequent events must finally be judged.

Nor were Nottingham's responses unique. Yet the ring-fenced intimacy of city politics, coupled with local circumstance, did produce a particular blend of reactions, compromises and later antagonisms which saw an unfeigned consensus turned upon its head within a decade and placed Nottingham in the upper divisions of local authorities notable for their political divisiveness and public intolerance. Paradoxically, it seems, this antipathy sprang from this very earlier agreement. Once compromise was discarded, once the parties no longer practised the broadly consensusal approach both had previously followed, and publicly continued to espouse, then disagreement on certain issues became absolute, irrevocable and, more importantly, highly contagious. Yet both parties did finally pull back from this local game of brinkmanship. Political consensus again became the norm, this time not built on the temporary foundations of reconstruction in a changing post-war world, but on a fully acknowledged and competitive bi-party system which still sought to minimise division. It was not a return to the past; it was a new beginning, a structure which for a further decade survived intact, aided by the unifying threat of local reorganisation. Yet at the same time, comparatively, it was a consensus built more around proscription than enterprise, on utility and efficiency more than vision. Like its post-war counterpart, in this too it was a product of its time.

Appendix

MEMORANDUM OF THE ARRANGEMENTS BETWEEN THE CONSERVATIVE AND LABOUR PARTIES ON THE NOTTINGHAM CITY COUNCIL AS TO THE ELECTION OF ALDERMEN AND OTHER MATTERS [SIGNED 1.1.1945].

Aldermen

As vacancies occur by death, resignation or expiration of office (subject as regards expiration of office as mentioned in paragraph 6 hereof) the Aldermanic Bench is to be made as far as possible to correspond with the strength of the recognised parties on the Council at the time of the vacancies being filled, subject to the following:-

1   This agreement shall terminate if either party hereto ceases to have at least six councillor members attached to it and a recognised Leader.

2   In calculating party strength for the purpose of filling Aldermanic vacancies only Councillors shall be reckoned.

3   For the purpose of calculating the proportion of the Aldermanic Bench to which a Party hereto is entitled, each member of a Party with less than three years service shall count as one, each member with three or more years service as two, and each member with six or more years service as three.

4   A fraction of an Alderman over one half shall count as one. Cases of equality shall be decided by lot. Where more then two parties are entitled to a fraction of an Alderman the Party entitled to the largest fraction shall select.

5   A councillor changing his Party shall not be reckoned in the above calculations until six months have elapsed from the date of notification to Party Leaders of the change.

6   (a) Notwithstanding the above provisions, an Alderman whose term of office has expired shall be re-elected, if his Party so desires, provided that he is (and for a reasonable time previously has been) doing active or material work upon or with the Corporation.

(b) Any question as to whether an Alderman is fairly entitled to the protection of the above proviso of this paragraph shall be decided by a Committee consisting of the Party Leaders and one representative selected by each of such Party Leaders respectively. Such Committee shall undertake to decide judicially and without reference to party matters.

(c) If either Party (other than that to which such Alderman belongs) would, but for this paragraph have been entitled to the seat, that Party shall be entitled to fill the first Aldermanic vacancy arising in such Alderman's Party irrespective of Party strength at such time.

(d) It is agreed that if either Party, which under the operation of this paragraph retains an Aldermanic seat not otherwise retainable, has any other Alderman not immediately subject to re-election who (if due for retirement) would not satisfy the proviso as to active or material work, such Party shall do everything

225

reasonably practicable to obtain the retirement of such last mentioned Alderman so as to permit of the due proportionate representation being maintained.

Mayoralty etc.

7   The right of choice of Lord Mayor and Sheriff shall be based as far as possible on the party strength (calculated as above, but with the inclusion of Aldermen), but so that any Alderman retained in excess of numbers under the provisions of paragraph 6. shall not count for voting purposes. The right of order of choice shall be decided for three years ahead and for a further three years ahead on or before 1st May 1945 and 1st May 1948 respectively.

8   The order of choice during the two three-year periods shall go in order of the calculated party strength. It is arranged that the Conservative Party are to take the Lord Mayoralties in 1945 and 1947, the Labour Party taking that in 1946. The Conservative Party are to take the Shrievalty in 1946, the Labour Party taking those in 1945 and 1947.

9   A Party having the right of choice may exchange with the party having the next or any subsequent right in the two three-year periods respectively.

10   It is understood that so far as the Party Leaders can exercise influence, the parties will do all in their power to ensure that a retiring Lord Mayor or retiring Sheriff due for re-election on the Council at the end of his term of office is not contested and it is also understood that, whilst not able to pledge all members of his party, each party leader has the support in this of a majority of his party.

Chairs, Vice Chairs and Committees

11   Subject as below mentioned and to paragraph 14 hereof, each Party shall be entitled to representation on Committees in proportion to Party strengths calculated on numbers only. The predominant Party shall be entitled to a majority on every committee but subject to such right changes shall only require to be made as vacancies occur unless the over-representation of either Party on a Committee exceeds two when a seat shall, if required, be provided for the Party then so under-represented.

12   Subject as below mentioned, each Party shall be entitled to Chairmanships and Vice-Chairmanships in proportion to Party strengths, calculated on numbers only and the predominant Party shall be entitled to select which Chairs and Vice-Chairs it will take as its proportion. Changes shall only be required to be made as vacancies occur, other than by usual annual retirements which shall not be regarded as vacancies for this purpose. The Old Age Pensions and Freeman's Committee shall be excluded from the operation of this clause.

In the event of any vacancy occurring in the Chair of the Finance and General Purposes Committee the Party with the largest Party strength under this paragraph shall be entitled, if it desires, to fill such vacancy and the next largest party shall be entitled in such case to take the Vice-Chair of such Committee.

13   The representation on Committees and in Chairs and Vice-Chairs to which any Party may become entitled under paragraphs 11 and 12 of this agreement shall be selected by the Party so becoming entitled and such selection shall be intimated through the Leader of such Party to the Leader of the other Party.

General

14   It is understood that the above arrangements have been approved by a majority of each of the parties concerned and are to be deemed binding on such parties accordingly.

15   A person elected to the Council who is not a member of the Conservative or Labour Parties, or an Alderman or Councillor who renounces his membership of either party shall be regarded as an unattached Member and shall be treated for the purpose of this Agreement as follows:-

(a) Every unattached Member shall be entitled to a seat on three Committees one (but not more) of which seats may be on the O.A.P. or Freeman's Committee.

(b) An Alderman or Councillor who becomes an unattached Member by renunciation during a municipal year shall retain his seat on Committees until the next Annual Meeting of the Council.

(c) An unattached Member elected to the Council during a Municipal year shall be allotted seats on three committees at the Council Meeting held next after his election such seats being provided by the Party which lost the by-election at which the unattached member was elected to the Council unless the Party Leaders agree otherwise.

(d) At every Annual Meeting of the Council, every unattached member shall be allotted seats on three Committees (not more than one being the O.A.P. or Freeman's Committee) and the total seats so allotted to unattached Members shall be provided by the Party Leaders in turn naming a seat on a Committee (the Leader of the majority party naming the first Committee) until the required number of seats has been made up. The seats then remaining shall next be divided among the Conservative and Labour Parties as laid down in paragraphs 11 and 13 of this Agreement.

(e) The distribution among the unattached members of the total seats allotted to them shall be made by the Party Leaders jointly. The Party Leaders shall have regard in such distribution to any wishes expressed to either or both of them by any unattached member but shall not be in any way bound to comply with such wishes. The provisions of this paragraph (14), whilst binding on the Parties hereto shall not confer any rights upon members to membership of any particular (or of any) Committees.

16   All the above arrangements shall continue in force until 31st December 1950.

17   Any question of doubt or difficulty arising as to the construction or carrying out of these arrangements in their true spirit shall be decided by the Party Leaders or if they cannot agree then by some person to be nominated by them.

MEMORANDUM OF THE AGREEMENTS BETWEEN THE CONSERVATIVE AND LABOUR PARTIES OF THE NOTTINGHAM CITY COUNCIL AS TO THE ELECTION OF ALDERMEN AND OTHER MATTERS [signed 29.1.1951]

As the 1945 agreements with the following provisos:

7   The right of order of choice shall be decided for the three year's ahead and for a further year's ahead on or before May 1st 1951 and May 1st 1954 respectively.

8   The order of choice during the two three-year periods shall go in order of the calculated Party strength. It is arranged that the Labour Party are to take the Lord Mayoralties in 1951 and 1953, the Conservative Party taking that in 1952. The Conservative Party are to take the Shrievalty in 1951 and 1953, the Labour Party taking it in 1952.

10   It is understood that so far as the Party Leaders can exercise influence, the parties will do all in their power to assure that an incoming or retiring Lord Mayor due for re-election on the Council at the beginning or end of his term of office, is not contested.

     A retiring Sheriff due for re-election on the Council at the end of his term of office is similarly not to be opposed. It is also understood that, whilst not able to pledge all members of his party, each party has the support in this of a majority of his party.

12   Subject as mentioned below, each Party shall be entitled to Chairmanships and Vice-Chairmanships in proportion to party strengths calculated on numbers only and the predominant Party shall be entitled to select which Chairs and Vice-Chairs it will take as its proportion. Changes shall only be required to be made as vacancies occur, other than by usual annual retirements which shall not be regarded as vacancies for this purpose. The Freeman's Committee [ditto clause 15a] shall be excluded from the operation of this clause.

     The chair of the Finance and General Purposes Committee shall be taken by the party with the largest Party strength, and the next largest Party shall be entitled to take the Vice-Chair of such Committee.

16   All the above arrangements shall continue in force until 31st December 1956.

Strictly Private and Confidential
MEMORANDUM OF THE ARRANGEMENTS BETWEEN THE CONSERVATIVE AND LABOUR PARTIES ON THE NOTTINGHAM CITY COUNCIL AS TO THE ELECTION OF ALDERMEN AND OTHER MATTERS [signed 2.4.1957]
Aldermen

1   On the death, resignation or expiration of office of any alderman his or her replacement shall be made in such a manner as to bring the total strength of the aldermanic bench most closely to correspond with the strength of the recognised parties in the Council at the time of the vacancy as follows:-

2   In calculating Party strength for the purpose of filling vacancies only councillors shall be reckoned.

3 A Party shall be entitled to one alderman for every three councillors. Two councillors above any multiple of three shall entitle a Party to a further aldermanic seat.

Lord Mayoralty and Shrievalty

4 Each of the two Parties with the greatest strength in the Council shall have the right to nominate to the office of Lord Mayor in each alternate year and to the office of Sheriff in each other alternate year. If however the proportionate strength of one of those Parties shall exceed three to two, the right of frequency of nomination to those offices shall be as nearly as possible in accordance with the respective strength of those Parties.

5 It is understood that so far as the Party Leaders can exercise influence, the Parties will do all in their power to assure that an incoming or retiring Lord Mayor due for re-election on the Council at the beginning or end of his term of office, is not contested.

6 A retiring Sheriff due for re-election on the Council at the end of his term of office is similarly not to be opposed. It is also understood that, whilst not able to pledge all members of his Party, each Party has the support of a majority of his Party.

Committees

7 Each Party shall be entitled to representation in Committees in proportion to Party strength in the Council, including Aldermen. The majority Party shall have a majority on every committee.

8 All the above arrangements shall be in force until 31st December 1961.

STRICTLY PRIVATE AND CONFIDENTIAL

Arrangements between the Conservative and Labour Parties on the Nottingham City Council [signed 24.5.1962]

1 *Aldermen.* Aldermanic seats shall be filled in equal numbers by nominees of the two parties to this agreement, and after such equal division, the Party in control shall be entitled to nominate the odd seat. The Party Leaders undertake to take all steps within their power to ensure that the arrangement shall become effective at the earliest possible date after any change in the balance of power, and shall continue to be effective.

2 *Lord Mayoralty and Shrievalty.* Each of the two Parties to this agreement shall have the right to nominate to the office of Lord Mayor in each alternate year and to the office of Sheriff in each other alternate year, subject to the provisos—
(a) That no Councillor shall be nominated for either office, except with the agreement of the Leaders of both Parties, if, at the end of his year or her year in such office, he or she would become due to stand for re-election to the City Council.
(b) If the proportionate strength of one of the Parties shall exceed two to one, the right of frequency of nomination to the said offices shall be subject of review.

3 Committees. Each Party shall be entitled to representation in Committees in proportion to Party strength on the Council, including Aldermen, but in any

interregnum period during which the transfer of an Aldermanic seat as provided for in Clause (1) hereof is pending, the representation of the majority Party shall be reckoned as though such transfer has in fact taken place. The majority Party shall have a majority on every Committee, and for the purpose in cases where the margin of the majority does not provide sufficient numbers the Chairman's casting vote shall be deemed to constitute the majority.

4   *Chairmanship and Vice-Chairmanship of Standing Committees.* The majority Party shall be entitled to nominate the Chairman, and the minority Party shall be entitled to nominate the Vice-Chairman of each standing Committee of the Council.

5   *Duration.* These arrangements shall continue in force until 31st December 1967.

STRICTLY PRIVATE AND CONFIDENTIAL

Arrangements between the Conservative and Labour Parties on the Nottingham City Council [signed 9.1.1968]

1   *Aldermen.* In the event of the number of Councillors being equal between the two parties, each party shall be entitled to nine aldermanic seats. If the number of Councillors is unequal then the Party having the largest number of Councillors shall be entitled to ten aldermanic seats, and that party with the smaller number of Councillors to eight aldermanic seats.

2   *Lord Mayor and Shrievalty.* Each of the two Parties to this agreement shall have the right to nominate to the office of Lord Mayor in each alternate year, subject, however, to the following provisions:-

(a) That, with the exception of the year 1968, when, due to the revision of Ward Boundaries all Councillors would, under this Clause, be disqualified from office, no Councillor shall be nominated for either office if, at the end of his or her year in such office, he or she would become due to stand for re-election to the City Council.

(b) That the Lord Mayor and Sheriff shall not, during their year of office, serve as Chairman or Vice-Chairman of any Standing Committee of the Council.

(c) If the proportionate strength of one of the Parties shall exceed two to one, the right of frequency of nomination to the said offices shall be the subject of review.

3   *Deputy Lord Mayor.* The retiring Lord Mayor's prerogative of nominating the Deputy Lord Mayor in the year immediately ensuing upon his or her appointment shall be subject to an undertaking to nominate such person as is sponsored by the Party not nominating the Lord Mayor.

4   *Chairmanship and Vice-Chairmanship of Standing Committees.* The majority Party shall be entitled to nominate the Chairman and the minority Party shall be entitled to nominate the Vice-Chairman of each Standing Committee of the Council.

5   *Committees.* Each Party shall be entitled to representation on Committees in proportion to party strength on the council, including Aldermen, but in any interregnum during which the revised allocation of Aldermanic seats as provided for in Clause (1) hereof is pending, the representation of the majority party shall

be reckoned as though such revised allocation had already taken place. The majority Party shall have a majority on every Committee, and for this purpose in cases where the margin of the majority does not provide sufficient numbers, the Chairman's casting vote shall be deemed to constitute the majority. In the event of the Parties being of equal strength, the allocation of Committee Chairmanships and Vice-Chairmanships shall be the subject of negotiation and if the Parties shall fail to agree the matter shall be decided by an independent arbitrator.

6   *Appointments by Council and Committees*. All appointments authorised by the City Council or its Committees shall be the subject of yearly discussions between the two Parties who shall resolve all representative appointments or nominations in proportion to Party strength, and any over-representation shall be adjusted at the expiration of the period of any appointment previously made.

7   *Duration*. These arrangements shall continue in force until 31st December 1973.

Bibliography

Manuscript Collections

Modern Records Centre
East Midlands Regional Labour Party (generally being Regional Organiser's Reports): MSS9.
TUC Correspondence Files: MSS292.

National Museum of Labour History
East Midlands Regional Labour Party: GS/EMRLP.
Morgan Phillips Papers.
National Executive Committee Minutes.
Separate files held on Nottingham's Constituency Labour Parties.

Nottingham Chamber of Commerce
Minute Books.

Nottingham Archives Office
Commonwealth Citizens Consultative Committee: DDCR.
East Midlands and Nottingham City Labour Party Correspondence, Minutes, Reports: LPC.
Market Ward Labour Party Minutes: LPC1.
Nottingham City Council: Committee and Council Minutes; Committee Reports; Local Enquiry into City Boundary: Ca ENQ/120.
Nottingham Journal Reference Books.
Nottingham Social Services Society: CSS 6.
St Mary's Ward Labour Party Minutes LPC 4.
South Nottingham Conservative Association Minutes: DDPP7.
South Nottingham Labour Party Minutes: DDPP7.

Nottingham Local Studies Library
Municipal Election Material: L34.32.
Nottingham City Council, *Epitome of Accounts*.
Nottingham and District Annual Trades Council Reports.

Nottingham University Manuscripts Department
Chambers Collection: Ch.
East Midlands Collection.

Nottingham City Council, *Epitome of Accounts* and Nottingham Corporation Accounts.
Nottingham and District Health Fund: Nh.
Nottingham Trades Council Correspondence, Minutes, Reports: TrM.
Robert Peers Papers: Pe.

Public Records Office
CAB 128, 129.
EL 3.
HLG 43, 79, 107.
HO 272.

Private Collections

Arts Council of Great Britain.
George William Dyer Papers, IAP.
Eric Foster Papers, IAP.
Oscar Watkinson Papers, held in his charge at Nottingham City Council House.
The Author's own research papers (interview notes and original/copy correspondence, Labour group minutes 1953–65, Labour party minutes, reports) to be deposited, with the Foster Papers, to form a collection at Nottingham University.
Oral History Collection based on interviews with the following: John and Jean Arnold, Jim Bagshaw, Hugh Bryan, Ken Coates, David Crane, Rex Fletcher, Eric Foster, Alan Griffin, Margaret Hurley, Brian Morley, George Powe, Fred Orton, Phillip Vine, Oscar Watkinson.

Official Papers and Publications

Census of England and Wales, 1911–1966.
Ministry of Labour Gazette (renamed *Employment Gazette*), 1918–67.
Hansard, *House of Commons Debates,* Fifth Series.
Hansard, *House of Lords Debates,* Fifth Series.
Registrar General's Statistical Review of England and Wales.
Report of the Royal Commission on Police Powers and Procedures (Cmd. 3297), PP (1928–29).
Report of the Committee on Electrical Distribution (1936).
Housing Returns: Appendix B (quarterly), 1945–67.
Housing (Cmd. 6609), PP (1945-6).

Temporary Housing Programme (Cmd. 6686), PP (1945–46).

The Gas Industry: Report of the Committee of Enquiry (Cmd. 6699), PP (1945–46).

Fifth Report from the Select Committee on Estimates (Sub-Committee C): Housing Expenditure, PP (1945–46).

The Housing Programme for 1947 (Cmd. 7021), PP (1946–47).

Economic Survey for 1947 (Cmd. 7046), PP (1946–47).

Temporary Housing Programme (Cmd. 7304), PP (1947–48).

Royal Commission on Population Report (Cmd. 7695), PP (1947–48).

Capital Investment in 1948 (Cmd. 7268), PP (1947–48).

Economic Survey for 1948 (Cmd. 7344), PP (1947–48).

Economic Survey for 1949 (Cmd. 7647), PP (1948–49).

Nineteenth Report from the Select Committee on Estimates: The Arts Council of Great Britain, PP (1948–49).

Reports of the Commissioners of the Inland Revenue (Annual), PP (1950–66).

Slum Clearance (England and Wales) (Cmd. 9593), PP (1955–56).

Royal Commission on the Police Minutes of Evidence, Vol. 11, 12, 15, 19, Appendix II (1961).

Royal Commission on the Police (Cmnd. 1728), PP (1961–62).

Government and the Arts 1958-64 (1964).

A Policy for the Arts: The First Step (Cmnd. 2601), PP (1964–65).

Department of Education and Science/Ministry of Housing and Local Government, Joint Circular (8/65) and (53/65), *A Policy for the Arts—Government Policy and the Need for Partnership* (June 1965).

Department of Education and Science, *Circular 10/65* (July 1965).

Report of the Inspector Appointed by the Minister of Housing and Local Government to Hear Objections to the Proposals of the Local Government Commission for the City of Nottingham and Surrounding Areas (1965).

Central Housing Advisory Committee, *Our Older Homes: A Call for Action* (1966).

East Midlands Economic Planning Council, *East Midlands Study* (1966).

Royal Commission on Local Government in England Minutes of Evidence—Vol. 12 (1967).

Royal Commission on Local Government in England (Cmnd. 4040), PP (1968–69).

Reform of Local Government (Cmnd. 4276), PP (1969–70).

Select Committee on Race Relations and Immigration, PP (1970–71).

Other Published Reports

Annual Report of the Arts Council of Great Britain (1945–67).

Arts Council of Great Britain, *Housing the Arts in Great Britain Part I* (ACGB, 1959).

Arts Council of Great Britain, *Housing the Arts in Great Britain Part II: The Needs of the English Provinces* (ACGB, 1961).

British Association for the Advancement of Science, *Report of the Annual Meeting, 1937* (BAAS, 1937).

R. Careless and P. Brewster, *Patronage and the Arts* (Conservative Political Centre, 1959).

The Conservative Party, *A Policy for Housing in England and Wales (A Report of the Conservative Housing Sub-Committee)* (Central Committee on Post-War Reconstruction, Jan. 1945).

P. Crane, *Enterprise in Local Government—A Study of the Way in which Local Authorities Exercise their Permissive Powers* (Fabian Society, 1953).

T. C. Howett, *A Review of the Progress of the Housing Schemes in Nottingham under the Various Housing and Planning Acts, July 1919 to December 1928* (Nottingham Corporation, 1928).

The Institute of Municipal Entertainment, *A Survey of Municipal Entertainment in England and Wales for the Two Years 1947/8 and 1961/2* (IME, 1964).

Institute of Municipal Treasurers and Accountants, *Return of Rates and Rates Levied per Head of Population (England and Wales)*, 1958–67.

The Labour Party, *Leisure for Living* (The Labour Party, 1959).

The Labour Party, *Report of the 38th Annual Conference of the Labour Party: Southport 1939* (The Labour Party, 1939).

The Labour Party, *Report of the 64th Annual Conference of the Labour Party: Blackpool 1965* (The Labour Party, 1965).

P. H. Mann, *The Provincial Audience for Drama, Ballet and Opera: A Survey in Leeds* (Arts Council of Great Britain, 1969).

Nottingham and District Trades Council, *Annual Report and Directory* (Nottingham, 1912–68).

Lord Redcliffe-Maud, *Support for the Arts in England and Wales* (Calouste Gulbenkian Foundation, 1976).

B. S. Rowntree and G. R. Lavers, *English Life and Leisure* (Longmans, 1951).

Newspapers and Periodicals

The Architect
Birmingham Post
Bulwell Dispatch

Daily Express
Daily Mirror
Daily Sketch
Daily Telegraph
The Economist
Local Government Finance
Manchester Guardian
Municipal Review
New Society
The New Statesman
News Chronicle
The Newsletter
Nottingham Citizen
Nottingham Daily Express
Nottingham Evening News
Nottingham Evening Post
Nottingham Guardian
Nottingham Journal and Express
Nottingham Guardian Trades Review
Nottinghamshire Guardian
Nottingham Journal
Nottingham Guardian Journal
Queen
Reynolds News
Sunday Pictorial
Sunday Times
Time and Tide
Tribune
The Week

Contemporary Published Material, Surveys and Autobiographies
(books published in London unless otherwise stated)

M. Abrams and R. Rose, *Must Labour Lose?* (Penguin, Harmondsworth, 1960).

W. J. Baumol and W. G. Bowden, *Performing Arts: The Economic Dilemma* (Twentieth Century Fund, New York, 1966).

F. J. Bayliss and J. B. Coates, 'West Indians at Work in Nottingham', *Race* 7 (1965), pp. 157–66.

F. Bealey, J. Blondel and W. P. McCann, *Constituency Politics: A Study of Newcastle-under-Lyme* (Faber and Faber, 1965).

B. Bernstein, 'Social Class and Linguistic Development' based on 'Some Sociological Determinants of Perception', *British Journal of Sociology* (June

1958), in A. H. Halsey, J. Floud and C. A. Anderson (eds), *Education, Economy and Society* (Free Press of Glencoe, New York, 1963).

J. Biffen, 'The Constituency Leaders', *Crossbow* 4/13 (1960), pp. 27–32.

J. Biffen, 'The Postwar Consensus (interview by Antony Seldon)', *Contemporary Record* 2/1 (1988), p. 16.

A. H. Birch, *Small Town Politics: A Study of Political Life in Glossop* (Clarendon, Oxford, 1959).

G. Block, *Party Politics in Local Government* (Conservative Political Centre, 1962).

J. Blondel, 'The Conservative Association and Labour Party in Reading', *Political Studies* 6 (1958), pp. 101–19.

J. Blondel and R. Hall, 'Conflict, Decision-Making and the Perceptions of Local Councillors', *Political Studies* 15 (1967), pp. 322–50.

J. M. Bochel, 'The Recruitment of Local Councillors: A Case Study', *Political Studies* 14 (1966), pp. 360–64.

T. Brennan, E. W. Cooney and H. Pollins, 'Party Politics and Local Government in Western South Wales', *Political Quarterly* 25 (1954), pp. 76–83.

H. Brooke, 'Conservatives and Local Government', *Political Quarterly* 24 (1953), pp. 181–89.

G. Brown, *In My Way* (Book Club Associates Edn., 1971).

I. Budge, 'Electors Attitudes Towards Local Government: A Survey of a Glasgow Constituency', *Political Studies* 13 (1965), pp. 386–92.

J. G. Bulpitt, 'Party Systems in Local Government', *Political Studies* 11 (1963), pp. 11–35.

J. G. Bulpitt, *Party Politics in English Local Government* (Longmans, 1967).

E. Burney, *Housing on Trial* (Oxford University Press printed for the Institute of Race Relations, 1967).

D. E. Butler, *The British General Election of 1951* (Macmillan, 1952).

D. E. Butler, *The British General Election of 1955* (Frank Cass, 1955).

D. E. Butler and A. King, *The British General Election of 1964* (Macmillan, 1965).

D. E. Butler and A. King, *The British General Election of 1966* (Macmillan, 1966).

D. E. Butler and R. Rose, *The British General Election of 1959* (Frank Cass, 1960).

R. A. Butler, 'Text of the Home Secretary's Address to the Police Conference, 10 June 1959, Torquay', *The Municipal Review* (Sept. 1959).

J. D. Chambers, *Modern Nottingham in the Making* (Nottingham Journal, Nottingham, 1945).

D. N. Chester, 'Council and Committee Meetings in County Boroughs', *Public Administration* 38 (1960), pp. 429–31.

D. N. Chester, 'The Independence of Chief Constables—Some Questions', *Public Administration* 32 (1960), pp. 429–31.

R. V. Clements, *Local Notables and the City Council* (Macmillan, 1969).

K. Coates, 'My Case Against Expulsion', *The Week*, 1965.

K. Coates, *The Crisis of British Socialism* (Spokesman, Nottingham, 1971).

K. Coates and R. Silburn, *Poverty, Deprivation and Morale in a Nottingham Community: St. Ann's* (Nottingham University, Nottingham, 1967).

C. A. R. Crosland, *The Future of Socialism* (Jonathan Cape, 1956).

C. A. R. Crosland, *The Conservative Enemy* (Jonathan Cape, 1962).

R. Crossman, *The Diaries of a Cabinet Minister. Volume One: Minister of Housing 1964–66* (Book Club Associates Edn., 1967).

E. Dell, 'Labour and Local Government', *Political Quarterly* 31 (1960), pp. 333–47.

D. V. Donnison and D. E. G. Plowman, 'The Functions of Local Labour Parties', *Political Studies* 2 (1954), pp. 154–67.

K. C. Edwards, *Nottingham and its Region* (Derry and Sons, Nottingham, 1966).

B. I. Evans and M. Glasgow, *The Arts in England* (Falcon, 1949).

M. Glasgow, 'Municipal Entertainment', *Municipal Review* (April 1948), p. 59.

R. Gosling, *Personal Copy: A Memoir of the Sixties* (Faber and Faber, 1980).

J. A. G. Griffiths, 'The Changing Shape of Local Government', *Adult Education* 31 (1958–59), pp. 167–86.

S. Hall, R. Williams and E. P. Thompson, 'Mayday Manifesto', in C. Olglesby (ed.), *The New Left Reader* (Grove Press, New York, 1969), pp. 111–43.

H. J. Hannan, 'The Organisation of the British Labour Party', *Western Political Quarterly* 9 (1956), pp. 376–88.

G. M. Harris, *Municipal Self Government in Britain: A Study of the Practice of Local Government in Ten of the Larger British Cities* (P. S. King, 1939).

F. A. Hayek, *The Road to Freedom* (Routledge, 1944).

T. E. Headrick, *The Town Clerk in English Local Government* (Allen and Unwin, 1962).

G. R. Hibbard, *The Neville Affair* (Nottingham Playhouse Action Group, Nottingham).

E. G. Janosik, *Constituency Labour Parties in Britain* (Pall Mall Press, 1968).

J. Jewkes, *Ordeal by Planning* (Macmillan, 1948).

P. M. Johnston, 'The Regional Housing Organisation of the Ministry of Local Government and Planning', *Public Administration* 29 (1951), pp. 236–44.

B. Keith-Lucas, 'The Independence of Chief Constables', *Public Administration* 38 (1960), pp. 1–11.

K. King and M. Baug, 'Does the Arts Council Know What It Is Doing? An Inquiry into Public Patronage of the Arts', *Encounter* 41 (1973), pp. 6–16.

F. W. Leeman, *Co-operation in Nottingham: A History of One Hundred Years of the Nottingham Co-operative Society Ltd.* (Nottingham Co-operative Society, Nottingham, 1963).

F. D. Littlewood, 'Municipal Theatres', *Municipal Review* (May 1946), p. 115.

R. T. McKenzie, 'The Wilson Committee Report and the Future of the Labour Party Organisations', *Political Studies* 4/1 (1956), pp. 93–97.

W. J. M. Mackenzie, 'Conventions of Local Government', *Public Administration* 29 (1951), pp. 345–56.

J. E. McColl and E. C. R. Hadfield, *British Local Government* (Hutchinson, 1948).

R. B. McCullum and A. Readman, *The British General Election of 1945* (Frank Cass Edn, 1964).

T. E. M. McKitterick, 'The Membership of the Party', *Political Quarterly* 31 (1960), pp. 312–23.

H. Maddick and E. P. Pritchard, 'The Conventions of Local Authorities in the West Midlands', *Public Administration* 36 (1958), pp. 145–55 and 37 (1959), pp. 135–43.

G. Marshall, 'Police Responsibility', *Public Administration* 38 (1960), pp. 213–26.

G. Marshall, *Police and Government: The Status and Accountability of the English Constable* (Methuen, 1965).

R. Michels, *Political Parties* (trans, Eden and Cedar Paul, Dover Publications, New York, 1959 Edn—first pub. 1911).

R. Miliband, *Parliamentary Socialism* (Monthly Review Press, New York, 1961).

C. A. Moser and W. Scott, *British Towns: A Statistical Study of their Social and Economic Differences* (Oliver and Boyd, 1961).

A. Popkess, 'The Racial Disturbances in Nottingham', *Criminal Law Review* (1960), pp. 673–77.

E. C. Rhodes, 'The Exercise of the Franchise in London', *Political Quarterly* 9 (1938), pp. 113–19.

E. C. Rhodes, 'Voting at Municipal Elections', *Political Quarterly* 9 (1938), pp. 271–80.

W. A. Robson, 'Labour and Local Government', *Political Quarterly* 24 (1953), pp. 39–55.

W. A. Robson, 'Post-War Municipal Elections in Great Britain', *American Political Science Review* XLI (April 1947), pp. 294–306.

R. Rose, 'The Political Ideals of English Party Activists', *American Political Science Review* 56 (1962), pp. 360-71.

S. K. Ruck, *Municipal Entertainment and The Arts in Greater London* (Allen and Unwin, 1965).

A. Sampson, *Anatomy of Britain Today* (Hodder and Stoughton, 1965).

L. J. Sharpe, 'The Politics of Local Government in Greater London', *Public Administration* 38 (1960), pp. 157–72.

L. J. Sharpe, 'Elected Representatives in Local Government', *British Journal of Sociology* 13 (1962), pp. 189–209.

L. J. Sharpe, 'Leadership and Representation in Local Government', *Political Quarterly* 37 (1966), pp. 149–58.

L. S. Sharpe (ed.), *Voting in Cities: the 1964 borough elections* (Macmillan, 1967).

A. Sillitoe, *Saturday Night and Sunday Morning* (Allen, 1958).

H. E. Smith, 'Party Politics in English Local Government', *Secretaries Chronicle* (March 1955), pp. 159–60.

M. Steed, 'A New Life for Local Politics', *New Society* (28 December 1967), pp. 922–24.

G. Thayer, *The British Political Fringe: a Profile* (Antony Blond, 1965).

W. Thornhill, 'Agreements Between Local Political Parties in Local Government', *Political Studies* 5/1 (1957), pp. 83–88.

E. P. Thompson (ed.), *Out of Apathy* (Stevens, 1960).

P. Townsend, 'The Meaning of Poverty', *British Journal of Sociology* 13 (1962), pp. 210–27.

J. H. Warren, *The English Local Government System* (Allen and Unwin, 1946).

J. Wickenden, *Colour in Britain* (Oxford University Press printed for the Institute of Race Relations, 1958).

H. V. Wiseman, 'The Party Caucus in Local Government', *New Society* (October 1963), pp. 9–11.

H. V. Wiseman, 'The Working of Local Government in Leeds: Part I. Party Control of Council and Committee', *Public Administration* 41 (1963), pp. 51–70.

H. V. Wiseman, 'The Working of Local Government in Leeds: Part II. More Party Conventions and Practices', *Public Administration* 41 (1963), pp. 137–56.

B. Wooton, *Freedom Under Planning* (George Allen and Unwin, 1945).

Anon., 'Red Faces at the Town Hall', *The Local Government Chronicle* (8th July 1961).

Secondary Works (books published in London unless otherwise stated).

N. J. Abercrombie, 'The Approach to English Local Authorities 1963–1978', in J. Pick (ed.), *The State and the Arts* (John Offord, Eastbourne, 1980).

T. Adams, 'Labour and the Erosion of Local Peculiarity', *Journal of Regional and Local Studies* 10/1 (1990), pp. 23–47.

P. Addison, *The Road to 1945: British Politics and the Second World War* (Quartet Edn., 1977).

P. Addison, *Now the War is Over: A Social History of Britain 1945–51* (Jonathan Cape, 1985).

D. H. Aldcroft, *The British Economy: Volume 1 The Years of Turmoil 1920–1951* (Wheatsheaf, 1986).

R. K. Alderman, 'The Conscience Clause of the Parliamentary Labour Party', *Parliamentary Affairs* 19/2 (1966), pp.224–32.

A. Alexander, 'The Decline of Local Government: Does Local Government Still Matter?', *Contemporary Record* 2/6 (1989), pp. 2–5.

J. Bailey, *A Theatre for all Seasons. Nottingham Playhouse: The First Thirty Years 1948-1978* (Alan Sutton, Stroud, 1994).

C. Barnett, *The Audit of War: The Illusion and Reality of Britain as a Great Nation* (Papermack Edn, 1987).

R. Baxter, 'The Working Class and Labour Politics', *Political Studies* 20 (1972), pp. 97–107.

A. Beck, 'The Impact of Thatcherism on the Arts Council', *Parliamentary Affairs* 42 (1989), pp. 362–79.

A. J. Beith, 'An Anti-Labour Caucus: The Case of the Northumberland Voters' Association', *Policy and Politics* 2 (1973), pp. 153–65.

C. Benn and B. Simon, *Half Way There: Report on the British Comprehensive School Reform* (Magraw Hill, 1970).

F. Berry, *Housing: The Great British Failure* (Charles Knight, 1974).

M. Blaug (ed.), *The Economics of the Arts* (Martin Robertson, 1976).

A. Blowers, 'Checks and Balances—The Politics of Minority Government', *Public Administration* 35 (1977), pp. 305–16.

N. T. Boaden, 'Innovation and Change in English Local Government', *Political Studies* 19 (1971), pp. 416–29.

N. T. Boaden, 'Local Elections and Party Policies', *New Society* (8 May 1969).

N. T. Boaden and R. T. Alford, 'Sources of Diversity in English Local Government Decisions', *Public Administration* 47 (1969), pp. 203–23.

M. Bowley, *Housing and the State 1919-1944* (Allen and Unwin, 1947).

J. Brand, 'Party Organisation and the Recruitment of Councillors', *British Journal of Political Science* 3 (1973), pp. 473–86.

B. Bravati, 'Campaign for Democratic Socialism', *Contemporary Record* 4/1 (1990), pp. 11–12.

A. P. Brier and R. E. Dowse, 'The Politics of the Apolitical', *Political Studies* 17 (1969), pp. 334–39.

S. Brooke, 'The Labour Party and the Second World War', in A. Gorst, L. Johnman and W. S. Lucas (eds), *Contemporary British History 1931–1961: Politics and the Limits of Policy* (Pinter, 1991), pp. 1–16.

S. Brooke, *Labour's War: The Labour Party during the Second World War* (Oxford University Press, Oxford, 1992).

S. Brooke, 'The Labour Party and the 1945 Election', *Contemporary Record* 9/1 (1995), pp. 1–21.

A. Bruce and G. Lee, 'Local Election Campaigns', *Political Studies* 30 (1982), pp. 247–61.

E. Bryson, *Portrait of Nottingham* (Robert Hale, 1974).

I. Budge and D. Farlie, 'Political Recruitment and Dropout: Predictive Success of Background Characteristics over Five British Localities', *British Journal of Political Science* 5 (1975), pp. 33–68.

J. G. Bulpitt, *Territory and Power in the United Kingdom: An Interpretation* (Manchester University Press, Manchester, 1983).

R. Burgess, 'Aspects of Education in Post-war Britain', in J. Obelkevich and P. Catterall (eds), *Understanding Post-War British Society* (Routledge, 1994), pp. 128–40.

D. E. Butler and D. Stokes, *Political Change in Britain: The Evolution of Electoral Choice* (Macmillan, Basingstoke, 1974 Edn).

S. Burgess, '1945 Observed—A History of the Histories', *Contemporary Record* 5/1 (1991), pp. 155–70.

A. Cairncross, *Years of Recovery: British Economic Policy 1945-51* (Methuen, 1985).

A. Calder, *The People's War* (Jonathan Cape, 1969).

D. N. Chester, *The Nationalisation of British Industry* (HMSO, 1975).

D. Childs, *Britain Since 1945* (Methuen, 1986).

J. B. Christoph, 'Consensus and Cleavage in British Political Ideology', *The American Political Science Review* 59 (1965), pp. 629–42.

R. A. Church, *Economic and Social Change in a Midlands Town: Victorian Nottingham 1815–1900* (Frank Cass, 1966).

P. F. Clarke, 'Electoral Sociology of Modern Britain', *History* 57 (1972), pp. 31–55.

P. F. Clarke, *The Keynesian Revolution in the Making 1924-36* (Clarendon Press, Oxford, 1988).

M. G. Clarke, 'National Organisation and the Constituency Association in the Conservative Party: the Case of the Huddersfield Pact', *Political Studies* 17 (1969), pp. 343–47.

K. Coates (ed.), *What Went Wrong: Explaining the Fall of a Labour Government* (Spokesman for The Institute of Workers' Control, Nottingham, 1979).

K. Coates and R. Silburn, *Poverty: The Forgotten Englishmen* (Penguin, Harmondsworth, 1970).

C. Cook, *The Age of Alignment: Electoral Politics in Britain 1922–1929* (Macmillan, 1975).

C. Cook, 'Liberals, Labour and Local Elections', in G. Peele and C. Cook (eds), *The Politics of Reappraisal, 1919-1939* (Macmillan, 1975).

C. Cook, 'Labour and the Downfall of the Liberal Party, 1906-14', in A. Sked and C. Cook (eds.), *Crisis and Controversy: Essays in Honour of A. J. P. Taylor* (Macmillan, 1976).

L. Corina, 'Elected Representatives in a Party System', *Policy and Politics* 3 (1974), pp. 60–87.

H. Cox and D. Morgan, *City Politics and the Press* (Cambridge University Press, 1973).

F. W. S. Craig, *British Parliamentary Election Statistics 1918-70* (Political Reference Publications, Glasgow, 1968).

T. Critchley, *A History of the Police in England and Wales 900–1966* (Constable, 1967).

J. B. Cullingworth, *Housing and Local Government in England and Wales* (Allen and Unwin, 1966).

R. Currie, *Industrial Politics* (Clarendon Press, Oxford, 1979).

J. Darke, 'Local Political Attitudes and Council Housing', in S. Lowe and D. Hughes (eds.), *A New Century of Social Housing* (Leicester University Press, Leicester, 1991), pp. 159–74.

M. J. Daunton (ed.), *Councillors and Tenants: Local Authority Housing in English Cities, 1919–39* (Leicester University Press, Leicester, 1984).

N. Deakin, '"Vanishing Utopias": Planning and Participation in Twentieth Century Britain', *Regional Studies* 19/4 (1985), pp. 291–300.

J. Dearlove, *The Politics of Policy in Local Government: The Making of Public Policy in the Royal Borough of Kensington and Chelsea* (Cambridge University Press, 1973).

P. Dunleavy, *The Politics of Mass Housing 1945–75* (Clarendon, Oxford, 1981).

R. Eatwell, *The 1945–1951 Labour Governments* (Batsford, 1979).

J. Elsom, *Post-War British Theatre* (Routledge and Kegan Paul, 1976).

D. Englefield and G. Drewry (eds), *Politics and Political Science* (Butterworth, 1984).

S. Fielding, 'What Did "the People" Want? The Meaning of the 1945 General Election', *Historical Journal* 35 (1992), pp. 623–39.

S. Fielding, 'The Second World War and Popular Radicalism: the Significance of the "Movement away from Party"', *History* 80 (1995), pp. 38–58.

C. H. Feinstein, *National Income, Expenditure and Output of the United Kingdom* (Cambridge University Press, 1972).

I. G. K. Fenwick, *The Comprehensive School 1944–1970: The Politics of Secondary Reorganisation* (Methuen, 1976).

P. Fletcher, 'An Explanation of Variations in Turnout in Local Elections', *Political Studies* 17 (1969), pp. 495–502.

M. Foot, *Aneurin Bevan—Vol. 2, 1945–60* (Davis Poynter, 1973).

T. Forrester, 'Anatomy of a Local Labour Party', *New Statesman* (5 October 1973).

D. Fraser, *Urban Politics in Victorian England* (Macmillan Edn, 1979).

C. Fudge, 'Winning an Election and Gaining Control: The Formation and Implementation of a Local Political Manifesto', in S. Barrett and C. Fudge (eds.), *Policy and Action* (Methuen, 1981).

C. Game and C. Skelcher, 'Manifestos and Other Manifestations of Local Party Politics', *Local Government Studies* 9/4 (1983), pp. 29–33.

J. H. Goldthorpe, D. Lockwood, F. Bechhofer, J. Platt, *The Affluent Worker in the Class Structure* (Cambridge University Press, 1969).

W. P. Grant, 'Local Councils, Conflict and the "Rules of the Game"', *British Journal of Political Science* 1 (1971), pp. 253–55.

W. P. Grant, '"Local" Parties in British Local Politics: A Framework of Empirical Analysis', *Political Studies* 19 (1971), pp. 201–12.

W. P. Grant, 'Size of Place and Local Labour Strength', *British Journal of Political Science* 2 (1972), pp. 259–60.

W. P. Grant, 'Non-Partisanship in British Local Politics', *Policy and Politics* 1 (1973), pp. 247–54.

D. A. Green, 'Inside Local Government—A Study of a Ruling Labour Group', *Local Government Studies* 6 (1980), pp. 33–49.

D. G. Green, *Power and Party in an English City: An Account of Single-Party Rule* (George Allen and Unwin, 1981).

G. Green, 'National, City and Ward Components of Local Voting', *Policy and Politics* 1 (1972), pp. 45–54.

R. Greenwood and J. D. Stewart, 'Towards a Typology of English Local Authorities', *Political Studies* 21 (1973), pp. 64–69.

R. Gregory, 'Local Elections and the Rule of Anticipated Reactions', *Political Studies* 17 (1969), pp. 31–47.

S. Goss, *Local Labour and Local Government* (Edinburgh University Press, Edinburgh, 1989).

J. Gyford, *Local Politics in Britain* (Croom Helm, 1976).

J. Gyford, *The Politics of Local Socialism* (George Allen and Unwin, 1985).

J. Gyford, 'The Politicization of Local Government', in M. Loughlin, M. D. Gelfand and K. Young, (eds.), *Half a Century of Municipal Decline 1935–1985* (George Allen and Unwin, 1985).

J. Gyford and M. James, 'The Development of Party Politics on the Local Authority Associations', *Local Government Studies* 8/2 (1982), pp. 23–46.

J. Gyford and M. James, *National Parties and Local Politics* (George Allen and Unwin, 1983).

W. Hampton, *Local Government and Urban Politics* (Longman, 1991, 2nd Edn).

C. Hardy and N. Arthur, *Nottingham at War* (Arthur Publications, Nottingham, 1986).

I. Harrington, 'Young Turks of the Town Halls', *New Statesman* (16 July 1971).

J. Harris, 'Did British Workers Want the Welfare State? G. D. H. Cole's Survey of 1942', in J. Winter (ed.), *The Working Class in Modern British History* (Cambridge University Press, Cambridge, 1983), pp. 200–14.

J. Harris, 'Political Ideas and the Debate on State Welfare', in H. L. Smith (ed.), *War and Social Change: British Society in the Second World War* (Manchester University Press, Manchester, 1986).

J. S. Harris, 'Decision-Makers in Government Programs of Arts Patronage: The Arts Council of Great Britain', *Western Political Quarterly* 22 (1969), pp. 253–64.

J. S. Harris, *Government Patronage of the Arts in Great Britain* (The University of Chicago, Chicago, 1970).

J. Hasegawa, *Replanning the Blitzed City Centre: A Comparative Study of Bristol, Coventry and Southampton* (Open University Press, Buckingham, 1992).

T. J. Hatton and K. A. Chrystal, 'The Budget and Fiscal Policy', in N. F. R. Crafts and N. Woodward (eds), *The British Economy since 1945* (Clarendon, Oxford, 1991), pp. 52–88.

N. J. Hayes, 'Tammany Hall Resurrected? Images of Labour Caucus Rule in Nottingham, 1956–60', *Transactions of the Thoroton Society* 98 (1993), pp. 136–44.

N. J. Hayes, 'Municipal Subsidy and Tory Minimalism: Building the Nottingham Playhouse 1942-1963', *Midland History* 19 (1994), pp. 128–46.

H. Helco, '"The Councillor's" Job', *Public Administration* 47 (1969), pp. 185–202.

P. Hennessy, *The Great and the Good: An Inquiry into the British Establishment* (Policy Studies Institute, 1986).

P. Hennessy, *Never Again: Britain 1945–51* (Jonathan Cape, 1992).

R. Hewison, *In Anger: Culture in the Cold War 1945–60* (Weidenfeld and Nicholson, 1981).

R. Hewison, *Culture and Consensus: England, Art and Politics since 1940* (Methuen, 1995).

G. M. Higgins and J. J. Richardson, 'Local Government and Public Participation: A Case Study', *Local Government Studies* 1 (1971), pp. 19–31.

D. M. Hill, *Participating in Local Affairs* (Penguin, Harmondsworth, 1970).

R. Hills, 'The City Council and Electoral Politics, 1901–1971', in C. H. Feinstein (ed.), *York 1831–1981: 150 years of Scientific Endeavour and Social Change* (Ebor Press, York, 1981), pp. 255–84.

A. Hilton, 'Economics of the Theatre', *Lloyds Bank Review* 101, (July 1971), pp. 26–38.

B. Hindess, 'Local Elections and the Labour Vote in Liverpool', *Sociology* 1, (1971), pp. 187–95.

J. Hinton, *Labour and Socialism: A History of the British Labour Movement 1867–1974* (Wheatsheaf, Brighton, 1983).

J. Holford, *Reshaping Labour: Organisation, Work and Politics—Edinburgh in the Great War and after* (Croom Helm, 1988).

M. Holmes, 'The Postwar Consensus', *Contemporary Record* 2 (1988), pp. 24–25.

C. Howard, 'Expectations Born to Death: Local Labour Party Expansion in the 1920s', in J. Winter, *The Working Class in Modern British History: Essays in Honour of Henry Pelling* (Cambridge University Press, Cambridge, 1983).

R. Hutchison, *The Politics of the Arts Council* (Sinclair Brown, 1982).

I. Jackson, *The Provincial Press and the Community* (Manchester University Press, Manchester, 1971).

P. W. Jackson, *Local Government* (Butterworth, 1967).

W. E. Jackson, *The Structure of Local Government in England and Wales* (Longman, 1966 5th Edn).

K. Jeffreys, 'British Politics and Social Policy During the Second World War', *The Historical Journal* 30/1 (1987), pp. 123–44.

K. Jeffreys, 'British Politics and the Road to 1964', *Contemporary Record* 9/1 (1995), pp. 120–46.

M. Jenkins, *Bevanism: Labour's High Tide. The Cold War and the Democratic Mass Movement* (Spokesman, Nottingham, 1979).

J. H. Jennings, 'Geographical Implications of the Municipal Housing Programme in England and Wales 1919–39', *Urban Studies* 8 (1971), pp. 121–37.

R. E. Jennings, 'The Changing Representative Roles of Local Councillors in England', *Local Government Studies* 8/5 (1982), pp. 67–86.

G. W. Jones, *Borough Politics: A Study of the Wolverhampton Town Council, 1888–1964* (Macmillan, 1969).

G. W. Jones and A. Norton (eds), *Political Leaders in Local Government* (Institute of Local Government Studies, University of Birmingham, Birmingham, 1978).

M. D. Kandiah, 'The Conservative Party and the 1945 General Election', *Contemporary Record* 9/1 (1995), pp. 22–47.

T. Karran, '"Borough Politics" and "County Government" Administrative Styles in the Old Structure', *Policy and Politics* 10 (1982), pp. 317–42.

I. Katznelson, 'The Politics of Racial Buffering in Nottingham, 1954–1968', *Race* 11 (1970), pp. 431–46.

I. Katznelson, 'A Reply to Letter by Miss Woods and Mr. Laird', *Race* 12 (1970), p. 238.

D. Kavanagh, *Thatcherism and British Politics: The End of Consensus* (Oxford University Press, Oxford, 1990 2nd Edn).

D. Kavanagh and P. Morris, *Consensus Politics from Attlee to Major* (Blackwell, Oxford, 1994 2nd Edn).

H. Keeble Hawson, *Sheffield: The Growth of a City 1893–1926* (Northend, Sheffield, 1968).

B. Keith-Lucas and P. G. Richards, *A History of Local Government in the Twentieth Century* (Allen and Unwin, 1978).

P. Kellner, 'Adapting to the Postwar Consensus', *Contemporary Record* 3/2 (1989), pp. 13–15.

A. F. Laird and D. Wood, 'Reply to Ira Katznelson on "The Politics of Racial Buffering in Nottingham 1954–68"', *Race* 12 (1970), pp. 237–38.

J. L. Lambert, *Police Powers and Accountability* (Croom Helm, 1986).

H. Laski, W. I. Jennings and W. A. Robson (eds), *A Century of Municipal Progress* (Allen and Unwin, 1935).

C. M. Law, *British Regional Development Since World War One* (David and Charles, Newton Abbot, 1980).

D. Lawrence, *Black Migrants, White Natives: A Study of Race Relations in Nottingham* (Cambridge University Press, 1974).

K. Laybourn, 'The Rise of Labour and the Decline of Liberialism: The State of the Debate', *History* 80 (1995), pp. 209–26.

C. H. Lee, *Regional Economic Growth in the United Kingdom since the 1880's* (McGraw Hill, Maidenhead, 1971).

J. M. Lee, *Social Leaders and Public Persons: A Study of County Government in Cheshire since 1888* (Clarendon, Oxford, 1963).

F. M. Levenstal, '"The Best for the Most": CEMA and State Sponsorship of the Arts in Wartime', *Twentieth Century British History* 1/3 (1990), pp. 289–317.

S. Lloyd-Jones, 'Working to a Plan—Committee Structure in Plymouth during Reconstruction and Subsequently', *Local Government Studies* (September/October 1980), pp. 29–36.

R. Lowe, 'The Second World War, Consensus, and the Foundation of the Welfare State', *Twentieth Century British History* 1/2 (1990), pp. 152–82.

R. Lowe, 'Welfare Policy in Britain 1943–1970', *Contemporary Record* 4/2 (1990), pp. 29–32.

R. Lowe, *The Welfare State in Britain since 1945* (Macmillan, Basingstoke, 1993).

L. Lustgarten, *The Governance of Police* (Sweet and Maxwell, 1986).

G. McCulloch, 'Labour, the Left, and the British General Election of 1945', *Journal of British Political Studies* 24 (1985), pp. 465–89.

L. J. MacFarlane, *Issues in British Politics since 1945* (Longman, 1975).

R. T. McKenzie, *British Political Parties* (Heineman, 1964 2nd Edn.).

D. C. Marsh, *The Changing Social Structure of England and Wales 1871–1951* (Routledge and Kegan Paul, 1958).

A. H. Marshall, *Local Government and The Arts* (Institute of Local Government Studies, University of Birmingham, Birmingham, 1974).

G. Marshall, 'Police Accountability Revisited', in D. E. Butler and H. A. Halsey (eds.), *Policy and Politics: Essays in Honour of Norman King* (Macmillan, 1978).

J. L. Marshall, 'The Pattern of Housebuilding in the Inter-War Period in England and Wales', *Scottish Journal of Political Economy* 15 (1968), pp. 184–205.

D. Marquand, *The Unprincipled Society: New Demands and Old Politics* (Jonathan Cape, 1988).

A. Marwick, 'Middle Opinion in the Thirties: Planning, Progress and Political "Agreement"', *English Historical Review* 79 (1964), pp. 285–98.

A. Marwick, *British Society since 1945* (Penguin, Harmondsworth, 1982).

A. Marwick, *Culture in Britain since 1945* (Basil Blackwell, Oxford, 1991).

A. Marwick, 'The Arts, Books, Media and Entertainment in Britain since 1945', in J. Obelkevich and P. Catterall (eds), *Understanding Post-War British Society* (Routledge, 1994).

T. Mason and P. Thompson, '"Reflections on a Revolution"? The Political mood in Wartime Britain', in N. Tiratsoo (ed.), *The Attlee Years* (Pinter, 1991), pp. 147–66.

R. C. O. Matthews, C. H. Feinstein, J. C. Odling-Smee, *British Economic Growth 1856-1973* (Clarendon, Oxford, 1982).

J. Melling (ed.), *Housing, Social Policy and the State* (Croom Helm, 1980).

C. Mellors, 'Local Government in Parliament—Twenty Years Later', *Public Administration* 52 (1974), pp. 223–29.

S. Merrett, *State Housing in Britain* (Routledge and Kegan Paul, 1979).

S. Merrett, *Owner Occupation in Britain* (Routledge and Kegan Paul, 1982).

K. Middlemass, *Politics in Industrial Society: The Experience of the British System since 1911* (Andre Deutsch, 1977).

R. Millward and R. Ward, 'The Cost of Public and Private Gas Enterprises in Late Nineteenth Century Britain', *Oxford Economic Papers* 39 (1987), pp. 719–37.

J. Minihan, *The Nationalisation of Culture* (Hamish Hamilton, 1977).

K. O. Morgan, 'Post-War Reconstruction in Wales, 1918 and 1945', in J. Winter (ed.), *The Working Class in Modern British History* (Cambridge University Press, Cambridge, 1983), pp. 82–98.

K. O. Morgan, *Labour in Power 1945–51* (Oxford University Press Paperback Edn, Oxford, 1985).

K. O. Morgan, *The People's Peace* (Oxford University Press, Oxford, 1990).

D. S. Morris and K. Newton, 'Marginal Wards and Social Class', *British Journal of Political Science* 1 (1971), pp. 503–07.

J. Myerscough, *The Importance of the Arts in Britain* (Policy Studies Institute, 1988).

A. A. Nevitt, 'Conflicts in British Housing Policy', *Political Quarterly* 39 (1968), pp. 439–50.

K. Newton, 'Turnout and Marginality in Local Elections', *British Journal of Political Science* 2 (1972), pp. 251–55.

K. Newton, 'Links Between Leaders and Citizens in a Local Political System', *Policy and Politics* 1 (1973), pp. 287–305.

K. Newton, *Second City Politics: Democratic Processes and Decision-Making in Birmingham* (Clarendon, Oxford, 1976).

M. Parkinson, 'Central Local Relations in British Parties—A Local View', *Political Studies* 19 (1971), pp. 440–46.

M. Parkinson, *The Labour Party and the Organisation of Secondary Education 1918–65* (Routledge and Kegan Paul, 1970).

N. Pearson, *The State and the Visual Arts: A Discussion of State Intervention in the Visual Arts in Britain, 1760–1981* (Open University Press, Milton Keynes, 1982).

H. Pelling, *The Labour Governments 1945–51* (Macmillan, Basingstoke, 1984).

P. E. Peterson and P. Kantor, 'Political Parties and Citizen Participation in English City Politics', *Comparative Politics* 9 (1977), pp. 197–217.

J. Pick, 'The Best for the Most' in J. Pick (ed.), *The State and the Arts* (John Offord, Eastbourne, 1980), pp. 9–20.

J. Pick, *Managing the Arts in Great Britain? The British Experience* (Rhinegold, 1986).

B. Pimlott, D. Kavanagh and P. Morris, 'Is the Post-War Consensus a Myth?', *Contemporary Record* 2/6 (1989), pp. 12–15.

B. Pimlott, *Harold Wilson* (Harper Collins, 1992).

S. Pollard, *The Development of the British Economy 1914–1988* (Edward Arnold, 1983 3rd Edn).

C. Price, 'Labour and the Town Halls', *New Statesman* (2 July 1971).

J. Ramsden, 'Adapting to the Postwar Consensus', *Contemporary Record* 3/2 (1989), pp. 11–13.

D. Regan, *Are the Police under Control?* (The Social Affairs Unit, 1983).

R. A. W. Rhodes, 'Hinterland Politics', *British Journal of Political Science* 1 (1971), pp. 123–28.

R. A. W. Rhodes, 'The Lost World of British Local Politics', *Local Government Studies* 1 (July 1975), pp. 39–59.

R. A. W. Rhodes, *Control and Power in Central-Local Relations* (Gower, Farnborough, 1981).

R. A. W. Rhodes, *The National World of Local Government* (Allen and Unwin, 1986).

J. H. R. Robbins, 'The Conservative Intervention in Doncaster Borough Politics', *British Journal of Political Science* 2 (1972), pp. 510–13.

N. Rollings, 'British Budgetary Policy, 1945–1954: A Keynesian Revolution?', *Economic History Review* 41/2 (1988), pp. 283–98.

N. Rollings, 'Poor Mr Butskell: A Short Life, Wrecked by Schizophrenia?', *Twentieth Century British History* 5/2 (1994), pp. 183–205.

R. Rose and I. McAllister, *Voters Begin to Choose: From Closed to Open Elections in Britain* (Sage, 1986).

D. Rubinstein and B. Simon, *The Evolution of the Comprehensive School 1926–1972* (Routledge and Kegan Paul, 1972 2nd Edn).

A. Sampson, *Macmillan: A Study in Ambiguity* (Allen Lane, The Penguin Press, 1967).

M. Savage, *The Dynamics of Working-Class Politics: The Labour Movement in Preston, 1880–1940* (Cambridge University Press, Cambridge, 1987).

M. Savage, 'The Rise of the Labour Party in Local Perspective', *Journal of Regional and Local Studies* 10/1 (1990), pp. 1–16.

M. Savage and A. Miles, *The Remaking of the British Working Class 1840–1940* (Routledge, 1994).

J. Saville, *The Labour Movement* (Faber, 1988).

H. Scarrow, 'Policy Pressures by British Local Government', *Comparative Politics* 4 (1971), pp. 1–28.

B. Schwarz, 'The Tide of History: The Reconstruction of Conservatism 1945–51', in N. Tiratsoo, *The Attlee Years* (Pinter, 1991), pp. 147–66.

J. Seabrook, *What Went Wrong: Working People and the Ideas of the Labour Movement* (Victor Gollancz, 1978).

A. Seldon, 'The Conservative Party since 1945', in T. Gourvish, and A. O'Day (eds), *Britain since 1945* (Macmillan, Basingstoke, 1991).

R. Shaw, *The Arts and the People* (Jonathan Cape, 1987).

J. R. Short, *Post-War Experience: Housing in Britain* (Methuen, 1982).

A. Sinfield, *Literature, Politics and Culture in Postwar Britain* (Basil Blackwell, Oxford, 1989).

J. F. Sleeman, *The Welfare State: Its Aims, Benefits and Costs* (Allen and Unwin, 1973).

R. Smith, P. Whysall and C. Beuvrin, 'Local Authority Inertia in Housing Improvement 1890–1914: A Nottingham Study', *Town Planning Review* 57/4 (1986), pp. 404–24.

R. Smith and P. Whysall, 'The Addison Act and the Local Authority Response: Housing Policy Formation and Implementation in Nottingham 1917–1922', *Town Planning Review* 61/2 (1990), pp. 185–206.

R. Smith and P. Whysall, 'The Origins and Development of Local Authority Housing in Nottingham 1890–1960', in S. Lowe and D. Hughes (eds.), *A New Century of Social Housing* (Leicester University Press, Leicester, 1991).

J. Stanyer, *County Government in England and Wales* (Routledge and Kegan Paul, 1967).

J. Stanyer, 'Why Does Local Turnout Vary?', *New Society* 17 (May 1971), p. 820.

H. J. Steck, 'Grassroots Militants and Ideology: The Bevanite Revolt', *Polity* 2 (1970), pp. 426–42.

B. Steel and Taketsugu Tsurutani, 'From Consensus to Dissensus: A Note of Post-Industrial Political Parties', *Comparative Politics* 18/2 (1986), pp. 235–48.

M. Stenton and S. Lees (eds.), *Who's Who of British Members of Parliament, Vol. IV 1945-79* (Harvester Press, 1981).

R. Stevens, '"Disruptive Elements"? The Influence of the Communist Party in Nottingham and District Trades Council, 1929-1951', *Labour History Review* 58/3 (1993), pp. 22–37.

J. Stevenson, *British Society 1914–45* (Penguin, Harmondsworth, 1984).

J. Stevenson, 'Planner's Moon? The Second World War and the planning movement', in H. L. Smith (ed.), *War and Social Change: British Society in the Second World War* (Manchester University Press, Manchester, 1986), pp. 58–77.

G. Stoker and D. Wilson, 'Intra-Organizational Politics in Local Authorities: Towards a New Approach', *Public Administration* (1986), pp. 285–302.

M. Swenton, *Homes Fit for Heroes: The Politics and Architecture of Early State Housing in Britain* (Heineman, 1981).

D. Tanner, *Political Change and the Labour Party 1900–1918* (Cambridge University Press, Cambridge, 1990).

D. Tanner, 'Elections, Statistics, and the Rise of the Labour Party', *Historical Journal* 34 (1991), pp. 893–908.

N. Tiratsoo, *Reconstruction, Affluence and Labour Politics: Coventry 1945–60* (Routledge, 1990).

N. Tiratsoo, 'Labour and the Reconstruction of Hull, 1945–51', in N. Tiratsoo (ed.), *The Attlee Years* (Pinter, 1991).

G. Trease, *Nottingham: A Biography* (Macmillan, 1970).

R. E. Tyrrell (ed.), *The Future That Doesn't Work: Social Democracy's Failures in Britain* (Doubleday, New York, 1977).

J. Vaizey (ed.), *Economic Sovereignty and Regional Policy* (Gill and Macmillan, Dublin, 1975).

M. J. Vipond, 'Fluctuations in Private Housebuilding in Great Britain, 1950–1966', *Scottish Journal of Political Economy* 16 (1969), pp. 196–211.

B. Waites, *A Class Society at War: England 1914-18* (Berg, Leamington Spa, 1987).

R. G. Walton, *The History of the Nottingham Chamber of Commerce 1860–1960* (Nottingham Chamber of Commerce, Nottingham, 1962).

F. A. Wells, *The British Hosiery and Knitwear Industry: Its History and Organisation* (David and Charles, Newton Abbot, 1972 revised Edn).

E. W. White, *The Arts Council of Great Britain* (Davis Poynter, 1975).

P. M. Williams, *Hugh Gaitskell: A Political Biography* (Jonathan Cape, 1979).

R. Williams, 'The Arts Council', *Political Quarterly* 50 (1979).

D. J. Wilson, 'Constituency Party Autonomy and Central Control', *Political Studies* 21/2 (1973), pp. 167–74.

D. J. Wilson, 'Party Bureaucracy in Britain: Regional and Area Organisations', *British Journal of Political Science* 2 (1972), pp. 373–81.

I. Wilton, 'Postwar Consensus', *Contemporary Record* 3/4 (1990), pp. 27–28.

G. D. N. Worswick and P. H. Ady (eds), *The British Economy 1945–50* (Clarendon, Oxford, 1952).

G. D. N. Worswick and P. H. Ady (eds.), *The British Economy in the Nineteen-Fifties* (Clarendon, Oxford, 1962).

C. Wrigley, *Lloyd George and the Challenge of Labour: The Post-War Coalition 1918–1922* (Harvester Wheatsheaf, Hemmel Hempstead, 1990).

P. Wyncoll, *The Nottingham Labour Movement 1880–1939* (Lawrence and Wishart, 1985).

K. Young, *Local Politics and the Rise of Party* (Leicester University Press, Leicester, 1975).

K. Young and L. Mills, *Public Policy Research: A Review of Qualitative Methods* (Social Science Research Council, 1980).

I. Zweiniger-Bargielowska, 'Rationing, Austerity and the Conservative Party Recovery after 1945, *Historical Journal* 37/1 (1994), pp. 173–97.

Unpublished Works

A. J. Burkett, 'Conventions and Practices in the Committee System in Selected Local Authorities in the East Midlands' (University of Nottingham, MA thesis, 1960).

N. J. Hayes, 'Nottingham 1945–66: Party Responses to Changing Political, Social and Cultural Expectations', (Open University, PhD thesis, 1992).

P. R. Shorter, 'Election Politics and Political change in the East Midlands of England 1918–35', (University of Cambridge, PhD thesis, 1975).

L. F. Wilson, 'The State and the Housing of the English Working Class, with Special Reference to Nottingham, 1845–1914', (University of California, PhD thesis, 1970).

Index

Addison, Dr Christopher 20
Addison, Paul 3, 6
Amalgamated Engineering Union (AEU) 106, 192
Amalgamated Society of Locomotive Engineers & Firemen (ASLEF) 105
Anti-Apartheid 207
anti-Labour demonstrations 118–19, 146
anti-Socialist pacts 13, 18, 21, 25–26, 94
Armitage, Sir Cecil 29, 31–33, 35, 79, 97
arts audiences 162–63, 167, 169, 172, 178, 181, 185
Arts Council of Great Britain (ACGB) 162–63, 165–66, 168–70, 173, 175–77, 180, 182, 184, 186
Association of Municipal Corporations (AMC) 59, 136, 163, 211
Atlee, Clement 4, 106; government of 9, 105

Ball, A. C. 54
Ball, Sir Albert 23, 33
Baxter, Tom 105, 109
Belgrade Theatre, Coventry 167, 176
Bestwood 56, 168
Bevanites 13, 76, 86, 94, 98–99, 109, 112
Bolshevism 21–22
boundary revisions 84–88, 207–11
Bowles, Herbert 17, 22, 24–25, 32–33, 35, 37, 45, 48–50, 59, 69–71, 84, 219
British Peace Council 99
British-Soviet Friendship Society 99
Brown, George 208
Broxtowe ward 108, 192
Bulpitt, Jim 14
Butler, Charlie 112, 141, 173, 175, 177–78
Butler, R. A. 117, 137, 145–49, 151, 158, 200
'Butskellism' 5–6
Byron ward 197–98

Callaghan, James 5
Callinan, Jim 111–12
Campaign for Nuclear Disarmament (CND) 113–14, 194
castle 83–84
Cattermole, Jim 101, 103, 105, 107–09, 112, 153, 192, 198, 201–02, 205, 208–09, 211
Caughtry, Jack 197–98
central-local relations 2, 6–7, 9, 12, 47, 51–52, 55–56, 58–59, 62, 64, 135–37, 139, 145–51, 197, 211, 216, 222
Chamber of Commerce 63, 100–01, 190
Charlesworth, Jack 99, 101–02
Churchill, Winston S. 5
Civic Restaurants 65, 72, 218
Civic Trust (arts) 168, 170
clean food campaign 101
Clifton 43–44, 51–52, 54–57, 81–82, 115, 168, 200
Clifton rebels 54–55
Coates, Ken 112, 193–94, 196–97, 199, 202–06, 208
Coffey, Chris 100–01, 105, 107–11, 119, 121–22, 138–40, 142, 148, 151, 154–55, 220
Coggan, Geoff 199
College of Arts and Crafts 44–45, 47
committee autonomy 23, 28–29, 36, 44–46, 55, 58, 67–70, 78, 83–84, 94, 213, 216–17, 220
Communists 100–01, 105–06, 192–93
concessionary fares 64, 218
consensus: national 2–5, 161, 223; in local government 6–7; in Nottingham 14–17, 21, 27, 93–94, 186, 213–224; inter-war period 14, 17, 28; wartime 29–31, 35; post-war bi-partisanship 44–52, 54–55, 57–63, 75, 78–80, 83–84, 92, 168, 173–74, 200, 207, 209–11, 213–14, 218–20; breakdown of 14–15, 17, 28,

64, 67, 73–91, 127–28, 213–21, 223; *rapprochement*in 1960s 104, 115, 122, 130, 132, 184, 187–90, 195, 214, 218, 222–24; and reconstruction 39–42, 44, 50–51, 78–81, 87, 92–93, 95–96, 215–18, 223

Conservative party and group: (pre-1914) 18–19; (inter-war) 19, 21, 23–28; arts and leisure 120, 160–61, 164–65, 167–68, 170–71, 173–86; and the caucus principle 14, 32–35, 54, 69, 82–84, 119–21, 127, 221; education 44–46, 60–61, 200, 219; 'minimalism' 26–28, 79, 96–98, 160, 165, 167–68, 171, 177, 185–86, 213, 218–19; attitudes to party discipline 33–34, 70, 71, 73, 84, 94–95, 216, 221; paternalism 21, 28, 79–80, 92, 96–97, 218; private enterprise 26, 51, 63–65, 79–83, 115, 181, 217, 219; rates 28, 47, 60–61, 63, 83, 160, 167–68, 175–76, 179, 181–82, 184–85, 191; reactionary 26, 76–77, 95; young conservatives 178

Co-operative Society (NCS) 49, 106, 165–66, 168, 172

corruption 118, 137, 140–44, 152–53, 157–58

Council for the Encouragement of Music and the Arts (CEMA) 162

Councillor autonomy 25, 29, 31–36, 54–55, 68–73, 82–84, 94–95, 98, 174, 213

Cox, William 31–32, 35, 72, 86–88, 94, 221

Crane, Sir William 23, 26–27, 29–30, 34, 42, 44, 46, 54–56, 79–80, 82, 90

Crosland, Richard 201, 203, 205

Crossman, Dick 124, 149

Daily Herald 105, 125

Daily Telegraph 154

Denman Street 82

Derbyshire, William 184, 210

Director of Public Prosecutions (DPP) 141–43, 157

Driberg, Tom 17, 120, 172

Dunnet, Jack 196

Dutton, George 109–10, 197

Dyer, William 35, 68–69, 126, 177, 179–80, 182

education: bilaterals 201–02, 205, 222; introduction of comprehensives 61–62, 199–206, 222; spending on 11, 60–61; technical 44–47, 215

elections: general (inter-war) 12–13, (1945) 1–2, (1951) 216, (1955) 95, (1959) 123–24; local (pre-1914) 18–19, (inter-war) 19–23, 25–26, (1945) 39–40, (1951 and 1952) 71, 73 (1954) 87–88, (1956) 117, (1958) 117, 175–76, (1959) 118, 123–24, 130, 142, (1960) 118, 125, 128–30, 132, 177, (1961) 130, 132

electricity (city) 10, 58–59, 62

Emmony, Harry 33–34

Employment, White Paper (1944) 5

Essential Works Orders 42

Finance Committee 28, 139–40, 151, 178–79

Finance and General Purposes Committee (F&GPC) 28, 41, 44, 64, 74–75, 83–85, 210

Finch, Robert 152, 157–58

Fire Brigade Committee (FBC) 74, 76–77

Fire Brigades Union (FBU) 77–78, 219

Flewitt, Jack 197

Forsyth, Cyril 165

Foster, Eric 16, 151–54, 156, 158–59, 178, 183–84, 188–90, 194, 197–98, 202–03, 206–10

Fraser, Sir Edward 18

Freemanships 158

Gaitskell, Hugh 117, 123

gas (city) 10, 58, 60, 62

Gas Fund Trust 174, 179–81, 184, 186

General Purposes Committee (GPC) 28, 173, 177, 181, 208–09

Glapton 82–83

Green, Roland 106, 118, 157, 177–80, 201–06

Green, William 30, 32, 35
Gregg-Herriot, Joseph 95
Gregory, Bob 198–99
Guardian Journal 16n, 85, 128, 149, 174, 195, 198, 204
Gyford, John 7–8, 119–20, 194

Halls, Walter 45–46, 78
Hallward, Bertrand 168, 179–80, 183–84, 186
Hanson, H. N. 54
Harris, R. Reader 77
Harrison, James 105
Hennessy, Peter 92
Heward, Noel 159
Hodgkinson, Joe 166
'Houses First' Committee and campaign 49–50, 70, 166–67
housing: (pre-1914) 19–21; (inter-war) 20–21, 26–28; completion rates 42–43, 56–57, 81, 196–97; consensus over 12, 19, 21, 26, 28, 40–44, 50–55, 80, 215; election issue 19–21, 40; 'garden city' influence 20, 27, 30, 52, 56; government restrictions 41, 55–56, 80–81; land shortages 51–52, 54–56, 81; 'no-fines' and prefabrication 42–43, 56, 81; rents 80, 104, 189; slums 20–21, 27, 40, 82, 196–97, 217–18, 222; spending on 11; waiting lists and housing shortfall 20, 40, 50, 52, 80–81, 196
Hucknall 208–09
Huntsman, Edmund 20–22
Hutchison, R. 164, 172

Independent Labour Party 18
Independent Party 31, 35, 49–50
Industrial Charter (1947) 6
inner ring road 48–49
inter-party agreements and patronage: (pre-1914) 18; (inter-war) 22–26, 28; (wartime) 29; (1945) 35–37, 39, 91–92; (1951) 37, 68, 91–92; (1957) 67, 89–92, 127–28, 213–14; (1962 and 1968) 91; arbitration clause 36, 67, 74–75, 78, 86; and member autonomy

25, 29, 31–36, 217; protection clauses 35–36, 86–90; full transcripts of 225–31
Ives, Tommy 72, 87, 103–05, 112, 121, 123–24, 141, 150–51, 154, 158–59, 170, 220–22

Jeffreys, Kevin 4
Janosik, Edward 98–99
Joint Consultative Committee (JCC) 100–03

Katznelson, Ira 120
Kavanagh, Denis 5
Kay, Constance 105
Keynesianism 95–96
Kenyon, John 72–73, 114, 126–27, 148, 151, 154, 156
Kirk, Bert 188, 193

Labour party and group: (pre-1914) 18–19; (inter-war) 19–24, 27–28; anti-left 98, 100–12, 190–96, 199, 204, 222, arts and leisure 161, 164–68, 170–72, 174–75, 178–79, 181, 184–86, 218, 222–23; caucus rule 13–14, 31–33, 67, 94, 98, 117–23, 127, 132, 140, 142, 213–14, 220–21; de-selection 106–07, 197–98, 205; direct works 65, 114–15, 222; education 44–46, 60–62, 199–206, 219, 222; 'extremism' 14–15, 67, 76, 86–87, 90–91, 94, 97–99, 118–21, 123, 125, 127–28, 146, 148–49, 160, 193–99, 220–23; greater pluralism 103–04, 113–15, 222; group discipline 29, 31–33, 54, 68–72, 84, 190, 220–21; housing 19–21, 27–28, 40, 44–49, 52, 54, 80–82, 122–23, 188–89, 196, 216–18, 222
Lee, Jennie 185
Liberal party and group: (pre-1914) 18–19, 49; decline of 25–26, 34–35; housing 20; anti-caucus campaigns 31, 33–35, 50, 132
Littlefair, Joseph 74–75, 84–85, 88–91, 96–97, 127, 158, 167, 173, 175–76, 179, 181–83, 185

Little Theatre 166
local authority responsibilities 7–11, 211
local authority spending 7; in Nottingham 10–11
Local Government Act (1948) 196
local government, apolitical ethos 2–3, 13
Lowe, Rodney 4
Lynch, Jeremiah 132
Lynch, Thomas 31

Market ward 107–08, 110
Marshall, G. 136
Marwick, Arthur 4–6, 161
Maud Report 209–11
Mayoral independence 71–73, 118, 128, 148, 151, 154, 177–80, 220–21
Meadows ward 106
Mechanics Institute 167, 173
Minihan, Janet 162
Ministry of Town and Country Planning 51–52
Minsk 113
Mitchell, Frederick 158
Mitchell, John 165
Mitson, Len 72, 202
Model Standing Orders 14, 70
Morgan, Kenneth 4, 6, 59
Moro, Peter 170, 172, 176–82, 185
Morris, Peter 5

nationalisation 9–10, 58–60, 62–63, 219
nationalisation of local politics 8–11, 12–13, 14, 47, 218
National Association of Blind Workshops 102
National Association of Labour Teachers 199
National Coal Board 52, 56
National Executive Committee (NEC) 107–09, 123, 194, 197–99, 206, 209
National Farmers' Union 52
National Federation of Building Trades Operatives (NFBTO) 114–15
National League for the Blind 102
National Union of Journalists (NUJ) 125–26
New Left 122–23, 188, 193–94, 199

New Statesman 166
Newton, Kenneth 15
Nottingham Central 106–07, 111, 123, 196
Nottingham Citizens Association 28, 31
Nottingham East 108
Nottingham Evening News (NEN) 16n
Nottingham Evening Post (NEP) 16n
Nottingham Guardian (NG) 16n, 73, 75
Nottingham Journal (NJ) 16n, 33
Nottingham Journal and Express 20, 21
Nottingham Peace Committee 111
Nottingham Playgoers' Club 164
Nottingham Theatre Trust 165, 167–68, 170–73, 176, 178–85
Nottingham Voice 195
Nottingham West 192
Nottinghamshire County Council 52, 209–10

O'Brien, Tom 146
Owen, Tom 54, 56, 68–69, 84–86, 138–41, 143–48, 149–50, 152–56, 172–73, 175, 177, 179, 181–83, 207–09, 220, 222

Pain, Sir Charles 96
Phillips, Morgan 105, 123, 132, 153, 159
Pick, John 161
Pimlott, Ben 2, 127
planetarium 138, 140–42, 143–44
Playhouse 15, 17, 98, 113, 120, 138, 165–87, 213, 223
police accountability 135–37, 145–47, 150–51
police housing 122, 138–39, 150; grant 147
Police Act (1964) 136
Police, Royal Commission 135–36, 145, 150
Popkess, Athelstan 98, 104, 110, 117–19, 122–26, 128, 135, 137–59, 177, 187–88, 190, 220, 222
Press: freedom of 98, 125–27, 148; political bias and influence 16, 94, 103, 117, 125–26, 128–30, 132–33, 149, 204, 222
Price, Peter 197–99, 206
progressivism 18–21, 26, 40, 215

Purser, Ernest 72, 94, 157

rates factor (political) 28, 47, 60–61, 63, 83, 160, 167–68, 175–77, 179, 181–86, 189, 190–91, 219
reconstruction 11–12, 29–30, 39–42, 44–48, 50, 78–81, 93, 95, 98, 164–65, 185, 215, 217, 221, 223
riots (1958) 196
Robbins, Jack 110
Rook, A. 54
Roper, Tom 107

Savage, Arthur 47
Savage, Mike 9
Scotland Yard 124, 140, 142, 144
Scott, Tommy 78
Sellars, A. E. 54
sewage farm 47
Sharp, William 46
Shaw, Bob 107, 110–11
Shaw, Robert 45
Sloma, R. T. 108–09
Smith, Ernest 159
Socialist Education Association 199, 203, 206
Socialist Fellowship 107
Socialist Outlook 108
sources 16
Steck, H. J. 112
Stevenson, John 9
Strelley 56

technical college 45–47
Thatcher, Margaret 5, 161
Thomas, Stanley 140, 142, 146
The Times 129
town meeting and polls 48–50
Trades Council 19, 43, 62–63, 78, 99–104, 106, 125, 151
traffic wardens 138–39, 150
transport (city) 10, 62–64
Tribune 125
Twells, George 32, 35, 132

USSR 113–14

Vigilante party 35, 132
Vietnam 195

Watch Committee 118, 125–26, 135, 137–40, 143–47, 150–56
water (city) 10
welfarism (local) 11, 61, 64, 65, 72n, 79–80, 96, 217–19
West, Arthur 192
Wigman, George 69, 71–72, 90, 107, 125–26, 138, 140–42, 149–50, 152, 157–58, 171–72, 220, 222
Willatt, Hugh 165, 168, 170, 172–73, 175–77, 182
Williams, W. E. 168–70, 175, 177
Winterbottom, Ian 107, 123
Wright, Sir Bernard 17, 23, 25, 29
Wollaton 81